PELICAN BOOKS

A 169

JOHN CITIZEN AN

RONALD F...

JOHN DOE and RICHARD ROE BROTHERS IN LAW !!

(From a print in the possession of Mr Stanley Rubinstein)

NOTE

John Doe and Richard Roe, who figure prominently throughout the work, and whose portraits appear in the frontispiece, are fictitious legal characters who have been dead for about a century. A brief account of their life history is given in an Appendix.

RONALD RUBINSTEIN

JOHN CITIZEN
AND THE
LAW

*

FOURTH EDITION EDITED BY
Christopher R. Rubinstein

PENGUIN BOOKS

Penguin Books Ltd, Harmondsworth, Middlesex
U.S.A.: Penguin Books Inc., 3300 Clipper Mill Road, Baltimore 11, Md
AUSTRALIA: Penguin Books Pty Ltd, 762 Whitehorse Road,
Mitcham, Victoria

—

First published by Penguin Books 1947
Second Edition 1948
Third Edition 1952
Reprinted 1955
Fourth Edition 1958

Made and printed in Great Britain
by Richard Clay & Company, Ltd,
Bungay, Suffolk

THIS BOOK

is dedicated in particular to my wife,
and in general to all those who
conscientiously read and digest the Preface
before they commence
Chapter One

ACKNOWLEDGEMENTS
(FIRST EDITION)

In addition to assistance given to me by members of my family (particularly my niece, Miss Joan Rubinstein), I desire to express grateful appreciation for the valuable help given or suggestions made to me by the following:

MR W. P. ALLEN

MR J. F. BEER, MISS L. BINNING

MR BERTRAM CECIL, MR R. A. CLARKE

MR HERBERT CREMER, MR J. W. GOLDMAN

MR MILNER HOLLAND, MR CLAUDE HORNBY

MR H. C. LEON, MR HAROLD LIGHTMAN

MR T. G. LUND, LORD MESTON

MR A. F. PULLINGER, MISS M. R. RAWLINSON

MRS A. B. ROSSITER, MR HARRY RUBENS

MR D. SACKER, MR W. A. STEINER

MISS I. TRISH, MR R. E. WILLIAMS

CONTENTS

FOREWORD

This book speaks for itself. It has already spoken to good purpose in the first three editions. The author Ronald Rubinstein was a most able member of the legal profession, and his early death was a great loss. He combined a wide knowledge of the law with much good common sense. He always mastered the details of his cases and was an excellent 'man of business'. His very extensive practice brought him into touch with problems of every kind. All this stood him in good stead when he came to write this book. Subject after subject – some of them specialist subjects – are treated with the easy style of a master. He picks out the salient points and makes them clear. It is a great boon to have the law thus explained in a way which laymen can understand – so long as it is also well understood that it is not wise for any man to attempt to be his own lawyer – and Mr Ronald Rubinstein explained this in his preface to the first edition.

The law does not, however, stand still, and a book of this kind needs revision from time to time to keep it up to date. It is gratifying to know that the author's son, Mr Christopher Rubinstein has been able to do it this time. This edition should prove a worthy successor to the first three editions. I hope it will have equal success.

DENNING

INTRODUCTORY NOTE TO THE
FIRST EDITION

'What is the use of a book,' thought Alice, 'without pictures or conversation?'

Alice in Wonderland

'JOHN DOE murdered. Man detained.' These arresting words catch the attention and excite interest.

'Be it enacted by the King's most Excellent Majesty, by and with the advice and consent of the Lords Spiritual and Temporal, and Commons, in this present Parliament assembled, and by the authority of the same, as follows. ...' These pompous and stilted phrases will attract nobody, and yet they introduce topics which will have a far greater effect on your daily life than the murder of John Doe, for they are the preamble to every Act of Parliament.

In this book I am anxious to excite interest in the law, because I believe it to be to the advantage of the community for each member to know something of the rules and regulations by which he is governed – a matter which normally arouses no interest, but is simply considered tedious.

This is not a book for lawyers, and I am fully conscious of the peril of an attempt to divulge legal magic to anyone who has not been trained in the subject. Indeed, lawyers may consider the book a menace, and it may well prove to be if it is misused. On the other hand, the dangers of ignorance and the injury you may individually suffer as a result of the total lack of knowledge of basic legal principles satisfy me that the effort is worth making. It is always pleasant to draw back the curtains in order to let in the light. However, I must give a preliminary caution in language which admits of no ambiguity and which cannot be misunderstood. You must not for one moment think that 'Every Man his own Legal Adviser' would be a suitable alternative title for this book. I would rather that the alternative title should be 'Why is this the Law?' for I have endeavoured in many instances to explain the reason why particular rules are made in particular cases. You must not commit the folly of believing that the book will give you the exact answer to your particular legal problem, or the best solution to any legal difficulty with which you may be faced, for even the Lawyer's Encyclopædia called *Halsbury's Laws of England*, consisting of thirty-seven volumes, each of some 1,000 pages, may not be able to do this. Moreover, that work is only an introduction to law, which refers you in each instance to the particular Law or legal decision upon which the text is founded. If you want to know all there is to be known about English law you must refer to the relevant Acts of Parliament and the relevant legal decisions which are contained in many thousands of volumes of Statutes and Law Reports. The matter does not even end there, for the complexities of our daily life produce problems to which there is no certain solution – a fact for which the lawyers are usually blamed – but that is a subject which I do not propose to pursue in this introduction.

It is unfortunate that any outline of English law (and this book deals only with the law in England and Wales, as distinct from Scotland) is bound to make liberal use of generalizations. Generalizations are, as a rule, very dangerous and very objectionable. They may be gunpowder in the hands of the unwary. They are safe only when they are recognized and approached with caution. In order to emphasize this point, may I say that neither the publisher nor the author will accept any responsibility if any foolhardy reader attempts to act on a decision at which he arrives by treating any generalization as applicable to the facts of his particular case. Rash and hazardous enterprise of this character is not to be encouraged. This volume gives you a sketchy outline of the law, and nothing more. Compare yourself with the man who is ignorant of the nature of the solar system and the stars. If he purchases a small telescope he will gain only very limited knowledge of the universe. Even large telescopes will fail to uncover more than a fragment of the galaxy of stars in the firmament. You may regard this work as a small telescope which may be focused on some of our day-to-day legal problems. It cannot pretend, however, to disclose more than a small segment of the legal system.

One thing is certain. A legal system, a respect for that system, and a reasonable certainty that it will be administered impartially, and without political prejudice, is essential to any civilized community. There are doubtless features of the English legal system which are petty and obstructive, and the fractious individual, who believes that Freedom means the right to snatch and grab what he wants, without consideration for the rights of others, is always ready to seize on them as an example of the tyranny of the law. Generally speaking, however, the English system is reliable and 'not so bad', and history has always proved that the absence of a reliable legal system means chaos and jungle law.

Of course, I am guilty of special pleading when I praise the law. My pride in the law is not, however, charged with complacency as to its imperfections. Nothing human ever is perfect, and I will gladly associate myself with any constructive proposals for improvements, bearing in mind that when a law meets the needs of 99·9 per cent of the community, but operates harshly on ten, a hundred, a thousand, or even ten thousand individuals, i.e. 1 in 40,000 of the population of England, there may not be adequate ground for revision, if the proposed alterations will do more injury than they cure.

'Law enters into nearly every relation of social and civic life from birth to death.' Bearing the cautions of this preface in mind, we shall be able in the following chapters to test the truth of this assertion, but you must be prepared to find that 'the tune is unfamiliar, and the end a note of interrogation'.

October 1946

INTRODUCTORY NOTE TO THE FOURTH EDITION

In her preface to the Third Edition, published in 1952, Miss Joan Rubinstein wrote, 'the body of our law grows and changes as imperceptibly but as continuously as a coral reef. And the justification for a new edition of this book is that charts must be brought up to date'.

The greatest single change in the law since 1952 is that involving Rent Restriction. The chapter in this edition is intended to give an outline of the more permanent sounding provisions of the new Act, which includes much that was already law. The innumerable other changes in the Law since the last edition have had a less restricted transforming effect, but I have tried to record faithfully those which took place up to the Spring of 1957, and which seem the most interesting and important.

My thanks are due to all those who have helped with the preparation of this edition, including the correspondents who have drawn attention to some aspect of the law which they have been privileged or unlucky enough to have experienced. A special word of thanks is due to Sir T. G. Lund, c.b.e., for the chapter on 'Legal Aid', which he wrote originally for the third edition, and which now appears with slight amendments.

WHAT IS LAW?

'O great and sane and simple race of brutes,
That own no lust, because they have no law.'
Tennyson

LAW has been defined as 'the just interference of the State in the interests and passions of humanity'. It will hardly be seriously disputed that it is necessary for the State to interfere in the affairs of the community to a greater or lesser degree, since community life would be a sad tangle if there were no laws or rules which had to be observed by all.

The average schoolboy will admit that his school would never function successfully without rules, and most boys prefer rules to be laid down with precision, for the more exact the definition, the better the boy understands his place in the school and the duties and obligations which he has to observe. Rules also help him to understand the meaning of co-operation, and even in schools which cater for the individual ego there is some limit to the latitude allowed to the children. They are not, for instance, permitted to murder their masters, or to set fire to the school buildings. As a rule, the guiding principle of such schools is that a child is entitled to freedom, so long as he does not abuse that freedom by injuring others, but it is doubtful if a narrow interpretation and the absence of discipline help the child to understand the importance of co-operation, as distinct from rugged individualism.

It seldom occurs to anyone that when children have left school it is equally desirable for them to learn something of the rules which govern community life. They are rarely instructed as to what they may or may not do, and they are usually ignorant of the procedure laid down for the adjustment of disputes between individual members of the community. Although, however, they know little or nothing of these rules, they rarely hesitate to grumble at them, particularly when they realize how easily they are infringed. On these occasions there is frequently a tendency to blame the Government. This is not necessarily reasonable. One of the duties of every Government is to protect the community, and this is done by rules and regulations which are known as laws. Those who regard the laws passed by a Socialist Government as examples of tyranny may not be able to appreciate that socialists entertain the same unfriendly feelings towards legislation created by Conservative Governments. The sort of rules which will be examined in this book, however, will have little to do with politics. For example, if you are out cycling after dark without a light, and a policeman stops you and lays his hand on your shoulder, his behaviour is not dictated by his political beliefs, even although you may be infuriated at this attack on your liberty. When, however, you appear in Court a few days later, charged with the legal offence of cycling after dark without a light, you are not charged with this offence because the Government is totalitarian or tyrannical. In fact, in a democracy, the Government consists of the lawfully appointed representatives of the people. The Government will not object if you wish to career round your garden at night on a bicycle without a light, for in such a case you will only be a danger to yourself. It is, however, the duty of a Government to protect the community from the antics of irresponsibility. It is too late to remedy the disaster when a pedestrian is knocked down and killed by a cyclist riding at night without a lamp, so it is the duty of the Government to look ahead and endeavour to forestall accidents of this character. It therefore requires cyclists to carry lamps at night because it has a greater duty to safeguard the community as a whole than to respect the freedom of the individual.

If, in fact, everyone respected the rights of every other member of the community, we should not require any rule or law to deal with or punish crime. As, however, crime is in our marrow, it is necessary to define the exact nature of every criminal offence and prescribe the punishment to be exacted for breaking any particular rule. Even the disappearance of crime would not, however, relieve the country of its obligations to make laws. We should still require rules to regulate our relations with each other. Rules are necessary in every phase of life, even if we are engaged only upon a game of ping-pong, although in such an event infraction of the rules may not involve legal consequences.

Many rules which involve legal obligations are made by Acts of Parliament, and they are then known as Statute Law. Statute-making became a regular practice in the thirteenth century. Before any rules derived from an Act of Parliament have the force of law today, the Government, or one or more Members of Parliament – i.e. the House of Lords or the House of Commons – must present a Bill setting out the proposed rules in exact terms. The Bill must be read and approved three times in the House of Commons, and also in the House of Lords, before it can receive the formal assent of the Sovereign. Thereafter it becomes law, and is placed upon the Statute Book. No law may be enacted without the direct or indirect approval of the House of Commons. As England is a democracy, and the Members of Parliament who constitute the Government are elected by the people, such laws may be said, accordingly, to represent the will of the people.

Statute Law, however, is applicable to only some of the problems which arise in the daily contacts which take place between individual members of the community. When, therefore, a dispute is brought before a tribunal for decision, and there is no Statute Law applicable, the Judge must find his solution to the problem by other methods. After he has heard all the relevant facts, he must consider what recognized legal principles are to be applied before he delivers his judgement. When a judgement is given in the High Court of Justice, a branch of the Supreme Court of Judicature in England, the judgement becomes almost invariably part of the law of the land, in the same way as a Statute. It is then known and described as part of the 'Common Law'. Common Law is therefore of an entirely different character from Statute Law, and the Common Law dates back to the Middle Ages, when Courts of Law were first firmly established in this country. From the outset, cases came for trial before the Courts which could not be decided by reference to any law on the Statute Book. For the sake of convenience, it therefore became the practice when a Judge delivered his judgement for such judgement to become what is called a 'precedent', and in this way the Common

Law was built up on precedent. In any other case which involved similar facts the Judge who tried it would generally deliver a similar judgement. Today every Judge is bound by precedent, and when a judgement is delivered in the House of Lords – the final appeal tribunal of the country – only Parliament, by the enactment of a new Statute, can re-make the law on the point in question. Frequently, in fact, laws are enacted which codify the existing Common Law, but many cases which are tried in the English Courts are still decided by the application of the principles of Common Law. The expression 'Common Law' is, accordingly, habitually used by lawyers to distinguish a class of case which is almost exclusively founded on 'precedent' as distinct from Statute Law, but the Common Law may never override Statute Law.

There is one other source which has greatly enriched our English legal system. It is known as 'equity' – i.e. 'right' or 'justice' – but we shall not stop to consider it here, because as a separate system it lost much of its importance over eighty years ago with the passing of the Judicature Act 1873. Lawyers still speak of 'equity' and the 'equitable jurisdiction' of the Courts, and a note on the subject is included in an appendix, for it has had such a powerful influence on legal history that no outline of English law could properly exclude a reference to the subject.

What does the average citizen mean when he says he is 'going to law'? He means that he intends to invoke the assistance of the Courts, in order to assert what he believes to be his legal rights. Since everyone is bound by the law, everyone is entitled to ask for its assistance against a defaulting member of the community.

A man goes to law because he believes the laws are fairly administered, and, subject to all-too-many human imperfections, he is not far wrong. He may rest assured that his complaint will be listened to with care. He will not run any serious risk of being told that he is in the wrong because of political or other improper influence. He will receive a fair trial, and the strict impartiality with which his complaint will be heard and considered is the foundation upon which the whole of our present ordered structure rests.

If this were not so, the result would be disastrous. Indeed, you would not bring an action – the technical way of 'going to law' – unless you felt assured of an impartial hearing of your case. You would not be so foolish as to waste your time and money, if you thought the result could be influenced by bribery or corruption, or if you feared that politics would enter into the case. You would in such circumstances hold the legal system in contempt. What, then, would be the result if you had no legal remedy for an injustice? Swindlers, already a burden on the community, would multiply in the same way as other rats. Most of them, at present, still act with a certain caution and respect for the law, but if they realized they could break agreements or commit fraud without fear of the consequences, all observance of the law would immediately cease. Under such conditions civil administration would collapse, and would be followed by unrestricted crime. When I can punch your nose with impunity because you are weaker than I am, and when a felon can break into a house and steal without risk, it follows that the thugs will do exactly as they please. When there is no punishment and no retribution, thieves and bullies will assume full control of the activities of the community. Nazi Germany provided an outstanding example of this calamity. After Hitler came to power, a Judge was rarely allowed to adjudicate on any dispute on its merits. He was compelled to give his decision according to the interests of the Nazi State. Unless the claimant was a National Socialist, he had no legal rights. Many German Judges would not accept these conditions and were compelled to resign. Others were at once appointed in their place, because Hitler could retain control only so long as the Judges were willing to carry out his instructions. 'Racks, gibbets, and halters were their arguments', and if a German Socialist or a German Jew had been entitled to a fair trial of his complaint on its merits, there would have been a speedy end to the Nazi regime. A strong and impartial judicial system is the first essential in any country which makes claim to be recognized as a civilized community.

Why, then, do people so often scoff at the law? There are, no doubt, a variety of reasons; but, of these, ignorance predominates. Very few people are able to appreciate the problems involved in their true perspective, and are far too tempted by the attractions of exaggeration. They will refer you to cases in which the law has been abused, or a criminal has escaped detection or conviction, and they will cite these cases as examples of the futility of the law. Alternatively, perhaps, they will give you particulars of cases of injustice, which are true and deplorable, and they will use these instances to prove our legal system is worthless. They fail, utterly and entirely, to recognize that the law in England has to cope with a population which exceeds 40,000,000 individuals. If 400,000 of these suffer from some injustice in a greater or lesser degree, it represents less than 1 per cent of the population, and it leaves 99 per cent of the people in a position to benefit from the protection given to them by the law. Far be it from me to be complacent at injustice to 400,000 – if this number were accurate. It is a terrifying total when each figure represents a human soul. On the other hand, lawyers are not superhuman, and do not claim to be so. They are not immune from the general shortcomings of mankind. The problem involved in the endeavour to make rules which are to be sufficiently flexible to be just to every member of a community of over 40,000,000 individuals is beyond human capacity. Our best efforts are bound to fall far short of perfection.

The machinery of law has, in fact, changed beyond all recognition in the past hundred years. It has moved with the times and has been modernized, and even though it still has so many imperfections, there is a genuine desire among the majority of lawyers to remove impediments to justice and to assist in providing legal machinery adequate to the involved needs of modern life. Justice must, however, always be uncertain, however lofty our intentions may be. Every Judge is himself John Citizen, a member of the community, and he is subject to the same limitations of human intelligence, and has all the failings of our common lot. Two judges may honestly arrive at two different opinions on identical facts. No man can say which of them, if either, is right. For this reason even trained lawyers are unable to forecast the result of a lawsuit. It is made more uncertain, since no one can say exactly what evidence will be given by the witnesses when they testify in Court, nor does anyone know how the Judge will react to the evidence of each witness. It is not the function of a Judge to decide a legal question until after the facts have been presented and analysed. Facts enable you to form a judgement, but as your neighbour's reaction to any given facts may be totally different from yours, you may each arrive at a totally different judgement.

You may be convinced in your mind that you performed a certain act on a certain day. If you are involved in litigation, and you give evidence to prove this fact, you may testify with complete honesty. Later, when your opponent gives his version of the case, he may tell a convincing story which is quite different from yours. This may not be due to any deceit on his part. He may feel as convinced as you do that he is telling the truth. The result, however, is that the Judge is confronted with two sets of facts which bear little resemblance to each other. Nevertheless, he must deliver his judgement. Since he is human, he will, of course, accept the evidence of the witness who has made the better impression. If he prefers the evidence of your opponent, and you are the disgruntled loser, you may leave the Court murmuring that there is no such thing as justice. This is very human, but very unreasonable. There is a loser to every lawsuit, and although there are many dishonest people, the majority of actions are contested by parties each of whom believes himself to be honest. When losers complain that it is the law which is at fault – that being the way of human nature – you learn of another reason why the law is unpopular. Many of those who hold the law in contempt never attempt to appreciate problems of this character, because critics are often as small-minded as those whom they criticize.

When you are willing to concede that the most honest legal system can never be infallible, you will the better understand the real purpose of this book, which deals with the legal obligations of members of the community, as well as their legal rights. An obligation is a duty, and whilst it is generally recognized that crime is a wanton breach of duty, we do not so readily realize the extent of our legal obligations in our ordinary day-to-day contacts with our fellows. As this book deals largely with these daily contacts, it will be more concerned with the civil, and less with the criminal, branch of the law.

When we appreciate the vital truth, that every legal right involves a legal obligation, many existing evils will disappear. If we ever realize that the real key to so many of our misfortunes is a failure to carry out these obligations, and a failure to observe the spirit as well as the letter of the law, we shall be on the way to Utopia. Nevertheless, this prospect places us in a predicament, for we shall achieve such an ambition only after our passions have become like the 'cold ash of an extinguished fire'. When that is achieved, we shall scarcely be justified in classing ourselves as 'human' beings, and Utopia may prove to be a dull affair.

2

LEGAL RIGHTS AND OBLIGATIONS

'Being asked the way to the Workhouse by a needy
looking man, I gave him a shilling. Judge of my surprise, as a local preacher and life-long teetotaller, when
he turned into the next "pub" into which I followed
in a useless effort to get my money back. What were
my legal rights?'

Letter in *John Bull* – quoted in 'This England'

THERE are many occasions when a man owes a duty – a legal
duty – to others, engaged upon lawful pursuits, not to cause
them harm or hurt by any negligent act, and every time you
are in contact with another man either one of you may be
guilty of a breach of that duty. It is, generally speaking, immaterial whether or not the breach of duty is intentional or
unintentional. All men are answerable for the natural and
probable result of every one of their actions. If, through lack
of caution, you have failed to consider the effect which may
follow from a particular act, and which would have been fore-
seen by a reasonable man, you may be legally liable for the
consequences. If these consequences result in injury to another
member of the community, you have committed a 'tort' (derived from the French word meaning 'wrong'), and when a
tort has been committed, a claim for damages may be made by
the injured party. Such a claim may sometimes be made even
if the aggrieved person is unable to prove that he has suffered
'special damage', as pecuniary loss is called. In such cases the
law awards damages because it assumes that the very nature of
the injury is bound to cause loss. In other cases it does so because no one is entitled to injure any other member of the
community with impunity. The word 'injury' must not be
taken in a literal sense as meaning physical injury. Every person who suffers damage to his person, his property, or his reputation as a result of an infringement of the law suffers a legal
injury. Compensation may frequently be recovered for damage
to property and to reputation, as well as for pain and suffering
due to physical injury. Many of these claims cannot be measured in actual money terms. It is for the Judge or jury to assess

the amount which may reasonably be estimated to reimburse the injured party for the loss which he has suffered as a result of the tort. Some general aspects of the principles upon which damages may be assessed are considered at the end of this chapter, but there are also many cases when there is no legal remedy for a financial loss, because it is not the result of any breach of a legal duty. If, for example, you are engaged in trade, and another trader opens a similar business on adjoining premises, you will suffer financial loss when he takes your customers from you. He does not, however, commit any legal wrong by his conduct, and the law, accordingly, will give you no remedy for your grievance.

A good picture of the meaning of a legal duty can be obtained if we examine the all-too-common case known to lawyers as a 'running down' case, when a pedestrian is knocked down by a car. Every motor-driver has a legal obligation not to drive 'negligently', and if his car has struck the pedestrian as a result of his negligence, he is guilty of a breach of this duty, and the pedestrian is entitled to compensation. It is, however, important to note – and there is considerable misconception on the point – that the driver is liable, and is liable only, if he has failed to comply with this legal obligation. Negligence is the crux of the matter, and if there is no negligence, there is normally no claim. Negligence in law is a failure, by the wrongdoer, to exercise the amount of care, in a particular case, which an average reasonable man would exercise in similar circumstances. The onus, or burden, of proving negligence is upon the person who makes the complaint. It is not necessary for a driver who injures a pedestrian to prove that he was not negligent. The law nearly always assumes that everyone has acted lawfully until the contrary is proved. If, accordingly, you have been knocked unconscious in an accident, and remember nothing of it, and if you are unable to trace any witness of the accident, you will not ordinarily be able to recover compensation, because you will not be able to prove that the driver was negligent. If, however, you remained fully conscious, you will be competent to give evidence as a witness in support of the allegation of negligent driving. If the driver denies his negligence – and he will usually do so – and if he claims that the accident was due to your own negligence or carelessness, your word is as good as his. If there is no other witness available, it will be for the Court to decide whether it will accept your evidence and reject that given by the driver. Remember, however, that if the driver's evidence is unsatisfactory, it will not necessarily enable you to succeed in your action unless your own evidence is convincing. The burden is upon you to PROVE that the driver was guilty of negligent driving. Facts can be proved in a Court of law only by evidence which is accepted by the Court as being the truth. Moreover, if you have yourself been negligent, and the accident has been caused partly by your own fault and partly by the driver's fault, and your negligent act was the proximate or decisive cause of the accident, you will not be able to recover full compensation. Indeed, a defence by a driver of 'contributory negligence' on the part of the pedestrian, if established in Court, had always been a complete answer to a claim for compensation, until the passing of the Law Reform (Contributory Negligence) Act 1945. This Act, which applied to all accidents occurring after its coming into force, achieved a long-overdue reform, as it provides (in relation to accidents) 'where any person suffers damage as the result partly of his own fault and partly of the fault of any other person or persons, a claim in respect of that damage shall not be defeated by reason of the fault of the person suffering the damage, but the damages recoverable in respect thereof shall be reduced to such extent as the Court thinks just and equitable having regard to the claimant's share in the responsibility for the damage'. This was a revolutionary doctrine for lawyers, who had been taught that a claimant was absolutely barred from recovering damages after an accident if he had been guilty of contributory negligence. It brought the law into line, however, with the practice observed in the case of claims arising as a result of collisions at sea, when damages have for long been apportioned according to the degree of responsibility of the parties to the accident.

Other considerations of law may also arise when a street accident occurs. If the driver was not himself the owner of the car, it may be necessary to consider if there was any legal relationship between the owner and the driver. In some instances an employer (whose relations to his employee generally are considered in Chapter 4) is liable for any tortious or wrongful act of his employee. One such instance occurs when the act is committed by the employee whilst he is lawfully carrying out his duty to his employer. In such a case the employer must bear the legal consequences of his employee's negligence. In other words, and in the case which we are considering, he will be liable if the employee is driving the car as part of his duty to his employer at the time of the accident. On the other hand, an employer is not, generally speaking, liable if the employee is engaged upon his own personal affairs at the time of the accident, or if he had taken out the car for a joy ride, and was driving it without authority.

The Crown and Public Corporations are in general liable for the wrongful acts of their servants to the same extent as any other employer, and if you are injured by the negligent driving of a Post Office van or of a National Coal Board lorry, you may sue the Postmaster-General or the National Coal Board as the case may be. The employees of Public Corporations are not servants of the Crown, and Public Corporations have never had any special immunity from legal proceedings. Government Departments, however, were before 1948 in a privileged position and could not be sued for the negligence of their employees. If negligence were proved, the Department concerned would usually pay compensation to the injured party, but this was done as a matter of grace, and the injured party had no rights against the Department. This legal anomaly was ended by the Crown Proceedings Act 1947, and, subject to a few exceptions, an individual can now sue a Government Department for the negligence of its servants without fear of being defeated by the principle of Crown immunity.

Yet a third matter for legal consideration in every street accident is the relationship which exists between the driver or owner of the car on the one hand, and his insurance company on the other hand. The law requires every driver of a motor car to be insured against 'third-party risks' – i.e. claims by members of the public for damages for negligence. Provided the driver was properly insured at the time of the accident, the question as to whether or not he was the owner of the car has usually been academic. However, the law which requires a driver to be insured does not automatically insure him. An organization called the Motor Insurers' Bureau has, however, been set up voluntarily by the insurance companies themselves to deal with the scandal of the uninsured driver. Accordingly, an injured party who is able to establish negligence against the driver of a car involved in an accident will receive the same compensation from the Bureau as he would have recovered if the driver had been properly insured. Proper notice (details of which are obtainable from every insurance company) must be given to the Bureau within a specified period after the accident.

If you wish to claim compensation after you have been involved in an accident, you do not ordinarily have any legal rights against the driver's insurance company. It is true that in cases in which the driver's policy is in order the compensation which may become payable, by compromise or under a judgement of the Court, will be paid to you by the insurance company. They will, however, make this payment to you because they agree with their policy-holder to do so by the terms of the contract or agreement with *him*, and not as a result of any legal obligation which is owing to *you*.

If a car which is in good running condition and has just had a new set of tyres, suffers an unexpected burst which throws the car out of control, and it injures a pedestrian, the victim may not be entitled to recover compensation from the driver, because the accident is not *prima facie* due to the latter's negligence. There might be a possibility of recovering damages against the manufacturer of the defective tyre, for manufacturers are under the same legal obligation to members of the community as others. In order, however, to establish a claim the injured man would have to satisfy the Court that the manufacturer had been negligent in his process of manufacture, and also that the manufacturer could not reasonably have expected examination of the tyre to have been made by any middle-man or dealer – formidable propositions, which in most cases would be very difficult of proof.

Many think that the driver of a car should always be liable for an injury which he causes, whether it occurs through his negligence or otherwise, since a motor car is so often a menace.

In support of their arguments, they point out, if they are learned in the law, that a person who owns or has charge of a dangerous object must not allow it to escape or break from his control. If he does so, he is liable for any damage which it causes, even without proof of negligence, and he will be able to avoid liability only if he satisfies the Court that the accident could not have been prevented, no matter what precautions had been taken, or, in truth, that it was an act of God. Be careful to note, however, that an act of God is a rare occurrence. Generally speaking, it applies only to acts which are unquestionably beyond human control, such as thunderbolts and earthquakes. It is no act of God when a motor car mounts the footpath, no matter what the cause may be, but even so, the driver is not necessarily liable, since a motor car is not, in fact placed in the category of objects legally considered to be dangerous. There the matters rests until such time as the law is altered, and changes in the law are ultimately promoted by the votes of the community, as much as by the lawyer.

Cyclists and pedestrians must never forget that they are under the same obligation as motorists to exercise care, and they must not meander along the roadway without regard to the safety of others. Careless cyclists and pedestrians are frequently responsible for serious accidents when cars swerve to avoid them. Foolhardy cyclists and 'jay walkers' may be as dangerous as a car, and where they are responsible for an accident may be sued for damages. Indeed, there is always a possibility that careless acts which result in injury to others may give rise to a legal claim for damages. When we consider the number of mistakes which each of us makes every day of our lives, we must feel grateful that so few of our errors involve us in legal complications.

Before leaving this 'chapter of accidents', you may note that, if an accident results in death, the representative of the estate of the deceased person (see Chapter 27) has the same right to recover compensation as if the victim had survived. This is subject always to the obligation to prove negligence against the defendant, for if it is not proved, the claim cannot succeed, and no damages will be recovered.

So much, for the moment, for torts. The other important

source of right and obligation, which is of a totally different character, is derived from express 'agreement' or 'contract'. For practical purposes, the two words may be regarded as synonymous.

Contracts are an incident of daily life, and many of us enter into them almost hourly. Frequently we may be quite unconscious of their existence, although, if we analysed the facts which are construed by the law as amounting to a contract, we would understand the soundness of the reasoning. For example, every time you travel on an omnibus there is, in law, a contract between the bus owners and yourself, for each of the three elements essential to every contract of this character it present, and each of the parties looks upon the incident as a business matter. The three essential elements of every contract, other than contracts 'under seal', which are referred to later are (1) an unconditional offer made by one party to the other, (2) an unconditional acceptance of the offer, and (3) 'consideration' to support the offer and the acceptance. Consideration imports the element of bargain into what might otherwise be a purely one-sided transaction. It is the *quid pro quo*, and it may be either in cash or in kind. Generally speaking, the law is not concerned as to the adequacy or inadequacy of the consideration in any particular case, as this is essentially a matter to be decided by the parties themselves. The law has the right to interfere only if the consideration is so small, or so excessive, as to give rise to a presumption of fraud. Consideration must, however, have direct reference to the bargain which is being made between the parties, and not relate to some past event. For example, if John Doe has voluntarily undertaken and completed some work for Richard Roe, which so pleases the latter that he tells John Doe that if he will call on the following day he will give him £5 in payment, John Doe could not sue Richard Roe if the latter subsequently changed his mind and refused to make the payment. The promise to pay would not be enforced, as it was based on what is called in law 'past consideration'. The promise could have been enforced as a contract only if Richard Roe had agreed with John Doe, before the work was undertaken, that if John Doe would do the work, Richard Roe would pay him £5 for it, or if the work had been undertaken expressly at Richard Roe's request.

There are some dealings which might appear to give rise to a contract, although they do not, in fact, do so. This is particularly the case when the parties do not intend to bind themselves legally. For example, if you ask a friend to tea, for 'discussion of philosophy and investigation of subtleties', and he accepts your invitation and you buy some 'cakes and ale' for the occasion, you are not entering into a contract which involves a legal obligation. It is an incident of social life, and neither party intends legal consequences to arise from subsequent cancellation of the arrangement.

The terms of every contract are either express or implied. The express terms are those conditions which are expressly agreed between the parties. The implied terms are those which are not expressly included. Except in cases in which an Act of Parliament deems terms to be implied in a contract, Courts are always slow to imply a term in a contract. They have no power to do so unless two conditions are fulfilled. Firstly, the Court must be satisfied that if both parties had been asked to include the term when the contract was made, they would both have agreed that the proposed term was essential to their bargain. It may frequently be said that it would have been 'reasonable' to include a certain condition, but this will not be sufficient. Secondly, it is necessary to satisfy the Court that the implied term is required in order to give efficacy to the contract, and that the contract would be incomplete without it. For example, when a visitor to a Turkish bath was injured by the collapse of a couch on which he was reclining, he was awarded damages for breach of contract. Although it was not an express term of the contract that the couch should not collapse, the Court drew the inference, from the facts, that if the matter had been previously discussed between the parties, both would have agreed that a couch supplied to bathers should unquestionably be fit to lie on. The Court accordingly decided that both the essential conditions had been fulfilled, and they treated the misfortune as being the breach of an implied condition of the contract, awarding the bather damages for the injuries which he had sustained.

There is a widespread belief that a contract has no legal significance unless it is in writing. This opinion is, as a general rule, erroneous. Certain classes of contracts, which are dealt with in the next chapter, have to be recorded in writing, but in other cases the phrase 'his word is as good as his bond' may be legally true.

When two parties negotiate as a preliminary to a bargain, there will be no contract between them until one party makes an unequivocal offer which is unconditionally accepted. For example, if John Doe offers in writing to sell Richard Roe a house for £1,000, there will be no contract if Richard Roe agrees to buy the house 'subject to a surveyor's report'. If this condition is imposed, neither John Doe nor Richard Roe is under any legal obligation to the other, for the acceptance is not unequivocal.

For the same reason, the law will not enforce an agreement to make an agreement. If John Doe accepts an offer of £1,000 made by Richard Roe for the house, but adds words, to a receipt given for the deposit, that the acceptance is 'subject to an agreement to be approved by his solicitors', there is no contract, and neither of the parties is under any obligation to the other, except as to a return of the deposit. When a purchaser is anxious to buy a particular house, it may frequently happen that he will willingly pay an estate agent a deposit of 10 per cent of the purchase price in the belief that he has secured a legal right to the house. If, however, he looks closely at his receipt, he will usually find it contains the words 'subject to contract'. All he has agreed to do is to enter into an agreement. The acceptance is not unconditional. The fact that he has paid 10 per cent of the proposed purchase money has no binding effect.

If two parties intend to enter into a contract, there will, generally speaking, be no enforceable bargain if it subsequently appears that there has been a genuine confusion as to the identity of the object which was to be the subject of the bargain. This does not mean that John Doe will necessarily be relieved of his obligations if he makes a foolish mistake and agrees to buy a pedal cycle in the mistaken belief that he is purchasing a motor cycle. If he has acted in a way which will lead the vendor to believe that he is proposing to buy a pedal cycle, and the vendor, as a reasonable man, does in fact so believe, the law may hold John Doe to his bargain. The law may say that he is 'estopped' by his conduct from denying that he has agreed to the purchase. Estoppel is a doctrine which we shall meet in other chapters. It is applied on fixed principles to prevent a man from repudiating his own acts or conduct, when a stranger has relied upon them, and shaped his own conduct accordingly. In such a case, the law does not permit repudiation, because it would be inequitable or unfair to do so.

When a mistake arises in a written contract, it is a general principle that every man is assumed to have read and understood the document which he has signed. No one should ever sign any document unless he has read and understood the contents, for if a man is foolish enough to sign a document which binds him to buy a pedal cycle when he intended to buy a motor cycle, he cannot normally escape from the consequences of his folly. He may, however, be able to do so if he has been induced to sign the document by misrepresentation. This might arise when he had signed a contract for the purchase of a *pedal cycle* without reading it, because he had been told by the vendor and believed that the document referred to the purchase of a *motor cycle*. Such an action would normally be based upon fraud, a subject dealt with in Chapter 12. Analogous to such a case is that of 'duress' or 'undue influence'. A party enters into a contract under duress if he is compelled to do so under threat of physical violence, or even, in some cases, oppressive action short of actual threat. In such a case the contract may be avoided. 'Undue influence' arises when there is a special relationship between the contracting parties, such as parent and child, solicitor and client, or doctor and patient. In such instances the Court may find that the power to dominate has been unfairly exercised, and the contract may be repudiated.

When a mutual mistake is made in reducing a verbal agreement into writing, or in recording the terms of an agreement, it is sometimes possible, when the error is discovered, to obtain 'rectification' of the contract – i.e. the Court will order the document to be altered so as to represent the true bargain between the parties. It is, however, necessary to emphasize that the mistake must be a mutual one. It is not possible to obtain rectification of a contract when there is a mistake by one party only.

The damage you may recover for a breach of contract is such damage as flows directly from the breach. In the case of a tort a more generous measure is adopted, for the law will usually do its best to place the injured man in the same position as he would have been in if the tort had not been committed. After a fatal accident damages may be awarded to compensate the family of the deceased for the pecuniary loss they have suffered, and funeral expenses may be recovered. By a rather curious twist of the law the administrator or executor can also claim a sum to cover the loss of expectation of life. This is an extremely difficult figure to assess, and the Court is permitted to award only a 'very moderate' sum. 'Moderate' is a relative term, and the amount is not an assessment based on age, financial, or social circumstances. The Court must consider the value of the loss of prospective happiness, and in the case of a child the amount is reduced on account of the uncertainties of childhood. As a rule, sums of between £100 and £500 are awarded under this heading. The additional sum for loss of expectation of life is claimed on behalf of the deceased's estate, and would be available for the payment of his debts, but in practice it will normally be added to the compensation which his family will receive.

There are limits beyond which damages may not be awarded, because the claim is too remote from the accident which occasioned the loss. For example, if you break your leg in a motor accident due to the negligence of the driver of the car, you may recover the expense and loss which you incur as a result of the injury, as well as compensation for your pain and suffering. If, however, you do not fracture a bone, but suffer from shock, and your doctor orders you to spend a week in bed in order to recover from the shock, you are expected to obey the doctor's order. You cannot claim extra compensation if you suffer a relapse because you keep an important business appointment when you ought to be in bed. If the result of your disobedience to the doctor's order is a six months' illness, the damage you suffer is too remote from the original accident. It is the result of your disobedience of the doctor. This is not the responsibility of the driver of the car.

Damages are of two kinds, 'special damage' and 'general damage'. The former consists of the financial loss which is, in fact, caused by the wrongful act, e.g. loss of salary or wages, after making due allowance for income tax which would have been payable, doctors' fees and other proper out-of-pocket expenses. General damage covers the loss and suffering which cannot be measured exactly in terms of money. The principles to which we have referred usually limit the amount of damages which may be recovered for a breach of contract to 'special damage' – i.e. the actual loss which the aggrieved party has suffered. A man is not entitled in such a case to recover general damages. For example, a man who was dismissed from his employment and claimed general damages, because the circumstances in which he had been dismissed were of an ignominious character, failed in the House of Lords to recover compensation on this footing. His damages were limited to the actual loss of salary which he suffered by reason of his dismissal. A Court which allowed an actress general damages for breach of contract when she was dismissed from the principal part for which she had been engaged, because it took the question of her reputation into consideration when the compensation was assessed, did not depart from this principle. It allowed such compensation on the footing that it was an implied term of the contract that she should be permitted to appear in the principal part for which she had been engaged, and it considered that the refusal of the management to allow her to play the part was a breach which was bound to damage her prospects of increasing her reputation.

Sometimes the contract itself will prescribe the amount of the damages which are to be paid in the event of a breach. For example, a contract for the sale of a business may contain a condition which restricts the vendor from carrying on a competing business within a specified radius. The contract may also include a clause binding the vendor to pay a sum of £100, or some other specified amount, for any breach of this condition. The Courts will not, however, necessarily enforce such a clause. The obligation to pay a fixed sum of £100 may be regarded as a 'penalty', and not a fair measure of the damage suffered by the other party to the contract. Whether an agreed sum payable on the breach of a condition is a penalty, or a fair measure of assessed damage, is a question of fact in each case. If, in the judgement of the Court, it is regarded as a penalty, it will not be enforced, as it is against the policy of the law to impose payment, on a breach of contract, of a sum which is palpably in excess of any damage which may have been suffered by the aggrieved party.

You will find some further observations on the subject of damages in several other chapters. The subject is a fascinating one for an expectant recipient. He should, however, approach the subject intelligently. If you are a claimant, and a reasonable compromise is proposed to settle your claim, you may be foolish if you are over-confident and reject the offer without serious consideration, merely because it does not come up to your expectations. You should not forget that Judge Doe may only award £200 damages in a case in which Judge Roe might have awarded £1,000. Moreover, there are many instances when an apparently unanswerable claim has failed, owing to some unforeseen difficulty, and when this occurs, the plaintiff not only loses all, but may also be heavily out of pocket. To reject the substance for the shadow is always foolish. Be careful, if occasion arises, not to become a victim.

Finally a word of caution to everyone who receives a letter which contains an unjustified claim may not be out of place. Never ignore it! Many of us dislike writing letters, but if you throw a baseless demand in the waste-paper basket, and litigation subsequently ensues, you are almost certain to regret your folly in failing to repudiate the charge when it was first made. If you are in doubt as to the correct reply, seek early advice. By this method you may save your pocket substantial sums at a later date. As a corollary, it is also equally unwise to ignore a well-founded claim because you are temporarily short of cash. If you are being 'dunned' for a debt, it is always more prudent to meet your creditor and place your position frankly before him. There will be few cases in which you can suffer as a result of doing so, for a creditor rarely wishes to make an honest debtor bankrupt. While, therefore, you may expect to be able to arrange a satisfactory settlement if you pursue a policy of frankness, you will deserve no consideration if you decide upon prevarication as your method of approach.

3

CONTRACTS

'How agrees the Devil and thee about thy soul, that
thou soldest him on Good Friday last for a cup of
Madeira and a cold capon's leg?'
King Henry IV, Part 1

THE essential features of every contract were outlined in the
preceding chapter. There is no reason why a cup of madeira
and a cold capon's leg should not be good consideration to
support a contract, but whether or not the Court would consider a contract by the Devil to acquire a man's soul to be
against public policy is another matter. It might, of course,
depend on the man.

When you enter the realm of contract, it is in some respects
like entering a large West-End store. Which of the many departments do you want? One branch of the law of contract
deals with the relations between employer and employee, a
second with principal and agent, a third with vendor and purchaser, and there are a number of others. Each department has
its own special regulations, most of them based on the Common Law, but some on Statute Law, whilst there are some
features which are common to all. These common features are
dealt with in this chapter. When you have read it, it will be
easier for you to find your way about each of the departments
in turn, and when you leave the store you will understand
some of the basic principles which guide the Common Law of
England. You will have a better idea of the function of the law
and the extent of its development. Ignorance of the law is
never an excuse for infringement, as everyone is supposed to
know the law, although, in fact, no one knows the law, nor is
it possible for anyone to do so. It is an 'unfinished symphony'
which must always develop to meet the changing social character of the community. The function of a Judge when a question of law arises is both to construe any relevant Act of Parliament and to construe and apply any existing precedent of the
Common Law which will help him to elucidate the problem.
A Judge does not make new law – he applies the existing law

according to the construction which he places on the meaning of words and phrases.

It has been stated that most contracts may be verbal – that is, by word of mouth – but there are some which cannot be legally enforced unless their essential terms and conditions are reduced into writing. In each case the terms of the contract must be clear and specific, or capable of exact construction. They must not be vague or indefinite. The three ingredients mentioned in the previous chapter – viz. offer, acceptance, and consideration – are essential to every contract except one which is under seal. To speak of an 'understanding' as an agreement is misleading. It rarely has any legal significance when you say of your dealings with another that it was 'understood' that he should do a certain act. Either it was, in fact, agreed between you or it was not agreed. In the former case it is not an understanding, but an agreement, and in the latter case it is without legal effect. When you speak of an 'understanding', you refer, as a rule, to something which you yourself understood. It does not follow that the other party to the negotiations had a similar understanding. You should therefore always be careful to avoid anything which may be referred to simply as an 'understanding'.

A 'promise' is another feature of daily life which has ordinarily no legal significance. It cannot be enforced in law, because there is no consideration involved in a promise. If consideration is given for a promise, it ceases to be a promise and becomes a bargain, and enforceable as such.

A 'gentleman's agreement' is equally without legal significance, since it only binds the parties morally. The term is frequently applied to an 'agreement' which relates to betting or gambling. Such agreements, discussed in Chapter 11, are not enforceable in law, but in the eighteenth and nineteenth centuries 'debts of honour' frequently ranked higher than legal obligations, and even today some people consider it more meritorious to pay a gaming debt than to pay a tailor's account.

The contracts, the terms of which must be recorded in writing, signed by the person to be charged (i.e. sought to be held responsible) before they may be enforced in the event of subsequent default, were originally set out in a Statute called the Statute of Frauds, passed in the year 1677.

Two classes of such contracts, contracts which cannot be performed within one year and contracts for the sale of goods to the value of £10 and over, need no longer be recorded in writing owing to the Law Reform (Enforcement of Contracts) Act 1954. The two remaining and important classes of contract referred to in the Statute of Frauds are:

(1) *Contracts Relating to Land.* These are of wide application, and any agreement which you make relating to land must be recorded in writing, or it cannot, generally speaking, be enforced. This class of contract is dealt with in Chapters 16, 17, and 18.

(2) *Contracts of Guarantee.* John Doe may wish for an overdraft from his bankers, but they may be unwilling to lend him the money unless someone of standing is prepared to guarantee repayment of the loan. If you are prepared to act as guarantor, and the Bank is willing to accept you as a citizen of integrity who honours his engagements, it will not suffice for you to tell the bank manager that he may lend the money to John Doe and that you will accept responsibility for repayment. You will be asked to sign a document which will place your guarantee on record. The Bank is making a business deal, and, however honest you may be, your promise to guarantee a debt is of no value in law unless it is in writing. The form which you will be asked by the Bank to sign will not only contain your undertaking to pay the debt on demand, if Mr Doe defaults, but will also contain provisions to enable the Bank to enforce its rights against you, which are as extensive as those which it has against Mr Doe. You will, accordingly, be well advised, if a friend asks you to guarantee payment of a debt, to refuse to do so unless you are ready and willing to pay in cash on demand the maximum sum due under the guarantee.

When we say it is necessary for such a contract to be in writing, it is really loose speaking. It is not essential for the actual bargain which has been struck to be in writing at the time it is made. It may be done at any time. For example, on 1 January 1952 John Doe may verbally agree to buy a house from Richard Roe for £1,500. Although this verbal agreement cannot be legally enforced, the written memorandum, required to record the agreement, in order to make it an enforceable bargain, may be made at any subsequent date.

In some instances there are exceptions to the rule which requires these specified contracts to be recorded in writing. One of these exceptions arises when there has been what is called in law 'part performance' of a contract, generally relating to land, or an act equivalent to part performance. Part performance is some step taken by the party against whom enforcement is sought, which affords evidence of his intention to take the benefit of the contract. In such a case it would be inequitable to permit repudiation of the bargain. For instance, if you have verbally agreed to take a lease of premises on certain agreed terms, and the landlord lets you into possession before the contract is signed, and accepts the first payment of rent, there may be sufficient part performance of the contract to prevent either you or the landlord from avoiding the agreement.

Written contracts fall into two classes. They may be either ordinary signed agreements, which are described as agreements 'under hand', or they may be agreements 'under seal', which are contained in a 'deed', a formal document bearing a seal and 'signed, sealed, and delivered' by repetition of the words 'I deliver this as my Act and Deed' with a finger placed on the seal at the time of signing. It is the practice to execute deeds and documents in the presence of a witness, although it is not usually essential. In the absence of a witness, however, it may always be difficult to prove due signature in the event of dispute at a later date. Although husband and wife are competent witnesses to the signature of each other, neither can be compelled in criminal proceedings to give evidence against the other. To avoid argument it is, therefore, preferable for the witness to be an independent person. These observations do not apply to wills, and special attention is called to Chapter 26, which sets out the formalities required for the execution of a will. The law has a 'superstitious reverence' for a seal, and the formalities which attend the 'execution' of the deed, as the signing, sealing, and delivering is called, involve important legal consequences, for the doctrine of 'estoppel', referred to in the previous chapter, may come into operation. 'Estoppel by deed' means that, in the absence of fraud or misrepresentation, a party to a deed is not entitled to repudiate its contents, for after he has signed it he must accept every statement which it contains as being accurate.

There is nothing illegal in making a verbal contract which falls within one of the categories which require a written contract. The disadvantage of the verbal agreement will become apparent only if it is repudiated or broken by one of the parties. In the absence of the written memorandum the injured party will then be unable to obtain any legal redress.

The class of contracts known as 'illegal contracts' are in quite a different category. They may be illegal because they infringe an Act of Parliament, or they may be illegal because they are contrary to public policy. There is no precise definition of public policy, but when one approaches the subject one treads on 'unsafe and treacherous ground'. Generally speaking, an act against public policy is an act which is contrary to the moral law and spirit in which the business of the country, as a well-ordered community, is from time to time conducted. Contracts made for an immoral purpose, or designed to cause legal injury to third parties, or the performance of which would be an affront to the 'comity of nations', are examples of illegal contracts. If Doe and Roe enter into an agreement with each other deliberately and fraudulently to represent a picture as having been painted by Rubens, with a view to its sale, it is an illegal agreement. If Doe and Roe subsequently fall out, and Doe refuses to pay Roe his share of the swindle, the law will refuse to enforce the contract between them. Indeed, they may also be prosecuted, for an agreement between two or more persons which is designed to cause legal injury to a third may constitute the offence of conspiracy, a crime punishable by imprisonment as well as being a civil wrong.

There is another class of contract which is not illegal but may nevertheless be unenforceable. It is called a 'voidable contract'. A voidable contract is a contract made with a person who is 'under a disability'. For example, a person of unsound mind is under a disability, and cannot be held to the terms of a contract which he has made. Persons of unsound mind receive very particular care and protection from the law. They should never be described as 'lunatics', for they are known to the Courts as 'patients'. If a person becomes unable to manage his affairs by reason of mental incapacity, the proper course for his relatives is to apply to the Court of Protection for the appointment of a receiver, who will be authorized to manage the affairs of the 'patient' under strict control. A contract made with a person of unsound mind is known as voidable and not void, because the receiver, on behalf of the patient, need not necessarily refuse to recognize its validity but may be authorized to accept it. If this is done, the contract is said to be 'ratified', and it then becomes enforceable. Unless, however, it is so approved it is of no legal effect, because the law will not bind a man to an agreement when he is not capable of understanding and appreciating the nature of his acts. Infants – i.e. persons under twenty-one years of age – are in a similar category to persons of unsound mind in this respect. Consequently a contract with an infant is not generally binding on the infant, and such contracts are considered in Chapter 23. Married women, previously under a disability and unable to enter into contracts, are now capable of contracting without legal restraint.

The remedy for the breach of a contract may be either by way of damages or by specific performance – i.e. an order from the Court directing the defaulting party to fulfil his obligations. The Court will, generally speaking, order specific performance of a contract only in a case in which damages would prove an inadequate remedy. If you agree to purchase a house, it is sometimes difficult to assess the compensation which it would be fair to award, if the agreement is broken by the vendor. No two houses are exactly alike, and you may accordingly ask the Court to order the vendor to complete the sale. If, on the other hand, you enter into an agreement with a decorator to repaint your house, and you stop him working when the house is half-painted, the law will not compel you to allow him to finish the work. The amount of damage which he has suffered can be exactly measured. It will be equivalent to any expense which he has incurred, together with the profit which he would have made if the contract had been completed. The Court may order you to pay that amount by way of damages.

A breach of contract may sometimes be restrained by the Court by granting an 'injunction'. An injunction is a peremptory order which restrains a person from committing an act which is a breach of his legal duty, or orders him to carry out a specific obligation. We shall meet the term again when we come to Chapter 13. The person against whom the injunction is granted will be guilty of contempt of Court if he disregards its terms, and he may then be committed to prison until such time as he is deemed to have purged his contempt.

A contract is said to be 'performed' or 'discharged' when all the obligations have been fulfilled on both sides. Sometimes it is not possible to complete a contract. If a fruit merchant agreed in 1938 to import 1,000 tons of bananas a year from Jamaica for each of the five following years, it would have been impossible to complete the contract because it became illegal to import bananas shortly after the outbreak of the war. In such circumstances the contract is said to be 'frustrated', and, generally speaking, neither party is under any obligation to the other after the date of frustration, although in certain cases payments which have already been made under the contract may be recovered. Again, the subject-matter of the contract may cease to exist. If your house had been destroyed by fire before the decorator had commenced to paint it, in accordance with the terms of his contract, there would be nothing left to paint. The contract has been frustrated, and if the fire was not due to any fault on your part, it will be discharged without further liability on either side.

A contract may also be brought to an end by repudiation. Repudiation is a refusal to be bound by the terms of the contract, or conduct which makes it clear that the defaulting party does not intend to fulfil his part of the contract, even before the date for performance has arrived. Some examples have already been given. Not every breach of a contract is an act of repudiation. When an employee is guilty of absenteeism, he may be breaking his contract of employment, which requires him to attend his work daily. He is not, however, as a rule, intending to repudiate the contract. He is absent one day, but comes to work on the following day, and he is not acting in a way which justifies a contention that he does not intend to fulfil the contract. If a condition of a contract is broken, it is a question of fact, in each case, as to whether the breach is of such a character as to justify a claim that the person in breach had no longer any intention of being bound by the terms of the contract. When a contract is repudiated, the other party may accept the repudiation, or may refuse to do so, and insist upon holding the defaulting party to the bargain. In either event he may claim damages for breach of contract.

The death of one of the parties to a contract will not normally affect its validity, except in the case of a contract for personal services, when the contract will be discharged or terminated. In other cases, the personal representatives of the estate of the deceased person will stand in his place, and the provisions of the contract may normally be enforced by either party.

It has been observed that contracts are a feature of daily life. It is doubtful, however, if the average man appreciates the extent to which they enter into his affairs.

He gets up in the morning, and after breakfast he leaves for his work by train, tram, or bus. Whichever method of travel he adopts, it involves a contract – an agreement by the transport organization to carry him to his destination in consideration of the payment of the fare. He arrives at his work, and his employment is regulated by contract. At midday he visits a restaurant or café for dinner – another act which involves a contractual relationship between the proprietor of the restaurant and himself, as the restaurant proprietor may learn to his cost if the customer subsequently suffers from an attack of food poisoning. After his meal he returns to his work, and perhaps he may make a telephone call, or write a letter to his Insurance Company enclosing a cheque for a renewal premium, which he later drops in the pillar-box. The cheque is drawn as a result of a contract between himself and his bankers, the payment of the renewal premium results from a contract between himself and the Insurance Company, while both the telephone connexion and the delivery of the letter are effected as a result of a contract with the Post Office. When our friend returns home in the evening he may do so by the same form of transport as when he set out, and finally, if he is a married man, he will find, when he arrives home, that during his absence his wife has been shopping – and every purchase she has made has involved business of a contractual character.

Every one of these contracts is regulated by conditions which are accepted by the parties. They are always at liberty to include any terms in a contract so long as such terms are not illegal or contrary to public policy. Every such contract involves legal rights and obligations which will be enforced by the Courts. However, there is a type of clause sometimes to be found in a contract often known as an 'exemption clause', which relieves a party from liability in the event of his committing a breach. Nearly everyone has, as we have seen, to enter into contracts which have to be taken as they stand with no question of arguing over the terms. When a breach of contract occurs, an exemption clause may prevent damages from being obtained. The Courts may sometimes prevent an exemption clause from taking effect, on the ground that the party relying on its protection has committed an act or caused a misunderstanding which can justly be held to lead to the clause being overriden.

When you seek advice and inquire as to your contractual rights against another member of the community, the answer must always be 'What did you agree? What were the terms of your contract?' When the terms of a contract are clear and specific, it will be easier to define the legal rights of parties if there is any subsequent disagreement between them. If, however, the parties fail to define the conditions of their contract in precise terms, it is not reasonable to blame the law for being unwilling and unable to do so.

4

EMPLOYER AND EMPLOYEE

'The wages of sin is death, but the wages of engineers
are worse.'
> Banner at Engineering Union Meeting
> reported by B.B.C. in 9 p.m. news on
> 23 March 1946

THE law which governs the relationship between employer
and employee is known as the law of Master and Servant – not,
perhaps, a very happy expression to describe the relations
which should exist between the owner of a business or industry and those who work in it and are expected to help to
establish its prosperity.

In most cases a man's employment is not governed by any
written document. Nevertheless, every such employment
necessarily implies a contract or agreement. A written agreement is not legally necessary, except in a few special cases.

When you apply for a job, you will, of course, be vitally
interested in the hours of work and the amount of the wages
or salary which you are to receive. As is generally known, the
law requires income tax to be deducted from all salaries or
wages before payment – a matter which is dealt with in Chapter 28. Manual workers must always be paid in cash, and the
cost of such things as meals in the works canteen cannot be
deducted from the wage packet without the written consent of
the worker to the deduction. In the absence of any agreement
to the contrary, you are entitled, unless you are engaged on
piece-work, to receive the agreed wage or salary during the
entire term of your employment. Your right to recover payment during periods when you are absent through illness or
other unavoidable cause is a question of fact which depends in
each case on the terms of employment. If nothing has been
said on the subject, the Court must draw an inference, from
the evidence, as to the intention of the parties. The obligations
of the employee include an obligation to attend to his work
during the prescribed hours, and if he deliberately stays away –
i.e. voluntary absenteeism – his employer is entitled to make a

claim for damages against him for breach of agreement. The amount of the damages, if such a claim is made, will normally be the loss which the employer has suffered as a result of the worker's absence, and may include the additional cost of any substitute employed to replace him. If you are a worker who is being paid by piece-work, you will not be entitled, in the absence of agreement, to receive payment during periods when you are away either through illness or other cause.

If you are injured when you are working, you are now entitled to receive compensation under the National Insurance (Industrial Injuries) Acts 1946 to 1957. These Acts replaced the Workmen's Compensation Acts, and apply to accidents occurring after 5 July 1948, the same date as the National Health Service came into operation. Under them the State accepts responsibility for compensation for industrial injuries, and makes it part of the country's system of social security. All persons employed in Great Britain under any contract of service or apprenticeship are insurable without income limit. In addition, compensation may be paid to other industrial workers, such as lifeboat crews, taxi-drivers, seamen carried in British-owned ships, and certain airmen employed in British aircraft, but most casual workers are not included. Both employer and employee are required to pay weekly premiums to provide for the fund out of which the compensation will be paid.

Compensation under the Acts falls into three classes: (1) injury benefit; (2) disablement benefit, which is sub-divided into two sections – (a) a disablement gratuity and (b) a disablement pension; and (3) death benefit.

'Injury Benefit' is payable to an insured person for every day of incapacity within six months from the date of the accident, but unless the disability lasts for twelve days, no benefit is payable for the first three days. The benefit, now 67s. 6d. a week for a single adult, is commensurately larger for a married claimant, and allowances for children and other dependants may be added. A recipient will frequently have to obtain further aid from the National Assistance Board.

'Disablement Benefit' is payable to an insured person who has not recovered within six months, but is suffering from physical or mental disability which is likely to be either of a permanent or substantial nature. The benefit may be varied from time to time in the event either of improvement in health or a relapse. If the disability is permanent, but less than 20 per cent in extent, the benefit takes the form of a gratuity instead of a pension. When the extent of disability is not less than 20 per cent, the pension payable is fixed according to the seriousness of the disability.

The local medical tribunal examines the disabled person and, as laid down in regulations, makes a provisional or final assessment of the percentage loss of mental or physical faculty. Blindness, deafness, and double amputation may provide examples of 100 per cent loss of faculty. The assessment is reached without referring to the claimant's individual circumstances, e.g. his capacity before injury for some highly skilled work, but is based on the physical and mental standard of the average person of the claimant's age and sex.

Both the Minister and the disabled person have a right of appeal against an assessment to a medical appeal tribunal which re-examines the claimant. In the case of a provisional assessment the claimant is barred from appealing within a period of two years.

'Death Benefit' is payable to certain classes of dependants when death results from the accident. A widow who was residing with the deceased or being maintained by him is entitled to a pension for life, or until re-marriage, and a gratuity on re-marriage equivalent to a year's pension. A widower, if he was wholly or mainly supported by the deceased, and permanently incapable of self-support, receives a life pension. Weekly allowances are payable for children of the deceased, and parents and dependent relatives, including an 'unmarried wife', are entitled to a small pension under prescribed conditions.

All these provisions relate to accidents. Regulations have, however, been made under the Acts for the payment of compensation when the nature of the insured's employment leads to disease, when that disease is on the Minister's list for the insured's occupation. Additions are not infrequently made to these lists.

To qualify for compensation in one of the three prescribed

classes the personal injury which the insured has received must have been caused by an accident 'arising out of and in the course of his employment'. This phrase, reproduced from the earlier Workmen's Compensation Acts, sounds easy and simple to construe. It has, however, been the subject of a great deal of litigation, and illustrates how apparently elementary language may present difficult problems of interpretation.

It is probable, however, that many of these difficulties no longer exist under the provisions of the present Acts, since clauses have been included which extend substantially the rights of the worker to compensation. For example, an accident is now to be deemed to arise 'out of and in the course of the employment', although at the time of the accident the worker may have been acting, in certain circumstances, without instructions, or even in defiance of regulations or orders actually given to him, provided that the accident would otherwise have been covered by the Acts, and further provided that the act was done for the purpose of and in connexion with the employer's trade or business. Moreover, for the purposes of the Acts, an accident arising 'in the course of' employment is now to be deemed also to have arisen 'out of' that employment, in the absence of evidence to the contrary.

Local insurance officers appointed by the Minister administer the Acts, and disputes are referred to special tribunals and sometimes where points of law are concerned to the High Court. The High Court has jurisdiction, where for instance the Minister's regulations, which have statutory force, are not properly followed.

The claim to compensation under the Acts is not necessarily the only remedy open to a man injured at his work, for irrespective of the right of an employee to recover compensation under the Acts, an employer owes a duty to his employee at Common Law not to do any act calculated to cause him injury. If he neglects this duty, and injury results, damages may be assessed on the same basis as they are assessed in any other case of negligence, only a partial allowance being made for the benefits likely to be received by the employee under the system of Industrial Injuries Insurance mentioned above. The negligent act may be a failure to exercise proper precautions.

The Courts have held that where a one-eyed man was employed on work involving danger to the eyes the employer should have been especially careful, because 'risk of greater injury is greater risk of injury'. Or it may be a breach of a statutory duty – i.e. a duty expressly prescribed by law. For example, the Factory Acts, generally speaking, require machinery to be fenced, in order to minimize danger to employees, and if, as a result of the employer's neglecting this duty, injury results to one of his employees, the employer may be sued. Although a man is working at an unfenced machine, however, he must be careful not to do any foolhardy act. Otherwise, in the event of an accident, his employer may plead that the foolhardy act was the immediate or proximate cause of the accident, and if he is able to prove this he may escape from liability.

It is a principle of the Common Law that the employer is liable for the negligence of his employee, but until 1948 he could generally escape liability if the person injured by the negligent employee was not an outsider but a fellow employee. An employee was deemed to accept the possibility of injury by a negligent fellow employee as one of the risks inherent in his employment. This escape for employers was sealed when the doctrine of common employment was abolished by the Law Reform (Personal Injuries) Act 1948, and an employer is now liable to pay damages to any employee who is injured by the negligence of a fellow employee in the course of his employment.

If an employee is engaged upon employment of a particularly hazardous character, and he meets with an accident due to the dangerous nature of the work, he may not be able to claim compensation, other than under the National Insurance Acts. The employer is entitled to contend that, as the worker has voluntarily undertaken the risk, he cannot recover compensation for an accident which work of that character may have been expected to entail.

This doctrine is, however, out of favour with the Courts, and an employer must consider each employee individually. The ordinary man must earn his living, and if the only work open to him is of a hazardous character, acceptance or refusal of it may involve little freewill. The doctrine will therefore be applied only when the acceptance of the risk is voluntary in the true sense of the word. For example, it would apply in the case of a cinema actor injured by jumping out of a burning building as part of a film. It did not, however, apply during the Second World War in the case of an engine-driver who drove his engine into a bomb crater. He was instructed to drive his engine cautiously after an air raid, and he did so. Nevertheless, it fell in the crater, and the driver was injured. The Court decided that the company had no right to order the driver to proceed in the circumstances, until proper steps had been taken by the railway officials to satisfy themselves that the line was clear. It was not a case in which the driver had voluntarily undertaken a hazardous risk, for an engine-driver does not expect to expose himself to such a risk when he undertakes to drive an engine.

When a man is dismissed from his employment, a question frequently arises as to whether or not he has received proper notice to terminate his employment. If there is a contract in writing, provision should be made as to the length of notice which is to be given on either side. If, however, the employment is verbal, and nothing is said at the time of employment as to the length of notice required, a man is entitled to receive and is required to give 'reasonable' notice. 'Reasonable' notice is a question of fact. In a few instances the length of notice deemed to be reasonable is established by custom. For example, a domestic servant who is paid monthly has established, by custom, the right to receive one calendar month's notice. At the other end of the scale there are cases in which an hour's notice only is customary. For the sake of good relations between employer and employee, and to reduce fear of unemployment and unofficial strikes, both equally damaging to the community, it may be hoped that the Government will introduce legislation to make it illegal for either party to end the contract at an hour's notice.

When there is no express agreement or custom, the question as to what is reasonable notice is one of fact. Each case must be treated on its merits. Generally speaking, if you receive your wages weekly, you are entitled to receive a week's notice, as this is a reasonable notice. If you are paid by the month, you are entitled to a month's notice. The principal factors which have to be taken into consideration when determining the question of reasonable notice are the importance of the work and the ease or difficulty with which the employee will be able to obtain other employment of a similar character, and with which the employer may be able to replace the employee.

If a man is guilty of wilful disobedience to a proper order given to him in the course of his employment, or if he is guilty of gross misconduct, his employer is entitled to dismiss him summarily – i.e. without any notice. If he is paid a fixed weekly wage, he is not, in that event, entitled to a proportion of his week's money. Each week is treated as a separate period of employment, and a man is not entitled to half a week's pay for half a week's work, if he is summarily dismissed for wilful misconduct in the middle of the week. An employer must, however, exercise his right of dismissal in such a case without delay. He cannot use the pretext of 'wilful misconduct' to dismiss a man summarily a fortnight after the alleged misconduct has come to his notice. Unless he acts promptly, and as soon as the misconduct is known to him, he loses his right of summary dismissal.

If a man is dismissed without proper notice, he is entitled to claim damages for wrongful dismissal. In that event, it is his duty to try to find other employment, so as to mitigate the damage which follows from the breach of contract. Wrongful dismissal of an employee, without notice, is on the same footing as any other breach of contract. If you are being paid £18 a week, and you are dismissed without notice, but can satisfy the Court that three months' notice would have been a reasonable notice, you will be entitled to claim £234 damages. However, it was decided by the House of Lords a few years ago that the actual damages awarded for loss of wages or income must not include an amount held to represent the income tax which might have become payable had the wages or income been received in the normal way. The amount of the reduction cannot be estimated exactly, since not even a Court of law can be expected to declare what might have happened had no ground for an action ever existed. The Court has to do its best to arrive at the most likely figure. The damages received will not be liable to tax. Nor is the sum deducted for the estimated tax paid over to the tax collector. Also, if you have obtained other employment during the three months in question, or if you could have done so if you had been diligent, you must give credit against the damages for the amount which you have earned or might have earned during that period.

There is a term implied in every contract of employment which requires the employee to serve the employer faithfully. The acceptance of a secret commission, or bribe, is a breach of that duty, and may also be a criminal offence. It is more specifically dealt with in Chapter 5. The employee is also under an obligation to obey all lawful instructions given to him by his employer which fall within the scope of his employment, and he must never disclose his employer's business secrets. Holidays are a matter for express agreement between the parties. In the absence of agreement, and subject to the rights established in certain trades, an employee's legal right to insist upon a holiday may be difficult to establish.

After the termination of his employment, a man is entitled to use, for his own benefit, any information which he has received which has improved his skill or knowledge of his trade. A former employee must not, however, make use of any secret process or invention which it was part of his duty to discover in the course of his employment. These belong to his former employer. He is also not entitled to remove any papers or documents which belong to his employer. There is, however, nothing to prevent him from approaching customers of his former employer and soliciting their custom, provided he has approached only those whose names he retains in his memory. He is not entitled to take their names from any list of customers which he has appropriated or copied. A contract that he shall not compete with, or help a competitor of his former employer, must not place an unreasonable restraint on his future work.

An employee is not entitled to require a reference from his former employer, but if the employer gives him a reference it must be fairly and honestly given, or the employee may have a right of action for defamation, a subject dealt with in Chapter 15.

Good relations between employer and employee are essential to the welfare of the community. Both parties may be to blame when they are lacking, for there are both bad employers and bad employees. Bad employers were responsible for the birth of the Trade Union movement, but we have made progress since the days when a Trade Union was regarded in law as being an illegal combination. Any worker in these days who does not join a Union which is applicable to his trade is weakening a system which has proved of inestimable value, for the work performed by the Unions in bettering the conditions of employment is beyond calculation.

No worker ought to criticize his Union because it requires its members to fulfil their legal obligations, and to give a proper notice before withholding their labour. The repeal in 1946 of the Trade Disputes and Trade Union Act 1927 placed the Trade Unions in the same powerful position as they were in before the General Strike of 1926, but their legal rights and obligations are still governed in many respects by Acts of Parliament and are still somewhat obscure.

In 1955 after many years of the contrary view being thought correct, the House of Lords, although not unanimous, decided that a registered Trade Union should be regarded as having an identity of its own apart from its members for the purposes of the law of contract. The precedent was established that a member of a Union who is wrongfully expelled may be able to claim damages against his Union for breach of contract. Such a contract is usually constituted by the rules of the Union, because subject to certain overriding statutory qualifications, the rules of a Union govern the rights of its members as between themselves and their organization.

In some respects Trade Unions may appear to be privileged. They are exempted by the Trade Disputes Act 1906 from liability for any tort committed by them. Strikes and threats of strikes are prevented from being unlawful, as they would otherwise be for being in restraint of trade and for interfering with contracts of employment. A Union's funds, essential for its bargaining power, are also safeguarded. Individual members of a Union are not, of course, exempt from liability for tortious acts, except in so far as they may be acts which are merely in restraint of trade or an interference with contracts of employment, done in contemplation or furtherance of a trade dispute and which are within certain limits. Peaceful picketing is, for instance, legal.

A trade unionist need not contribute anything towards his Union's political fund, if he does not so wish, since he has a statutory right to refuse to pay the political levy which is a prominent feature of nearly all the sizeable Unions.

5

PRINCIPAL AND AGENT

'Our friend has exceeded his instructions again.
So much the worse for him.'
The Man of Property

AN agent is a person who is authorized to carry out an act for and on behalf of another man, who is called the principal. The primary duty of the agent is to act in good faith towards his principal, and to devote to the interests of his principal such care and attention as a man of ordinary prudence bestows on his own affairs. Sometimes the agency business may be carried out in the name of the agent, but usually it is carried out in the name of the principal. In most cases the agent must himself carry out the duties for which he is appointed. He is not allowed to delegate them to other parties, unless he is specially authorized to do so.

You may have dealings with agents several times in the course of a day. In many cases the contracts referred to in Chapter 3 are made with agents. When you travel by bus, the conductor to whom you pay your fare is an agent, as well as an employee, of the transport organization. He is authorized, as an agent, to accept your fare and to issue you with a ticket. When you telephone, the telephone operator is the agent of the Postmaster-General. If you instruct a solicitor on a business matter, which involves negotiations or dealings with a third party on your behalf, he carries out those negotiations or dealings as your agent.

If Richard Roe, as an agent for John Doe, enters into a written agreement with you, he will usually do so in the name of John Doe. He will sign the agreement 'For and on behalf of John Doe, Richard Roe'. Alternatively, he may sign 'John Doe, p.p. Richard Roe'; 'p.p.' means *per procurationem*, or by the agency of Richard Roe. If Richard Roe signs in a way which makes it clear that he is signing as an agent, and not on his own account, he cannot, generally speaking, be held personally liable on the contract. So long as he has acted within the scope of his authority, John Doe will be the only person bound by the contract. If there is a subsequent breach of the contract, you may only make a claim against John Doe. On the other hand, the agent may be made personally responsible, if he has exceeded his instructions.

If you are going abroad, you may wish to appoint an agent to manage your business affairs for you during your absence. In that event, you may give him a document under seal called a 'power of attorney', in which you appoint him to be your attorney or agent, and authorize him to carry out specified acts on your behalf and in your name for a specified period. There will be a clause in the document by which you agree to ratify and confirm everything your attorney does on your behalf within the scope of his defined powers. It is necessary to make the power irrevocable for a specified period, as otherwise any person proposing to deal with your attorney would have no assurance that the power was still operative. During the currency of the power of attorney you are bound by every act done by your attorney within the scope of his authority. Even if you die before the specified period has elapsed, the power is not revoked unless notice of your death has come to the knowledge of your attorney and to any person who is dealing with your attorney. If your attorney conceals your death and continues to act on the power, strangers, acting in good faith, are entitled to rely upon it and to make a claim against the personal representatives who are dealing with your estate after your death.

After the expiration of the specified period, the power of attorney may still be effective. After that time, however, anyone dealing with your attorney should ask for evidence that the power has not in fact been revoked. He should satisfy himself that you are still living and that it is still in force. If he does not do so, you or your estate may not be bound, if in fact you have revoked the power, or have died.

Usually, an agent acts under less extensive powers than those conferred on him by a power of attorney. If, for example, you wish to sell or let a house you will probably instruct an estate agent. He is an agent of a particular class who deals with the buying and selling of properties. You give him a limited authority to negotiate the sale or letting of your house for a specified purchase price or a particular rent. It is his duty to endeavour to obtain a purchaser or tenant in accordance with your instructions, and he must not do any act which is in conflict with this duty. He must not try to persuade you to accept a lower price for the house, because it will be more advantageous to him to sell it quickly, before it is sold through another agent. As a general rule, estate agents do not receive remuneration except when their efforts have led to success, and they are then paid on a commission basis. If you have notified the agent that you have appointed other agents to find a purchaser, and that you will pay a commission only to the agent who introduces the purchaser, he will naturally be anxious to strike a bargain as quickly as possible. He must not, however, allow this to influence his duty to you, even though he will receive no remuneration or commission for the trouble he has taken, if the purchaser is introduced by another agent.

If an agent negotiates the sale of your house for less than the figure you have authorized him to obtain, you are not bound by the transaction. He will not only have been guilty of a breach of his duty to you, but will also have laid himself open to an action for damages by the prospective purchaser of the house.

If you appoint more than one agent to find a purchaser for your house, you may become liable to pay commission to any agent who has given an order to view to the purchaser. To avoid this risk, you should notify each of the agents at the time when you give them your instructions that you will pay only one commission if the house is sold, and that any dispute as to which agent has introduced the purchaser must be adjusted between the agents themselves.

If you appoint an agent as a sole agent for a limited period, it will give him greater incentive to find a purchaser for your house, as it gives him a better chance of earning his commission. At the same time you will be irrevocably committing yourself to the payment of a commission to that agent if the property is sold by him or any other agent during the period of his sole agency, as sole agency means an unqualified right to act on your behalf during the period of the agency. Accordingly, if you sell the house through another agent, it will be a breach of your obligation to the sole agent. He will be entitled to claim the commission which he would have earned if it had not been for the breach of your agreement appointing him as sole agent.

The commission charged by an estate agent varies according to the price of the property sold, or the rent of the property let. Particulars of the recognized scales laid down by the Institute of Auctioneers and Estate Agents are appended at the end of this chapter. Additional charges may be made when the property is offered for sale by auction.

If an agent asks you to sign a written authority for him to act, you should read the authority carefully before you sign it, and satisfy yourself that it does not provide for commission in excess of the recognized scale of the Institute. An estate agent is not bound to work on the Institute scale if he can find members of the public who are willing to pay him excessive fees.

An estate agent is not usually entitled to his commission unless he has introduced a purchaser who in fact completes the purchase of the property. The question as to whether the agent has earned his remuneration is in every instance a question of fact, which depends on the terms of the contract between the agent and his client. If his client withdraws the property from the market after he has found a purchaser, but before the binding contract is made, he may be deprived of his commission, and may have no claim for remuneration.

If you are a prospective purchaser, and obtain particulars of a house from an estate agent, you must remember he is not your agent. He is the agent of the seller of the house. He does not ordinarily owe you, as the prospective purchaser, any duty. An estate agent will owe a duty to a purchaser only if he has received express instructions from the purchaser to find a house, and if he is to receive remuneration for so doing. Otherwise, a purchaser must not rely upon the agent to volunteer any information about the house. He must make his own inquiries. This does not mean that the agent is entitled to furnish a purchaser with untrue or misleading particulars about the property. If the agent makes untrue representations, as a result of which the purchaser agrees to purchase the property, the latter may be able to repudiate the contract. If there was no deliberate intention to mislead, and the erroneous particulars were furnished innocently, the purchaser's rights are usually limited to rescission of the agreement. If, however, the false or misleading particulars were given recklessly or deliberately, the purchaser may also be able to claim damages for fraud.

When an agent is appointed for a specific purpose, he is usually entitled to carry out the work in his own time. He has no fixed hours, and, subject to any express agreement to the contrary, he is entitled to use his own methods to carry out his duties. He is not at the beck and call of his principal, and he is not required to carry out any duty which is outside the scope of the purpose for which he has been appointed as agent.

This liberty of action does not, however, necessarily apply when an agent acts in a dual capacity, and his principal is also his employer. A London bus conductor who collects your fare does so as an agent of the London Transport Executive. He is also an employee of the Executive. He has to work fixed hours, and the terms of his employment are strictly regulated. His freedom of action as an agent is of very limited scope. He may collect your fare at any time while you are on the bus, but otherwise he has no real discretion as to the method of carrying out his duty as an agent. A railway booking clerk who issues tickets has even less scope. Nevertheless, he is acting as an agent of the Transport Commission every time he issues a ticket. When you have dealings with Richard Roe as an employee of John Doe, you do not as a rule treat with him as an employee, but as an agent. The fact that he is an employee of John Doe as well as his agent is, generally speaking, irrelevant, so far as you are concerned.

When John Doe sends his servant, Richard Roe, to purchase groceries from the local Stores – and a bottle of whisky – the relation between John Doe and Richard Roe is that of master and servant, but Richard Roe is the agent of John Doe for the purpose of making the purchases. If John Doe has no account with the Stores, and the groceries are paid for in cash, neither the question of employment nor of agency is likely to arise. The manager of the Stores will not know, and will not be interested to know, whether Richard Roe is purchasing the groceries and whisky for his own account or for John Doe. If, however, the transaction is not a cash transaction, and John Doe has a credit account with the Stores, different considerations will arise. These considerations will usually be based on the laws which govern the relationship of principal and agent. The Stores will have no greater and no lesser right because Richard Roe happens to be also the employer of John Doe, and when Richard Roe orders the groceries on credit, he will do so as the authorized agent for John Doe. It follows that, if the latter fails to pay the account, the Stores will not be able to make any claim against Richard Roe.

Transactions of this character seldom result in complications, but difficult legal problems arise when an agent does an act which is outside the scope of his authority, or if he acts fraudulently. If Richard Roe is dishonest, he may obtain whisky from the Stores for John Doe's account without any authority from John Doe. If he misappropriates the whisky, the question of John Doe's liability to the Stores for payment is likely to arise.

The general legal rule is that a principal is liable for the fraud of his agent if the fraud is committed within the scope of the agent's actual or implied authority, but he is not liable if the fraudulent act was outside the scope of his actual or implied authority. It is therefore necessary in each instance to examine the relevant facts.

If John Doe has established a practice of sending his servant Richard Roe to purchase grocery and whisky from the Stores on credit, he will have held out Richard Roe to the Stores as his agent authorized to make the purchases for him. Ordering and fetching goods will accordingly be within the scope of his actual authority. If, therefore, Richard Roe, in fraud of his principal, keeps back a bottle of whisky which he has received, John Doe will usually be liable to the Stores for payment.

A similar result will follow if John Doe terminates Richard Roe's authority to purchase goods, but fails to notify the Stores that the authority has been revoked. In that case, when Richard Roe continues to order goods, he will be acting within the scope of his apparent or implied authority. The Stores will have no means of knowing that the actual authority has been terminated unless they are informed of this by John Doe.

On the other hand, if it has been the practice for Richard Roe to take a written order to the Stores each week, and if, contrary to this usual practice, the Stores foolishly deliver goods to Richard Roe without a written order, they cannot make John Doe pay the account in the event of Richard Roe's misappropriating the goods. As it was outside the scope of his actual or implied authority to take delivery of goods on a verbal order, the Stores must bear the loss if they cannot recover payment from Richard Roe.

There is much common sense in these principles, which are based on the general legal doctrine that when two innocent parties have been victimized by the fraud of a third party, the innocent party who by his conduct has enabled the fraud to be perpetrated must bear the loss. If your agent has defrauded the Stores through no fault of their own, it is, generally speaking, more reasonable that you should have to bear the loss than the Stores. You appoint your agent, you make inquiries as to his integrity, and you have an opportunity of judging his reliability. The Stores, who have been in the habit of carrying out your instructions through his agency, have no means of investigating these matters, and it is not their business to inquire. If, on the other hand, the manager at the Stores is imprudent enough to give your agent goods on a verbal request, although he has always received your written orders, it would be unfair if the loss were to fall on your shoulders. The Stores suffer a loss because their manager, as their agent, has failed to carry out your instructions to supply goods on a written order. Moreover, when two people transact business together over a prolonged period, each is entitled to assume that the normal course of dealing will be continued, unless and until any variation is notified to the other. If you lull a person into a certain state of belief by a particular course of conduct, it is proper you should notify him of any change in your arrangements. If you do not do so, it is logical for the law to say you are 'estopped' by your conduct from relying upon facts which have not been expressly brought to his notice, and to hold you responsible for any consequent loss or damage which he may have suffered. From a practical point of view, you should have the same consideration for the rights of others as you expect them to have for your rights. If, accordingly, you terminate your relations with an agent, you should notify every person who has had dealings with him, in order to make certain that you will be relieved of responsibility for his further actions.

It should be added that Richard Roe would himself be liable for payment of the goods, which he has fraudulently failed to deliver to his principal. In many cases he might not be in a position to meet the liability, and in some instances a criminal charge might be preferred against him for the fraud. If the acts done by Richard Roe, as an agent, fall short of fraud he may still be sued for damages in any case in which he has claimed without authority to act as agent. By his conduct he is said to have 'warranted' himself as having authority to act on behalf of John Doe – i.e. he has held himself out as having such authority. A claim will then lie for damages for breach of 'warranty of authority'. The Stores would be entitled to claim as damages the amount of the loss which they have suffered as a result of his breach of warranty.

There are many occasions when you have to consider the relation of principal and agent. Chapter 2 included a brief survey of the legal liability of the employer for his employee's negligence in certain cases. The principles there referred to are, generally speaking, equally applicable in the case of principal and agent. In Chapter 24 reference is made to the right of a wife, in certain circumstances, to pledge her husband's credit for necessaries as an 'agent of necessity'. In Chapter 7 the question of agency in connexion with partnerships is considered, for every partner in a firm is an agent of the firm for certain purposes. Limited liability companies, explained in Chapters 19 and 20, also introduce many agency problems, for each of the directors of a limited liability company may be an agent of the Company, when he contracts with a third party on behalf of the Company.

Among many other classes of agents mention must be made of a broker, who is an agent who carries out negotiations for the sale of various types of goods and chattels, and also stocks and shares. A broker may act in a dual capacity, for he is entitled to enter into a binding contract, on behalf of both the vendor and the purchaser, in respect of the subject-matter of the deal. This contract is frequently made in a recognized form, customary in that class of transaction. For example, a contract for the sale and purchase of shares will usually be effected by a stockbroker, who is a member of a Stock Exchange, and the contract, in a standard form, will be declared to be subject to the rules and regulations of the Stock Exchange.

Sometimes the agreement by which the principal appoints an agent is in writing, and sometimes it is verbal. In most cases, unless the agency is of simple character, it is preferable to have a written agreement. The contents of such an agreement must, of course, vary according to the nature of the agency, but here are some points to be observed in the case of an agency for the sale of goods – a very normal type of agency:

(1) The exact scope of the agency should be described.

(2) The duration of the agency should be specified. Normally, the death or bankruptcy of the principal or the agent will terminate the agency.

(3) The remuneration to be paid to the agent for his services should be stated. If he is to be paid on a commission basis he will be known as a commission agent. He may also be entitled to receive either a fixed allowance in respect of expenses or reimbursement of expenses actually incurred by him. In cases in which an agent is employed for a special purpose, at a specified remuneration, he is, generally speaking, entitled to his remuneration only if the special purpose is fulfilled.

(4) The basis upon which any commission is to be calculated should be defined with exactness, if disputes are to be avoided. If it is a percentage of the profits, the word 'profit' should be accurately defined, since there are various methods by which profits may be calculated. The agreement should also make it clear whether the commission is to be paid on orders obtained, orders accepted, or orders paid for – three very different things. It should also be made clear whether commission on repeat orders, or on orders received after the termination of the agency, is to be paid.

(5) The principal may seek to include a clause in the agreement by which the agent agrees not to solicit the principal's customers after the termination of the agency. If a clause of this

character is included, the agent should be careful to insist upon the right to continue to solicit any of his personal customers. Otherwise, the agent may find, after the agreement has been terminated, that he has parted with his entire connexion without any compensation. He will then have to start his business life afresh. 'Restraint clauses', as they are called, are not popular with the law, but, if they are reasonable and do no more than give the principal fair protection, they will be upheld. If, however, they are unreasonable in any way, either in length of time or as regards territory or the nature of the actual restraint itself, the whole restraint clause, unless it can be distinctly severed, may be held to be bad. If you are entering into a contract containing a restraint clause, whether as a principal or an agent, you will be imprudent if you do not take legal advice as to its probable effect and validity before you sign the contract.

(6) The agreement should provide for accounts to be rendered by the principal to the agent at periodic intervals, to show the commission he has earned. It should also set out the dates on which he is to receive payment of his commission, or other form of remuneration.

(7) The principal will usually reserve the right, by the terms of the agreement, to accept or reject orders. He will also take upon himself the responsibility for inquiry into the financial status of a new customer. The agent must not, however, recklessly accept an order from a man who he knows, or ought to know, is of bad financial standing, unless he discloses the fact to his principal. If he does accept such an order, it might be held that he had not acted in good faith, and he might make himself liable for any loss which ensues.

It will be unnecessary to include a clause in the agreement by which the agent agrees not to accept a secret commission. A person acting in the capacity of an agent must never accept a secret commission from a third party to whom he is selling or from whom he is buying. If he does so – i.e. if he 'corruptly accepts or obtains for himself or for any other person any gift or consideration as an inducement or reward for doing or forbearing to do any act or business, or for showing or forbearing to show favour to any person in relation to his principal's affairs', he commits a criminal offence under the Prevention of

Corruption Act 1906, and may be sentenced to a term of imprisonment. In such a case the principal is also entitled forthwith to terminate the agency, and to take proceedings for recovery of the bribe. The principal is further entitled to sue the third party for any loss which he has suffered. For example, if the principal has paid an inflated price for goods, because the seller has increased the price of the goods by the amount of the bribe paid to the agent, the principal may claim, as damages, the difference between the price which he has paid and the price which he would have paid if there had been no bribe.

The law attempts to keep the community straight, but it can be successful only when the community is ready and willing to co-operate. If large numbers of the community break the rules, it not only brings the law into disrepute, but also diminishes its efficiency. It is, however, unreasonable to blame the law when this occurs.

SCALE OF CHARGES APPROVED BY THE INSTITUTE OF AUCTIONEERS, SURVEYORS, AND ESTATE AGENTS

SALE OF PROPERTY

5 per cent on first £300
2½ per cent on next £4,700
1½ per cent on excess of £5,000

with an addition of 5 per cent on £500 and 2½ per cent on the excess of £500 in respect of sums paid by the purchaser for chattels, fixtures, fittings, trade-stocks, and other movable effects, timber, and tenant rights.

LETTING OF PROPERTY

Unfurnished premises (excepting flats and offices with liability to repair, or farms and agricultural land):

5 per cent of the rent if letting is for one year or less;
7½ per cent of one year's rent if letting is for more than one and less than five years;
10 per cent of one year's rent if letting is for five years or upwards.

Flats or offices or parts of a building when tenant is liable for repair or redecoration:

> 10 per cent on one year's rent irrespective of duration of letting.

Furnished Premises (including collection of rent):

> 7½ per cent on rent payable.

A commission of 5 per cent on the first £1,000 and 2½ per cent on the excess is also payable on any premium, consideration, or goodwill.

6

SALE OF GOODS

*'A silk suit which cost me much money, and I pray
God make me able to pay for it.'*
Samuel Pepys, 1 July 1660

WHEN you purchase goods from a trader and you have received and paid for them, the liability of the trader in respect of the transaction is not necessarily at an end.

If, for example, you purchase a bicycle, and a month later, when you are cycling, it collapses and you fall and break your leg, you may under certain conditions have a legal remedy against the seller.

A number of factors must, however, be considered before it is possible to decide whether or not a man is entitled to make a legal complaint if an article which he has purchased proves at a later date to be defective. It is essential to ascertain, in particular, in every instance, the express and implied conditions of the sale.

When a dealer or a trader sells goods, he frequently makes representations as to the nature or quality of the goods he is selling. He may, for example, sell you a watch with a guarantee that, if kept under proper conditions, it will be an effective time-keeper for a specified period of years. A trader does not, however, necessarily describe the nature and quality of his goods. When you purchase a bicycle, nothing may be said on either side as to its condition. In such a case, however, and even though no word on the subject is exchanged between the buyer and the seller, the law will in certain cases deem or imply certain representations to have been made by the seller, unless such representations are expressly excluded by the terms of the bargain or contract.

Reference was made in Chapter 2 to the general rule which makes a Court reluctant to imply a term in a contract which has not been expressly agreed between the parties. The Sale of Goods Act 1893 has, however, provided a number of exceptions to the rule in the case of a sale of goods to which the Act applies. The Act put a severe brake on the application of the maxim, *Caveat emptor*, or 'let the purchaser beware', the common maxim when goods are purchased. When the Act applies, certain representations are deemed to be included as a term of every contract of sale, unless they are expressly excluded by the terms of sale.

When I sell you a bicycle and tell you before you buy it that it has new tyres, I am said to make a representation as to the state of the tyres on the bicycle. Representations of this character fall into two classes when they are made sufficiently emphatically, or in such circumstances, as to show they are meant to be *included* in the contract – e.g. when the contract is in writing they too should generally be in writing. They may either be *conditions* or *warranties*, and there is an important distinction between the two, for the breach of a condition goes to the root of the contract, and may vitiate the whole transaction, while a breach of warranty does not affect the validity of the contract as a whole, but gives rise to a claim for damages only.

The distinction may best be explained by an example. If I sell you a cycle and tell you it has new tyres, this is, as we have said, a representation that the tyres are new. It will depend on the circumstances in which the representation was made as to whether it is a condition or a warranty of the sale – or, conceivably, not part of the contract at all. If you buy the cycle because I have made the representation as to the state of the tyres, and you had made it clear to me that you did not wish to purchase the cycle if its tyres were old, the state of the tyres becomes a condition of the contract, and as soon as you ascertain the tyres are old, you may claim to rescind the contract. If, on the other hand, your principal object in purchasing the cycle is to buy that cycle and no other, because it is the particular type for which you have been looking, then my representation that the cycle has new tyres may be only incidental to the purchase, and such a representation will at best amount to a warranty. In that case you will not be entitled to rescind the contract, but will have a claim for damages for breach of warranty, and the amount of the damage you have suffered, and which you will be entitled to claim, will be the cost of obtaining new tyres, less any allowance you receive for the old ones.

The essential conditions and warranties implied in every contract of sale to which the Sale of Goods Act applies may, as stated, be expressly excluded. Most dealers in second-hand goods, in fact, expressly exclude all conditions and warranties from their terms of sale. If they did not do so, many of them would become bankrupt. Unless, however, they are so excluded, a purchaser of goods is entitled to rely upon them. They are four in number, and are as follows:

(1) There is an implied representation by a man who sells goods that he has a legal right to sell the goods. They must be his absolute property, or he must have been lawfully entrusted with their sale. If John Doe has sold you a stolen cycle you might be ordered by the Court to return the cycle to the owner, and you would then have a claim against John Doe for the return of your money. You would also be entitled to claim any expense which you had properly incurred in reasonably defending proceedings brought against you for the return of the cycle. It would not, however, be reasonable to defend an action for its return if the thief had been prosecuted and convicted for stealing the cycle. In such a case cogent evidence of ownership would have been produced to you. If, on the other hand, John Doe refuted the allegation that the cycle was stolen and claimed that he had a good title or right to sell you the bicycle, it would be reasonable to defend the proceedings brought against you in order that the Courts might decide the issue. If John Doe was impecunious, it would not, of course, necessarily be wise to rely upon his assurances, unless you were yourself satisfied that they were well founded. If you resist a claim and lose an action, you usually have to pay your opponent's costs of the proceedings, as well as your own. If John Doe was a man of straw, your subsequent claim against him for reimbursement of the costs might be valueless.

An exception to the general rule which requires a purchaser to return stolen goods arises on a sale and purchase in what is known as 'market overt' – i.e. open market. An open market is an established public market, and if the sale takes place during authorized days and hours, a purchaser in good faith of goods which prove to have been stolen is under no obligation to return them until the thief has been prosecuted to conviction.

(2) There is an implied representation when a dealer sells goods by description that they shall, in fact, correspond with that description. I may purchase a clock which I see described in a catalogue as 'an eight-day clock', and on its arrival I find that it requires winding every twenty-four hours. It does not correspond with the description, and as 'eight-day' is a representation which goes to the root of the contract, it is a condition of the contract, and its breach entitles me to reject the clock and demand the return of my money. Alternatively, I may demand from the seller what he had offered to sell and I had agreed to buy – viz. an eight-day clock – and if the seller fails to deliver a clock of this character I may sue him for damages. My damages would normally be the difference between the price of an eight-day clock which is as near to the seller's description as I am able to procure and the advertised price in the catalogue.

(3) A dealer, generally speaking, is not obliged to disclose the defects attaching to any particular article which he sells. The purchaser must look after his own interests. If, however, I inform a trader who specializes in the sale of a particular class of goods that I require goods of that class for a particular purpose, I am entitled to rely upon his skill and judgement and there is an implied condition that the goods will be reasonably fit for that purpose. For example, I may wish to start in the business of dog-breeding. If I communicate with a breeder, and inform him of this desire, I am entitled to assume that any bitches I purchase from him are suitable for breeding purposes. If, on their arrival, I ascertain he has sold me mongrels and not pedigree bitches, they would be useless for breeding, and I might return them. He is not entitled to 'sell me a pup'.

A similar responsibility is imposed upon a trader who deals in a particular class of goods, and in such a case there is an implied condition, when the goods are sold by description, that they shall be of 'merchantable quality'. For example, if you purchase a cycle recommended to you by a cycle dealer, the law requires the cycle to be fit for the road, and if it collapses under you when you are out cycling, and you are injured, you are entitled to claim compensation. If, however, you see a bicycle in a shop window, and you say to the cycle dealer: 'I want that bicycle which you have in your window,' and he replies: 'Very good, sir; thirty pounds, please,' it is not a sale by description, and it is a case to which the maxim *Caveat emptor* will apply. You will note, however, that the obligation applies only to a trader who makes it part of his general business to deal in such goods. If you purchase a second-hand bicycle from a private seller you have no remedy if the bicycle is defective. Moreover, a trader may also be exempt from liability if he sells you goods under a trade name, or goods which he himself had no reasonable chance to examine. For example, a grocer would not normally be liable to the purchaser of a branded food product called, say, 'Roedoe', if the contents of a particular tin brought on an attack of ptomaine poisoning. He could disclaim responsibility, both because the sale took place under a trade name, and also because he had no reasonable chance of inspecting the contents of the sealed tin. Liability might, however, arise if the seller had expressly recommended the purchaser to buy the goods sold under the trade name, and the exemption would not extend to the manufacturer, who might in certain circumstances be sued with reasonable prospects of success.

(4) The fourth representation is deemed to arise only when there is a sale by sample. In such a case there is a condition that the bulk shall correspond with the sample in quality, and the buyer must be allowed a reasonable opportunity of comparing the bulk with the sample. If you select material from a pattern shown to you by a tailor, he is not subsequently entitled to sell you a material which has an identical design, if it is not also of the same quality, at any rate in so far as normal inspection may reveal quality. If he does so, you may reject it.

The *quantum*, or amount, of the damage which you are entitled to claim upon a breach of any of these implied conditions or warranties, and which may be either additional or alternative to your right of rejection, is assessed in the manner described in Chapter 2. Before, however, you embark upon the good ship Litigation you should remember that there is always danger of storms and tempests, and you may have a rough passage before you are able to bring your cargo of damage safely into port, even if the ship does not founder or turn turtle in mid-ocean.

The sale or purchase of an article is effected in two stages. The first stage is the agreement to buy and sell, and the second stage is the actual delivery of the article.

The two acts may sometimes be simultaneous, but are not necessarily so. You may agree to buy a cycle, and the dealer may agree to effect certain necessary repairs to the machine before delivery. The first stage is the agreement to purchase. An object in a shop window with a price label attached is not regarded by the law as an offer of sale, and there is no enforceable contract until trader and customer have agreed to all the terms. When a contract has reached the first stage, but has not been completed by delivery of the goods, it is said to be 'executory'. The contract is completed, or executed, when the goods agreed to be purchased, or the documents of title to the goods, are delivered, and delivery means a formal acceptance after tender – i.e. a formal offer for acceptance.

A common case in which documents of title are delivered, instead of the goods themselves, occurs when goods are shipped to the purchaser. In such a case the documents of title are called Bills of Lading, and they are either made out in the name of the purchaser or endorsed over to him or to his order. When these bills are tendered to the purchaser, and he accepts them, the legal consequences are the same as if he had taken actual delivery of the goods. Further references to 'delivery' of goods in this chapter include, accordingly, the delivery of the documents of title in relevant cases.

When you agree to purchase goods, many things may happen to them between the date of the agreement and the date of delivery. They may, for instance, be destroyed by accidental fire or other unavoidable cause. The burden of the loss between the vendor and yourself in such a case depends on whether the legal ownership in the goods has passed to you or still remains with the vendor. This is partly a question of law and partly a question of fact which turns on the circumstances of each individual case.

For example, when you agree to make a purchase of goods, such goods may consist of an article or articles which are identified, or they may consist of merchandise which cannot be immediately identified. If you agree to buy a specified piano, it is identified immediately the agreement is made. If, on the other hand, you agree to buy 3 cwt of coal to be delivered to you on the following day, you cannot go into your coal merchant's yard and identify the particular 3 cwt of coal which is to be assembled to satisfy the agreement. The identification can take place only after the coal has been gathered in sacks, or loaded on a van for delivery.

Identification of goods agreed to be purchased has a very important bearing on the question of legal ownership, because such ownership normally depends on whether or not the goods have been 'appropriated' to the contract of sale. Unidentified goods cannot be appropriated, but the general rule is that goods agreed to be sold are appropriated to the contract as soon as they are identified, and as soon as they are appropriated the property in them passes to the purchaser, and he becomes the legal owner.

In these circumstances the accidental loss of goods destroyed after an agreement to purchase, and before delivery has been effected, normally falls upon the vendor in the case of unidentified or unappropriated goods, but the purchaser must bear the loss in the case of identified or appropriated goods.

These rules do not necessarily apply if the goods are destroyed or damaged as a result of negligence, as distinct from unavoidable accident. In such a case the usual rules applicable to negligence may be applied. Even though the property has passed to the purchaser, and he is therefore the legal owner, he may claim from the seller, as damages for negligence, an amount equivalent to his loss.

Goods are not always paid for in cash, and in the case of credit transactions questions may arise as to the legal rights of an unpaid seller. What is the legal position if you have agreed to sell a piano to John Doe, and before the piano is delivered, or before you have been paid the purchase price, John Doe is made bankrupt? Are you bound to deliver the piano, or may you keep it until your account has been paid? You will not be able to contend successfully that it is your piano. The property in it has passed to John Doe as from the date when the piano was 'appropriated' to the contract. You are not normally entitled to retain property which belongs to a third party, and if you do so you may be sued for delivery up of the property and also for damages for detinue, i.e. its detention, or for damages for conversion, which is legally defined as being any act in relation to property which is inconsistent with the rights of the true owner. Must you, then, deliver the piano, although you may have no prospect of receiving payment? The answer may be in the negative, for you may have what is legally termed the 'lien of an unpaid seller'. Lien is a subject which is considered in Chapter 8. Although you are no longer the legal owner of the goods, the law entitles you to retain them in your custody, in this instance, until you have been paid the purchase price.

Your lien or right to retain the goods as an unpaid seller may even be enforced by you after you have parted with the piano, if it has not actually been delivered to the purchaser. You may re-claim the piano if it is in the hands of the railway or any other carrier in process of delivery, because it is 'based on the plain reason of justice and equity that one man's goods shall not be applied to the payment of another man's debts'. The right of the unpaid seller to a lien may, however, be set up only against the purchaser personally. If John Doe is the purchaser of the piano, but you have been instructed by him to deliver it to Richard Roe, because he has resold it, you cannot reclaim it, in order to enforce the lien, after it has left your premises.

If you have sold a piano to John Doe, but he does not want it delivered to him until he moves into a new house, he cannot later repudiate the bargain if he changes his plans and does not acquire his new house. In such a case you would be entitled to maintain an action for the price of the piano, and it would remain John Doe's property to be held by you to his order. If, however, you prefer to accept the repudiation, you are at liberty to do so. In that case you would be entitled to keep the piano and maintain an action for damages for any loss you may have suffered. Your normal loss would be the loss of the profit which you would have earned if John Doe had carried out his contract, less any profit you receive on a second sale.

The provisions of the Sale of Goods Act 1893 which have been considered do not, in general, apply to hire-purchase agreements.

Goods are frequently sold on agreements known as hire-purchase agreements. The essence of a hire-purchase agreement is that the goods are on hire only, and that the property in them is not to pass to the customer or hirer until the final instalment of the purchase price has been paid. Until the final instalment is paid the goods are the property of the stores who have hired them to the customer.

The law relating to hire-purchase was drastically altered shortly before the Second World War. Formerly some traders had abused their rights under hire-purchase agreements. They re-claimed goods and retained all money paid under the hire-purchase agreement when default was made by purchasers in payment of a single instalment of the agreed purchase price.

For example, if John Doe had bought a piano on hire purchase for £80, and had paid £75 by instalments, he might have lost the piano and his £75 if he had defaulted in payment of the final instalment of £5. It was the practice for the trader to retain this right under the terms of his agreement with John Doe, and an unscrupulous trader would readily avail himself of it. There were also cases in which a grossly inflated purchase price was charged for goods purchased on hire purchase. A customer might be attracted by a suite of furniture worth £40. The trader would have been willing to sell it for £40, but as the customer was buying on hire purchase, the price asked might be £2 a month for three years. £2 a month for a suite of furniture sounds a modest figure to a person who is not mathematically minded. Calculation shows, however, that a regular payment of £2 a month amounts to £72 in three years. The customer accepting such an offer would accordingly pay £72 for goods which he might purchase in cash for £40.

These abuses were countered by the sweeping provisions of the Hire Purchase Act 1938. The chief defect of that Act at the time was that it applied only to transactions which even then might have been considered modest. The Act of the same name of 1954 has raised the price ceiling, above which transactions are not affected, to correspond with increases in prices since 1938, and has slightly improved the position of a hirer brought to court for failing to pay instalments.

The Act applies to all hire-purchase agreements and 'credit sale' agreements where, in the case of all goods except livestock, the hire-purchase price or total purchase price does not exceed £300. In the case of livestock the figure is £1,000. A 'credit sale' agreement is defined as an agreement in which the purchase price is payable by five or more instalments.

Under the provisions of the Act, if you propose to purchase a piano for £200 by instalments, the trader is obliged, before making any hire-purchase agreement, to inform you in writing of the price at which you may purchase the piano in cash. There must also be a memorandum signed by all parties which sets out the hire-purchase price, the cash price, the amount and date of each instalment due, a schedule of the goods sold, and a notice which sets out clearly the more important rights of both parties to the agreement. A copy of this memorandum must be supplied to the hirer within seven days of the making of the agreement. If the owner does not comply with these conditions he may forfeit his rights under the agreement. Conditions of a similar character are made in the Act regarding credit sales agreements.

In the case of a hire-purchase agreement, the hirer has a right by the Acts to terminate the agreement on payment of the instalments due, together with such sum, if any, as will make his total payment not less than one-half of the total hire-purchase price, unless a lesser sum is specified in the agreement, and if the owner includes any provision in the agreement for a larger payment, such a provision is void. The hirer is, however, liable to pay damages if he fails to take reasonable care of the goods, and the Court may order him to deliver up the goods if he retains them wrongfully.

A number of provisions which had frequently been included in hire-purchase agreements are in future declared to be void. They include provisions which entitled the owner to enter premises for the purpose of seizing the goods, and which imposed additional liabilities on the hirer.

The owner is required to supply the hirer at any time on demand, and on tender of the sum of 1s., with the fullest information regarding the agreement and the balance still due under the agreement. If the owner fails to comply with this demand he may substantially lose his rights under the agreement, and may be subject to a penalty of £10. The hirer is subject to a similar penalty if he fails to reply to the owner's request for information as to the whereabouts of the hired goods.

Further protection is given to the hirer by the provision that if he has paid a sum equal to or in excess of one-third of the hire-purchase price, the owner must not take any step to recover possession of the goods in the event of default, except through the Courts, or unless the hirer has terminated the agreement. If the owner acts illegally in this respect the agreement is treated as being at an end. The hirer can then recover all payments made by him under the agreement.

The commercial potentiality of hire-purchase and credit-sale trading has been increasingly appreciated by retailers and the public, and finance companies frequently supply ready money to retailers who would otherwise have to wait until the customer had paid all his instalments. Many commodities such as cars, motor-cycles, television sets, household goods, and furniture are purchased mainly under hire-purchase or credit-sale arrangements. The nation's standard of living may be considerably affected by the Government regulating the percentage of the cash price paid as a deposit and the duration of the period over which instalments may be paid. Rental agreements under which the customer never has more than the loan of the property concerned may similarly have restrictions placed upon them.

7

FIRMS AND PARTNERSHIPS

> 'The ugliest of trades have their moments of pleasure.
> Now, if I were a grave digger, or even a hangman,
> there are some people I could work for with a great
> deal of enjoyment.'
>
> D. W. Jerrold

IF you decide to 'run a business', you may open it in your own name, or you may do so in the name of a firm. You may operate it as an individual, or you may do so in partnership with one or more of your friends or business acquaintances. You may also organize it in the form of a limited company, and become a director. In that event the Company will in some respects occupy the same position as if it were your employer, and as a director of the Company you will, generally speaking, be its agent, even although you may have complete control over its operations. The structure of a limited company is dealt with in Chapters 19 and 20.

If you decide to carry on business in your own name you may do so without particular formality, but if you carry on business in a name other than your own, you must, by the provisions of the Registration of Business Names Act 1916, register particulars of the business in the office of a Government official called the Registrar of Business Names. You must also have your name printed as the owner of the business on all your business communications, including invoices. These provisions are designed to enable every person to know the name of the individual with whom he is dealing. The Register of Business Names, which is normally kept in London, may be inspected by any member of the public on payment of a small fee. If you enter into a contract with 'John Doe and Company' you are entitled to know if you are making a bargain with John Doe, or with Joan Doe, his wife. Before the Register of Business Names was established, it was easy for John Doe to lead his creditors to believe he was the owner of a business which belonged, in fact, to his wife. In such a case a creditor might have sued John Doe, believing him to be the proprietor of the business, and, after he had obtained judgement and had attempted to enforce the judgement by an 'execution' levied against the assets of the business – a subject dealt with later in this chapter – Joan Doe would claim all these assets. The creditor would then have to withdraw the execution, and in many instances he lost his money.

The particulars furnished to the Registrar must now, however, disclose the name of the owner of the business. If a supplier is unable to obtain payment for goods supplied, he is then able to sue the owner, and he is able to enforce his judgement against the assets of the business which belong to the owner.

When John Doe does not wish to disclose his identity as the owner of a business, he may purchase it in the name of a third person, who is said, in law, to be his nominee. Sometimes the fact that a man is acting as a nominee, and the name of his principal, are both concealed. At other times he is openly identified as a nominee, but the name of his principal is not disclosed. The principal who appoints the nominee may have no improper motive in wishing to conceal his identity, but the practice of trading anonymously through a nominee lends itself to abuse.

If you and John Doe carry on business as greengrocers a few doors away from each other, there will, no doubt, be legitimate competition between you. You may be in the habit of purchasing your supplies from a wholesaler called Richard Roe. You have no means of knowing that John Doe is, in fact, a nominee of Richard Roe. A wholesaler will frequently open a retail business in the name of a nominee, and in this instance it will mean you are purchasing your supplies from a rival trader. Imagination can suggest who will obtain first priority when goods are in short supply, and if you knew the facts, you would, no doubt, seek another market for your purchases. You may consider it unfair for Richard Roe to carry on both a wholesale and a retail business in this way. There is, however, nothing illegal in his doing so.

It is a common practice for a shareholder in a limited company to purchase shares in the name of a nominee, so that the public will not be able to identify his interest in the Company.

A Government committee appointed to consider Company

Law reform, which published its report in 1945, strongly criticized certain features of nominee shareholdings. Many of the Committee's recommendations were embodied in the Companies Act 1948, but their recommendation on nominee shareholding was not accepted in full, and the Act merely gives to the Board of Trade power to order disclosure of the owner behind the name in the register of shareholders if such disclosure is required in the public interest. This provision is designed to prevent large-scale fraud, and does not really help the individual who wants to know the identity of the persons with whom he is dealing when he enters into business relations with a limited company.

When you open up a new business you watch it, week by week, with some anxiety, to observe whether or not it is going to prosper. You are relieved if you see the takings increase progressively, and will be satisfied if you are able to claim, at the end of a year, that the business is firmly established.

When this occurs, you have created something of value by your personal efforts. If, as a result of some misfortune, you are unable to carry on the business, you will not necessarily have to close it down, and lose the fruits of your efforts without compensation. You will be able to sell it to a purchaser and require payment for it. The payment would be made for what is called 'goodwill'. It may have a great value in the case of an old-established business, but if you are the purchaser, and not the seller, there are many pitfalls you must avoid when you buy the goodwill of a business. Some of these are dealt with in Chapter 12. There is no yardstick to be applied in assessing the value of goodwill. It must depend on a large number of factors, and if you propose either to sell or to buy a business, the only safe course to adopt is to place all the facts and figures relating to the business before a qualified accountant. After he has considered them, he may be in a position to express an opinion as to a fair value which ought to be paid or received for the goodwill.

If you are proposing to purchase a business you should be aware that numerous statutory provisions, regulations, and by-laws will affect you; your trade association and local chamber of commerce should be able to supply you with information.

In Chapter 12 reference is made to the necessity of having a proper agreement, when you purchase a business, to safeguard yourself against a vendor who might desire to open a competing business on adjoining premises after the completion of the sale.

If you are the owner of a business and occupy your own business premises under a lease or a tenancy, there are important provisions in Part II of the Landlord and Tenant Act 1954 which will affect you. Broadly speaking, if the business had been carried on at the same premises for six months or more or under a lease or tenancy agreement granted in the first place for not less than three months, the tenant is entitled, if he receives notice from his landlord to quit the premises, to demand a new lease of the premises. A landlord cannot, of course, serve any notice to quit to take effect before the time stipulated under the tenancy. If the tenancy in question were granted in the first place for a term exceeding a year the tenant may take the first step under the Act to obtain a new lease. The tenancy must not be one which is protected under the Rent Restriction Acts, or excluded from their scope only through the rent charged being too low. Agricultural and most licensed premises are not covered, and there are other special cases where the Act does not help.

If neither side makes any move, the tenancy will automatically continue under the Act. The landlord may serve a written notice on the tenant between six and twelve months prior to the date specified in such notice for the tenancy to come to an end. The tenant may give notice to apply to the County Court for a new lease to be granted on reasonable conditions for a term not exceeding fourteen years.

The landlord may oppose the grant of a new lease for essentially four different reasons, assuming that the tenant has complied with his obligations under his old lease. (1) He may offer the tenant reasonable alternative accommodation; (2) he may have the genuine intention either of reconstructing or demolishing the premises; (3) he may have the genuine intention of combining them with others to obtain a higher aggregate rental; (4) he may wish to re-occupy them in limited circumstances for his own use. In the last three cases the landlord must pay compensation to the outgoing tenant amounting to the rateable value; in some cases, where the uprooted business has been carried on for a long time, twice the rateable value. The Act also contains provision for a tenant to be compensated by his landlord for improvements which he has effected and has to abandon.

As with the Acts dealing with Rent Restriction the rights given to the tenant cannot for the most part be taken away by agreement, and again as with the Rent Acts, the stipulations governing the parties' rights are highly technical. The Act provides more comprehensive cover for tenants than its predecessors, being intended as a permanent measure. The Landlord and Tenant Act 1927 however, continues to affect business tenancies among others, and for this see Chapter 17.

If you decide to start a business jointly with a friend or business acquaintance, he will generally be known to the law as your partner. Partnership is the 'relation which subsists between two or more persons carrying on business in common with a view of profit'. Partners also have to share losses. If you are inexperienced, and your friend is equally lacking in knowledge of the particular trade you have both selected, you are more likely to suffer losses than to make profits, and unless you are cautious you may find your steps leading you to the Bankruptcy Court. Enterprise should never be discouraged, but enterprise and experience are usually essential 'partners' for success.

Partnership is a contractual relationship – i.e. it is founded upon an agreement between the partners to carry on business together under specified terms and conditions. The individuals who have entered into partnership with each other are called collectively a firm. The name under which their business is carried on is known as the firm name. A firm must comply with the requirements of registration under the Registration of Business Names Act 1916. It must disclose the names of the partners, unless the firm consists of all their names without other addition. John Doe and John Doe, Junior, his son, may trade under the firm name of 'John and John Doe' without registration. If, however, they trade under the name of 'John Doe and Son' or 'John Doe and Company' they must register.

Except in those cases dealt with in Chapters 19 and 20 when a company is a corporation and must use the word 'Limited' or 'Ltd' as part of its title, the word 'company' used as part of a trading name is without legal significance. 'John Doe and Sons' and 'John Doe and Company' are both names under which a firm may operate, and when we speak of 'Company Law' we do not refer to business firms of this character.

Moreover, although we speak of a partnership as a 'firm', the law does not recognize a firm as having any legal existence, beyond a power to sue and to be sued in the firm name. It is only a matter of convenience to refer to the rights and liabilities of a firm. The rights are legally the rights of the owner or of the partners collectively. The liabilities are legally the liabilities of the owner or of the partners individually. It is essential to remember this whenever reference is made to 'a firm'.

The mutual rights and obligations of partners and their responsibility individual and collective to their customers and members of the public are important matters.

John Doe and Richard Roe have entered into the partnership business of outfitters, and trade as John Doe and Company. John Doe and Richard Roe have agreed between themselves that Richard Roe will purchase all the supplies which are required by the business. In breach of this agreement John Doe interviews a traveller and purchases some shirts ostensibly for the firm, but in reality for himself. If he fails to pay for them, can the traveller require the firm to do so? In order to obtain the answer you must apply the rule which would be relevant if similar circumstances arose in the case of a principal and agent. You will recollect from Chapter 5 that the principal is, generally speaking, responsible for the acts of his agent committed within the scope of his actual or implied authority. Every partner is an agent of the firm and has express or implied authority to enter into contracts on behalf of the firm. Therefore, if John Doe defrauds his partner in this way, the partner and not the traveller must suffer. Provided the latter has acted in good faith, he can require the firm to pay him for the shirts. At the same time, Richard Roe could, of course, require John Doe to reimburse him the loss which he, Richard Roe, has suffered when the firm has been required to pay John Doe's personal debt. On the other hand, the same firm would not normally be liable if John Doe, as one of its partners, purchased some groceries in the firm name. Such a purchase would not be within the apparent scope of the partnership business of outfitters, and the responsibility of a firm for acts done by any one of its partners is strictly confined to business transactions. The firm is not liable for a partner's private debts, contracted outside the actual or apparent scope of the business.

By application of the same principles, the firm would be compelled to deliver shirts which had been purchased by a customer, if John Doe had received payment from the customer for the shirts, but had failed to account to the firm for the purchase price. Payment to a partner in a firm for a debt owing to the firm is almost invariably a good discharge for the debt.

John Doe can involve his firm in financial loss in many ways additional to those already considered. They not only arise when he acts in breach of his primary obligation to act faithfully towards his partner. They may also occur when he is acting in good faith. For example, if John Doe is delivering goods in a car which belongs to the firm, and in the course of his journey he knocks down and injures a pedestrian as a result of negligent driving, John Doe and Company may be liable to pay compensation. This subject was discussed in Chapter 2. John Doe and Company will not, however, be liable if John Doe was engaged on his own private affairs at the time of the accident, and was not driving on the firm's business, for the firm is liable only for the consequences of any act of negligence by one of its partners which is committed within the scope of his duty as a partner.

If a creditor makes a claim against a firm, and subsequently obtains judgement against them, he may enforce it against the assets of the firm. He is not, however, compelled to do so. He may sometimes enforce the judgement against a partner personally, for a partner is always liable to the full extent of his private assets for any debts of the partnership. The judgement may be enforced against a partner either when he has entered an appearance to any legal proceedings and has admitted he is a partner, or when he has been served with a writ or a summons and has not denied his status as a partner. If one partner pays up the full amount of a debt due from the firm out of his own pocket, he is entitled to call upon each of his partners to repay him, by way of contribution, a proportion of the amount which he has paid.

If a creditor decides to enforce a judgement against the firm, and not against an individual partner, he may instruct the sheriff's officer to take possession of all plant, machinery, stock in trade, or office furniture which belongs to the firm. This process of instructing the sheriff's officer is called 'levying execution'. The creditor is also entitled to take bankruptcy proceedings against the firm, and if it is made bankrupt, all the assets of the firm will pass to the Trustee in Bankruptcy. The Trustee will sell these assets, in order to pay the debts, but if they do not realize enough to pay all the creditors in full, the Trustees may call upon each partner to make up the deficiency out of his private assets. If a partner fails to do so, he may, in his turn, be made bankrupt. The subject of bankruptcy is dealt with in Chapter 21.

If a partner retires from the partnership, he should notify all those who have had dealings with the firm that he is no longer associated with it. If he fails to do so, he may find himself estopped by his conduct from repudiating liability for the debts of the firm, incurred after he has ceased to be a partner, and he may be called upon to meet them. If members of the public have been trading with the firm of 'John Doe and Company', knowing John Doe is a partner, they are entitled to believe that he remains a partner and, accordingly, liable for the debts of the firm, until such time as they are notified of his retirement. If the business continues to be carried on in the name of John Doe and Company, John Doe will, however, not be under liability to an old customer for any debts arising from new contracts made with the firm after the customer has received notice of his retirement, or to any new customer who deals with the firm for the first time after the date of his retirement.

Although a written agreement is not essential to establish the terms of a partnership, and a verbal agreement is legal and enforceable, it is desirable for the express rights and obligations of each of the partners to be defined in writing. If they are not so defined, but are left to be inferred, it substantially increases the risk of subsequent disagreement. Haphazard business methods are in many cases responsible for litigation, and the greater the care taken to define business relations, the less will be the probability of subsequent friction.

Many of the terms of an agreement between partners will be dictated by common sense. What is to be the scope of the partnership business? What is to be the function of each partner? How much capital is to be employed in the business? In what proportions are the partners to contribute the capital? In what proportions are profits and losses to be shared? Who is to keep the necessary books of account? Who are to be the bankers of the partnership? How often are the accounts of the partnership to be prepared? How long is the partnership to last? What right is each partner to have to terminate the partnership? What are to be the rights of the survivor in the event of the death of a partner? What steps are to be taken to wind up the affairs of the partnership after dissolution? These are some of the important questions which ought to be considered by the partners before the partnership begins.

If there is no express agreement between the partners, the Partnership Act 1890 defines to a certain extent their respective legal rights. The relevant provisions of that Act, which operate in the absence of agreement, entitle each partner to share equally in the profits and losses of the business, and make each partner liable for an equal contribution towards the capital. Subject, also, to the terms of any agreement, each partner is entitled to take part in the management of the business, and if there are more than two partners, the majority may arrive at a decision which is binding on the minority.

There is one type of partnership seldom met in practice, called a limited partnership. In the case of a limited partnership, the rights of one or more of the partners are of a specified limited character. In all other cases a partner has certain statutory rights and obligations of which he cannot be deprived even by agreement. These include: (1) the right of access at any time to the books of account, which must be kept at the place of business of the partnership; (2) the right to make copies of any entries in the books; (3) the obligation to render a true

D

account of his dealings to each of his partners, so far as such dealings relate to the affairs of the partnership business; (4) the obligation to give each of his partners full relevant information; (5) the obligation not to employ the assets of the firm for his own private use without the consent of his partners, with a liability in the event of default to pay over to the firm any profit, and suffer personally any loss.

These rights and obligations arise from the legal responsibilities which rest upon every individual who owns, or partly owns, a business. It is, for example, obvious that a partner could not comply with his legal obligation to make proper income-tax returns if he did not have access to the books of the partnership. Moreover, an offence is committed under the Bankruptcy Act if a bankrupt has not kept proper books of account. Apart from these considerations, however, each of these points is fundamental to the existence of the mutual trust which should prevail between partners.

If an agreement between partners does not specify the duration of the partnership, it will continue for such time as all the partners are in agreement. In the event of disagreement, any partner may dissolve the partnership at any time without previous notice, while if the partnership has been formed with the object of carrying out some express purpose it will come to an end when that purpose has been fulfilled. A partnership which continues after the time originally agreed is determinable at any time by any partner, but a partnership for a fixed term, which has not expired, can only be terminated either by the death or bankruptcy of a partner, or by agreement, or by an Order from the Court. If the dissolution follows death or bankruptcy, the assets of the deceased or bankrupt partner may be utilized towards making good any deficiency in the assets of the firm, in respect of debts incurred by the firm, prior to such death or bankruptcy.

Subject to the terms of any agreement, the accounts of a partnership are usually taken annually. After a dissolution, the accounts must be made up to the date of the dissolution. If the partners are in agreement, they may themselves appoint a Receiver who will wind up the partnership affairs; otherwise the Court has power to make the appointment. It is the duty of the

Receiver to collect and realize all the assets of the firm, to discharge the liabilities, and thereafter to distribute any surplus among the partners according to their respective shares.

There are a number of circumstances in which the Court has power to order a dissolution of partnership. These include the following:

(1) When a partner is permanently incapable of performing his duties as a partner.

(2) When a partner has been guilty of conduct calculated to injure the partnership business.

(3) When a partner has persistently or wilfully broken the partnership agreement.

(4) When a partner has so conducted himself in partnership matters that it is not reasonably practicable for his partners to continue to carry on business with him.

(5) When the partnership can be carried on only at a loss.

The Court also has a general jurisdiction to dissolve a partnership whenever it is 'just and equitable' that it should do so. The Court will usually exercise this power if the partners have disputes of such a serious character as to make it virtually impossible for the partnership business to continue.

To avoid the necessity of litigation, partnership agreements frequently contain a clause by which the partners agree, in the event of a dispute arising between them, that such dispute shall be referred to arbitration. The subject of arbitration is dealt with in Chapter 31.

This chapter should help you to appreciate that if you enter into a partnership you are undertaking a serious responsibility. A dishonest partner, as well as an incompetent one, can bring you to ruin. It is therefore of vital importance not to enter into any partnership without careful thought. It is rarely wise to buy a share in a partnership in answer to an advertisement, or to advertise for a partner. If you adopt the method of advertisement, it is difficult to satisfy yourself beyond reasonable doubt of the honesty of your proposed partner. There are some dishonest persons who make a practice of inserting and answering advertisements for partners. The results are always disastrous for the unfortunate individuals who have dealings with them. If you wish to enter into a partnership, you should choose as your partner a man of experience whom you have known for many years. You should be in a position to trust him of your own personal knowledge, and to know that if you start business together you will be setting sail in a fair wind.

8

TRAVELLERS, CARRIERS, INNKEEPERS, LIENS, AND INSURANCE

'Jonas acquired some reputation by travelling abroad, but lost it all by travelling at home.' [On Jonas Hanway, who followed his *Travels to Persia* with *An Eight Days' Journey from London to Portsmouth*.]

Samuel Johnson

IN this country the fare-paying traveller usually makes his journey by train or public-service vehicle, i.e. by omnibus or coach. Railways were nationalized by the Transport Act 1947, and the property of the former railway companies was transferred to the British Transport Commission. The Commission is the body with whom the traveller comes into contact in much the same way as he came into contact with the railway companies prior to nationalization.

When you travel by railway, bus, or tram a contract is made with the railway or other undertaking when you receive your ticket. Quite clearly the terms of the contract cannot be discussed with the booking clerk or conductor before the ticket is issued. There would not be time, and the transport system would come to a stop, or the vehicles would be mostly empty, if every passenger had to be, or insisted on being, acquainted with the terms upon which he is about to be transported. Therefore, the acceptance of a ticket 'clinches the deal'.

If, however, the passenger is conveyed subject to any conditions (it is rare nowadays if he is not) he must have this fact brought to his notice by suitable wording on the face of the ticket. For example, a typical railway ticket states on the face not only the destination but such words as 'for conditions see over', and on turning the ticket over there will be found: 'Issued subject to the Regulations and Conditions in the Commission's Publications and Notices applicable to British Railways.' Similar words appear on the tickets issued by the various road-transport undertakings, drawing attention to conditions, by-laws, and regulations which, although only to be found elsewhere, are nevertheless binding upon the passenger. They are 'terms of the contract', although he has never seen them.

By-laws have to be reasonable, and must not be repugnant to the law of the land. Their validity in these respects is subject to challenge in the courts. The railways have had common by-laws for many years. They may be seen posted up at railway stations, but under a power obtained by the British Transport Commission they will, if and when the Commission make fresh by-laws, be obtainable for inspection only on application to the booking clerk, unless you prefer to buy a copy for a shilling.

Railway by-laws cover such miscellaneous matters as travelling without a ticket, defacing tickets, smoking in non-smoking compartments, entering or leaving a train in motion, damaging property, and taking a loaded gun into a train or station. The Minister of Transport has made Regulations covering similar matters in respect of public-service vehicles.

Of course, very few people take the trouble to read the closely printed notices posted up at stations, and still fewer to ask the booking clerk – they are only too anxious to get their tickets and be away. Passengers are, therefore, sometimes surprised when, on making what appears to them a legitimate claim, they find that some condition of which they were totally unaware debars them. Liability for injury is, for example, not admitted in the case of passengers holding free passes. However, the Passengers Charges Scheme 1954, which has statutory force, has abolished the distinction between the rights of holders of cheap and ordinary tickets in accident cases.

If there is no exclusion of liability a legal obligation to pay damages to injured persons will normally arise after a collision, as the usual rule which requires an injured person to prove negligence is reversed. The law will assume, without legal proof, that the accident is due to a failure of an employee of the railway to exercise proper care, and there is no obligation to prove negligence. This assumption is based on the doctrine known as *Res ipsa loquitur* – i.e. 'the thing speaks for itself'. If, in fact, there is evidence to prove that the accident was not due to any fault on the part of the railway, e.g. if a trespasser had deliberately interfered with the signals, the assumption may be rebutted, but normally this is not an easy matter, and the railway does not attempt it. You may accordingly guess the reason for the announcement frequently made by British Railways after an accident that it will meet all claims. This does not mean that you will be entitled to claim compensation if you are injured when you get out of the train when it is in motion, or if you lean your head out of the window and are struck by an object projecting on to the line. You have no right to act in this way, and it is negligent to do so.

When you deposit your luggage in a railway cloak-room and pay a fee for the deposit, you may nevertheless be met with the following condition if your luggage is lost and you make a claim for compensation:

'The (Commission) shall not be liable for loss, misdelivery, or detention of or damage to

'(*a*) Any article or property which separately or in the aggregate exceeds the value of £5, unless at the time of deposit the true value and nature thereof shall have been declared by the depositor and a charge (as scheduled) paid for each day or part of a day in addition to the ordinary cloak-room charges, and such loss, misdelivery, detention, or damage shall be proved to have been occasioned by the negligence of the (Commission's) servants.

'(*b*) Any articles or property which separately or in the aggregate do not exceed the value of £5, unless such loss, misdelivery, detention, or damage shall be proved to have been occasioned by the negligence of the (Commission's) servants.'

This means that although the Transport Commission exacts a payment for the cloak-room charge, it will not pay you any compensation if it loses your luggage unless you are able to prove that the loss was due to the negligence of the Commission's servants, and unless, in addition, where the luggage is worth more than £5, you have complied with conditions of which nearly every passenger is wholly ignorant.

When you have goods conveyed by rail, water, road, or air, the carrier of the goods must assume certain legal obligations. Carriers of goods are classified by the law either as being 'common carriers' or 'private carriers'. Railways and most other transport undertakings are included in the former category, and a common carrier must carry the goods of any person who is willing to pay his proper charges, unless there are valid grounds for refusal. His proper charges must be reasonable, and he is not entitled to show priority to or preference for one customer over another. If the goods are duly delivered to him for carriage in the course of his business, he must take them by the most direct route that is practicable and without unnecessary delay. When he has received the goods, it is his obligation to deliver them in the same condition as that in which they are received. It is not necessary for the claimant to prove negligence, if the carrier fails to deliver the goods or delivers them in a damaged condition. The law implies a warranty on his part to carry them safely and securely, and to deliver them in accordance with the obligations of the contract. He is relieved from this obligation only if the failure to deliver arises from an act of God or the Queen's enemies, or if it is due to an act of the consignor or sender, or inherent defect or the nature of the thing carried.

It is, however, the duty of the consignor to declare the nature and value of the goods when they are such things as precious stones, articles of gold or silver, stamps, furs, lace, paintings, glassware, etc., and the value of the consignment exceeds £25 in the case of railway and £10 in the case of road transport. The carrier may, if he exhibits a suitable notice at his receiving office, charge an additional sum, by way of insurance, over and above the cost of carriage for taking the risk of conveying such articles. If the articles are not declared to the carrier at the time they are offered for transport, he is not liable for their loss or damage even up to the value of £25 or £10, as the case may be.

A common carrier is entitled to include special conditions disclaiming liability in his contract of carriage, but in the case of the Transport Commission they must be just and reasonable, or they will not be enforced. The question of what is 'just and reasonable' is one that must not be asked when the terms and conditions are the standard ones settled by the Transport Tribunal under powers granted by Act of Parliament. For terms and conditions other than standard ones to qualify as 'just and reasonable', the Commission must offer a 'fair alternative' to carriage at owner's risk.

A private carrier is a carrier who carries goods in special circumstances and not as part of his general trade or business. For instance, if you ask a friend to take a parcel with him on his journey to London for delivery on your behalf, he would be legally regarded as a private carrier.

The legal expression for the delivery of goods to common carriers or private carriers, or for the deposit of goods with third parties, is 'bailment', and the person who receives the goods for carriage or deposit is called the 'bailee'. There are many types of bailment, and the liability of a bailee for loss or damage may vary, or, in each instance, be defined by express contract between the parties. If there is no express contract, the law has laid down the degree of responsibility which the bailee must assume in each instance according to the nature of the case.

The friend who takes your parcel to London for you is described as a 'gratuitous bailee' – i.e. he does not expect to receive any payment for his services. A gratuitous bailee is not as a general rule liable for loss or damage except in the case of gross negligence. As he does not receive any reward for his services, he is not under any obligation to use special care. He must, however, avoid gross negligence. It is difficult to define 'gross negligence', and it has been suggested that it is the same thing as negligence with a vituperative epithet. But it has a generally accepted meaning. If your friend leaves your parcel in the train, it would almost certainly be regarded as 'gross negligence', and you might make a claim against him for compensation. From time to time we all leave parcels in trains. Before making a claim against a friend who has volunteered to carry a parcel, we must search our own conscience and decide whether or not we would wish to be charged with 'gross negligence' on these occasions.

A gratuitous bailee must not, of course, make use of articles deposited with him and employ them for his own purposes, for if he does so, and they meet with mishap, he may be liable for the loss. On the other hand, you may deposit an article with a friend and give him express permission to make use of it, and if you do so there is a different degree of responsibility in the event of damage. For example, if you give a friend permission to use your bicycle, and he meets with an accident as a result of his negligence, he must make good any damage at his own expense. He may, however, be excused from liability if the bicycle is damaged as a result of an accident beyond his control.

If you are taking a holiday, and have surmounted the dangers and risks to which you and your luggage have been exposed, further legal relations arise when you arrive at your destination. The liability of a hotel towards its guests may be subject to special conditions, which are laid down in the Hotel Proprietors Act 1956. This provides a code for hotel-keepers, and the regulations under the Act apply to every hotel or inn which undertakes to receive, lodge, and feed travellers. A public-house which does not lodge travellers is excluded from its provisions, as is also a boarding-house or private hotel which caters for 'boarders' as distinct from 'travellers', and does not claim to open its doors to every bird of passage. Furnished apartments are also outside the scope of the Act, since they do not undertake to provide food.

A hotel under the Act is compelled to accept every traveller if accommodation is available and the traveller is able and willing to pay, and is not obviously objectionable. The proprietor has a special duty to keep in safety the luggage on the premises of all guests who engage sleeping accommodation, and this duty may extend from the midnight preceding a guest's arrival to the midnight following his departure. The guest's motor-car or luggage left in it will not however have to be specially safeguarded by the proprietor, who in any case may limit his liability for loss of or damage to luggage by exhibiting a specified notice in a conspicuous position on his premises.

The notice the proprietor exhibits will result in his liability under the Act to any one guest being limited to £50 in the case of loss or damage to any article and to £100 in the aggregate. These upper limits will not apply if the visitor's property, if necessary in a fastened or sealed container, has been expressly deposited for safe custody with the management, or if such safe custody is not possible through some default of the staff. Nor will they apply if the property is stolen, lost, or damaged by reason of the negligence or deliberate act of the proprietor or one of his servants.

If property is deposited with the proprietor in the manner mentioned he will be responsible without limit unless the loss or damage occurs as a result of an act of God or the Queen's enemies. He is not, however, liable for goods which are stolen or destroyed through the visitor's own negligence, and, except in a case of negligence by him or his servants, he is probably not liable for any injury which may be suffered by the visitor.

Under the now repealed Innkeepers' Liability Act 1863, the hotel proprietor used to receive, in return for his obligations to his guest, the privilege of detaining his luggage if the bill were not paid before he left. He was said to have a 'lien' over it. A lien is a peculiar right of the English law. It allows a man to retain property, although it does not belong to him. It is applicable only in special circumstances, either by Act of Parliament or by custom.

A craftsman, or any man who in the course of his business executes repairs on an article, is entitled, in the absence of agreement to the contrary, to exercise a lien over the goods on which the work has been done, and to retain them in his possession until his charges have been paid. The Disposal of Uncollected Goods Act 1952 has given to this class of persons a qualified right of sale of such goods, which they did not have previously. The right of sale may only be exercised if the goods when ready for delivery after repair are neither paid for nor collected. In addition, the craftsman or shop-keeper must comply with the requirements of the Act in giving the proper notices to the defaulting customer, and he will not lawfully be able to sell the goods until twelve months have elapsed from the date of the first notice. Any balance over from the proceeds of sale after payment of all charges, including those for storage, will have to be paid over to the customer on demand.

In other cases when a right of lien arises, it is a mere right of possession – a right to retain the article over which the lien extends, until payment of the relevant debt. An unpaid seller of goods also has a lien in circumstances which were referred to in Chapter 6. With few exceptions, there cannot, however, be a right to exercise a lien unless the person claiming the right has in his possession the goods over which the lien is to be exercised, and also unless the amount of the debt is certain.

When we speak of goods being in the actual possession of the man who exercises the lien, it means the actual goods over which the right of lien arises, and it does not extend to other goods. For example, if a furniture store effects repairs to furniture, it may exercise a lien and retain the furniture in its possession until its bill for the repairs has been paid, or eventually, it has been able to exercise its statutory right of sale. The lien would not extend, however, to goods which may have been deposited with the store for safe custody, for there is no lien over goods deposited for storage. Of course, a furniture store may make a special contract with the owner of the goods, and include a term in the contract which entitles it to retain the stored goods until the account has been paid. This, however, is not an example of a lien. It is a right to retain property as a result of a contract. In practice, every warehouse usually insists on including a clause in the contract which gives it this right, before it will receive goods into store. Conditions imposed by furniture depositories are frequently arbitrary, and if you propose to store furniture, you should read with great care the contract placed before you by the warehouseman. You will find that the warehouseman will disclaim responsibility for loss which may arise under a variety of conditions, and if you wish to secure yourself against such loss, your remedy is to take out an insurance policy to cover the risks involved.

Insurance is, unfortunately, one of many subjects which must be dealt with all too briefly in this survey. A few particulars must suffice to indicate some of its salient features.

Fire, burglary, and theft are three of the more usual types of risk against which insurance is sought. Life insurance is also almost a habit, whilst marine insurance is the everyday experience of those who have to deal with ships and shipping. There is one feature common to every class of insurance – viz. that it is always based on contract. In each case the terms of the contract – i.e. the conditions under which payment will be made, if the misfortune occurs in respect of which the insurance has been taken – are fully set out in a document called an insurance policy. Insurance policies are issued by insurance companies, or you may in almost every case, except in respect of life insurance, insure with a curious but large and influential body in London, called 'Lloyd's'. This consists of a series of groups or syndicates, each of which is composed of a number of 'underwriters' – i.e. men who undertake or 'underwrite' the particular risk against which the individual wishes to insure.

When you take out an insurance, you will pay a sum, called a 'premium', to the insurers, and in return they will compensate you, if you suffer a loss, on the terms and conditions of the insurance policy which they issue. Before you insure, you must, as a rule, answer a number of questions on a form, called a 'proposal form'. You must be particularly careful to answer these questions accurately, or to see that the replies are correct, if an agent fills in the form, for the answers are intended to act as a guide to the insurance company as to whether or not they will agree to insure you. If, accordingly, there is any untrue or misleading answer, you may find, if you subsequently make a claim, that the Company will be entitled to repudiate liability.

Generally speaking, insurance is a matter of 'indemnity'. It is not a trade or business out of which the insured is entitled to profit. He may recoup himself for a loss, and nothing more. Life insurance is an exception in this respect, since a man whose life may be considered by the community at large to be worthless may, nevertheless, insure it for £10,000, and on his death this sum will, normally, be paid to his personal representatives. On the other hand, if you insure a brooch against loss by theft for the sum of £1,000, when it is worth only £500, and it is subsequently stolen, you are not entitled to recover £1,000, but only the actual value of the brooch at the date of the theft.

Another salient feature of all insurance is that the insured must have what is called an 'insurable interest' in the subject-matter of the policy. This means that you are not entitled to insure another man's property, or another man's life, unless you have some definite financial stake at issue. You are, however, entitled to insure another man's property if you have lent him money on the security of the property, and you would also be entitled to insure his life if he owed you money, and you desired the policy to secure repayment of your loan in the event of his death before he had repaid you.

When a loss occurs it is a frequent and bitter cause for complaint that the insurance policy covers everything but the loss in question. This is not altogether the fault of the insurance company. We are given eyes and intelligence in order that we may read and understand, and if we are too lazy to read our insurance policies, or to ask for an explanation of any technical expressions which are used in the conditions, and which we do not understand, we must accept a share of the blame. On the other hand, insurance companies are also not free of fault in this respect. They usually issue their policies in a form which is not easily intelligible. The conditions of the policy are frequently printed in small type, and no trouble at all is taken, as a general rule, to make the policy comprehensible to the man in the street. It is a matter in respect of which reform is long overdue.

There are few contingencies against which it is not now possible to insure, always bearing in mind that a policy must not be taken out as a mere gamble – e.g. you are not entitled to insure against the risk of the failure of the favourite to win the Derby or of your premium bonds turning out unlucky. If you pay a premium to secure yourself against loss in either case, you would be risking it on a contingency in which you have no active interest, beyond the loss or recovery of your money, and we shall see from Chapter 11 that this is illegal.

Details of National Insurance may be obtained from any Post Office.

9

BANKERS, BILLS OF EXCHANGE, AND PROMISSORY NOTES

'I note I am overdrawn by £7 5s. 10d., and as I have a
spare cheque form, I enclose a cheque for this amount.'
Letter from Joan Doe to her Bank Manager

THE relationship between a banker and his customer is that of
debtor and creditor. It is governed by the law of contract. If
you open an account you agree to lend the Bank your money.
It may do what it likes with it, provided it pays it back to you,
or to your order, in accordance with your instructions. These
instructions are usually given on a document supplied by the
Bank which is called a cheque. A cheque is a negotiable instrument, which means that it may be negotiated or transferred
from one person to another, in a manner to be described in this
chapter. It bears a twopenny stamp, as this is the Revenue duty
payable on all orders which require Banks to pay money on
demand. There is no foundation for the general belief that a
cheque may not be dated on a Sunday.

The conditions upon which the Bank will accept your account are matters of agreement between the Bank and yourself,
but there are some implied conditions which are in accordance
with the practice or custom of Banks. One of these is that the
Bank will treat your affairs as private and confidential, and another is that when you draw a cheque the Bank will honour it,
if you have sufficient funds standing to your credit to meet the
cheque or have made arrangements for an overdraft.

When you have insufficient funds in the Bank to meet a
cheque, the Bank is entitled to return it unpaid, and when it
does so it may mark the cheque in various ways. It may be
marked 'Insufficient funds' or 'Refer to Drawer', colloquially
known as 'R.D.'. Sometimes it may be marked 'Refer to
Drawer Effects not cleared'. This might occur, for example, if
John Doe pays in a £12 cheque for the credit of his account,
and at the time of such payment his credit balance is only £2.
On the following day a £10 cheque, drawn by John Doe and
payable to the order of Richard Roe, is presented to John

Doe's Bank for payment. As the £12 cheque has not yet been 'cleared', John Doe's account has insufficient funds to its credit with which to pay the £10 cheque. By the time the cheque is re-presented, a day or so later, the Bank will know the fate of the £12 cheque. If this has been cleared, and no other funds have been drawn from John Doe's account, the £10 cheque will be paid when it is presented a second time. If, on the other hand, the £12 cheque has been dishonoured and no further funds have arrived for the credit of John Doe's account, the £10 cheque may be returned to Richard Roe marked for the second time 'Refer to Drawer'.

Sometimes a cheque may be returned by a Bank marked 'Orders not to pay'. This means that the drawer has given instructions to his Bank that it is not to be paid. A customer gives such instructions to his Bank at his peril. A cheque not paid on presentation is a dishonoured cheque, irrespective of the circumstances of dishonour. If a man has once signed a cheque he may be liable for payment of the amount for which it has been drawn, and it will not necessarily relieve him of liability if he stops payment of the cheque, unless the cheque or his signature was obtained by fraud. Even in such circumstances he may still sometimes be liable, if the cheque has come into the hands of a third party who has given value for it without any knowledge of the fraud, unless the cheque had been crossed 'not negotiable'.

If your Bank wrongfully fails to pay a cheque which you have drawn, although you have funds in your account to meet it, you may have a claim for damages for breach of contract. You will remember, however, that you may normally recover damages for breach of contract only if you have suffered actual pecuniary loss, and as a general rule nominal damages only will be recovered in an action on a dishonoured cheque drawn to pay a private debt, as distinct from a business debt.

Cheques may be either 'crossed' or 'open'. A crossed cheque either has the name of a Bank or two lines across its face, and the significance of the crossing is that it must be passed through a banking account. An open cheque may always be cashed at the branch of the Bank of the customer who has drawn it, but if you receive a crossed cheque you cannot cash it. If you have no banking account or Post Office savings account, you must take it to a friend or acquaintance who has a banking account, and after you have 'endorsed' it in the manner described below, he may pay it in to the credit of his own account, and give you the cash for it.

Unless a cheque is cashed across the counter at the branch of the Bank on which it has been drawn, there are almost invariably two Banks involved in the collection and payment of every cheque. The Bank which receives the cheque from the holder is known as the 'collecting Bank', and the Bank on which the cheque has been drawn and which must pay the amount of the cheque is known as the 'paying Bank'.

When a cheque is paid into an account, it will be stamped by a crossing stamp with the name of the collecting Bank, and this enables the Bank to be identified at any future date. The words '& Co.' may also be written between the lines of a crossed cheque. This practice dates back to the period when a Banking Company was accustomed to trade with the words '& Co.' as part of its title. Some Banks, such as 'Hoare & Co.', the oldest English Bank, still retain this phrase.

There are many advantages in crossing a cheque. For example, if it is stolen, the thief is not able to cash it across the counter, as he may do with an open cheque. It must, as stated, always be passed through a banking account, and this facilitates detection.

When John Doe draws a cheque payable to 'bearer' it requires no 'endorsement'. If it is payable to Richard Roe, it must be signed or endorsed on the back by Richard Roe or his authorized agent. An endorsed signature must correspond exactly with the name on the face of the cheque. If Mr Doe receives a cheque drawn to his order, but with his name incorrectly spelt as 'John Dough' he must endorse it 'John Dough' and add his correct signature. If the cheque is made payable to Mrs John Doe she must endorse it 'Joan Doe wife of John Doe'. The person in whose favour the cheque is drawn is called the 'payee'.

Cheques which are payable to bearer and cheques which have been properly endorsed are known as bearer instruments. This means that they may be negotiated and cashed by anyone who holds them, in the same way as a bank note. If a bearer cheque has been stolen, no subsequent holder is required to repay the amount of the cheque to the true owner, unless it is crossed 'not negotiable', provided he has given value for the cheque in good faith and without knowledge of the theft.

There are, however, a number of ways in which either a drawer or a payee of a cheque may protect himself against loss by theft. If you make a cheque payable to the order of John Doe and write the words 'Account payee only' in the crossing, no Bank would accept it other than for the credit of John Doe's account. If you write the words 'Not negotiable', it means that no person can have a better title to the cheque than that of the person from whom he has taken it.

Even without this type of crossing, however, an order cheque which has been stolen before endorsement is usually of no value in the hands of the thief. It cannot be negotiated until it has been properly endorsed, and it cannot be properly endorsed, as the payee or his authorized agent are the only persons who may make a proper endorsement. If the thief forges the endorsement, the cheque becomes a nullity, and if the holder of a forged cheque is able to cash it before the forgery is discovered, he may be sued by the true owner for damages for conversion, as defined in Chapter 6. The damage suffered in such a case is usually the amount of the stolen cheque.

It is, of course, impossible for bankers to know if a particular cheque has been stolen, or if it bears a forged endorsement, when it is presented for payment. The Bills of Exchange Act 1882 and other Acts have accordingly given bankers a limited protection against claims for damages for conversion. If a banker pays an *open* cheque in the ordinary course of business and the endorsement appears to be in order, the banker is protected even although the endorsement is a forgery. If a banker pays a *crossed* cheque, he is also protected against a forged endorsement provided he has acted without negligence. In *collecting* a cheque a banker is protected against a claim for conversion provided (1) the cheque is crossed, (2) collected for a customer as distinct from a non-customer, and (3) the banker has acted without negligence and in good faith. When a claim arises, good faith is generally assumed, but the claimant usually relies upon negligence. Negligence in this connexion has been defined as an omission to exercise due care in the interests of the true owner. For example, the Bank must see that all endorsements are apparently correct. It must not accept for a private account a cheque which indicates that the holder is in possession of it as an agent, or in an official capacity, or as an employee of a firm or limited company, or for partnership purposes. Moreover, a Bank is not usually entitled to accept a cheque for the credit of John Doe's account if the cheque is drawn to the order of his employer, Richard Roe, or if John Doe is a director or employee of Richard Roe & Co., Ltd, and the cheque has been drawn to the order of that Company. To enable a Bank to claim protection, it is also essential that it has had no personal interest in the transaction. It must have acted strictly as a conduit pipe or agent for its customer. It loses the protection of the Act if it receives and applies the cheque for the purpose of reducing any overdraft due from its customer, but this does not mean that the Bank is not entitled in proper cases to claim against other parties through whose hands the cheque has passed.

A Bank receives no protection from the law if it pays a customer's cheque when his signature has been forged. A Bank is presumed to know the signature of its own customer, and however clever the forgery, the Bank will not usually be able to escape from its obligation to repay its customer any money paid out on a forged cheque. Exceptions may arise if the customer has actively assisted or deliberately acquiesced in the forgery, or has, by his own acts, hindered or prevented the Bank from recovering payment from the forger, or, in certain circumstances, if the customer has been guilty of such gross negligence as to justify a contention that he has made a substantial contribution towards the fraud.

A Bank may also have to re-imburse its customer for his loss if an alteration has been fraudulently made which increases the amount for which the cheque was originally drawn. If John Doe draws a cheque for 'Four pounds' and this is altered by fraud to 'Fourteen pounds', his Bank may be required to refund the difference if it pays out £14 to the holder of the cheque. The Banker's duty is to honour its customer's mandate. If the customer has only authorized the Bank to pay £4, the Bank is not entitled to debit him with £14. If, however, John Doe has been guilty of contributory negligence, by leaving space for fraudulent manipulation, the Bank may escape liability.

When John Doe receives a cheque payable to his order, he may send it to Richard Roe with the endorsement 'Pay Richard Roe. John Doe'. When Richard Roe receives the cheque, he must endorse it before it can be further negotiated. He may in his turn endorse it to a third named payee, if he so desires. There is no limit to the number of endorsements which may be made on a cheque. Every endorser, however, makes himself liable to the ultimate holder for the amount of the cheque, if it is dishonoured on presentation, unless at the time of endorsement he disclaims liability by the addition of the words 'sans recours' (without recourse) to his signature. When the holder of a dishonoured cheque wishes to enforce his legal rights against the endorsers, he must notify every endorser without delay of the dishonour. If an endorser has paid the amount of the cheque to the holder after it has been dishonoured, he may claim repayment of such amount from all prior endorsers, or, of course, against the drawer of the cheque.

The account which a customer normally keeps with his Bank is called a current account, and the money is 'on call' – i.e. payment may be demanded at any time. He may also keep a deposit account. When money is on deposit, the account-holder cannot require repayment on demand, or draw cheques on the account. It is usual for a Bank to require notice before repaying money on deposit. Interest is usually allowed on deposit accounts.

If a customer wishes to borrow money from his Bank, he should make an agreement either for an overdraft or for a loan, and the Bank may require security, either in the form of stocks and shares, title-deeds to property, a guarantee from an approved third party, or a life policy.

The interest which a customer receives on his deposit account is less than that which he will have to pay on a loan or overdraft, because a Bank is in business for the purpose of making a profit, while the customer deals with the Bank for his own convenience. Not only is it part of the business of a Bank to lend money, but it has to meet the expense of operating its customers' accounts, and also overhead charges and the costs of the services which it renders gratuitously to its customers. It must also keep large funds in hand with which to meet day-to-day demands.

The Bills of Exchange Act 1882 defines a cheque as being 'a bill of exchange drawn on a banker, payable on demand'. A bill of exchange is therefore closely allied to a cheque, and the same Act defines a bill of exchange as 'an unconditional order in writing addressed by one person to another, signed by the person giving it, requiring the person to whom it is addressed to pay on demand, or at a fixed or determinable future time, a sum certain in money, to or to the order of a specified person or to bearer'.

The following example will help to clarify this legal definition. John Doe owes Richard Roe a sum of £100. John Doe has no ready cash, but he has a sum of £100 owing to him by Robert Brown, who has agreed to pay him the debt in three months' time. He explains this to Richard Roe, and Richard Roe agrees to wait for three months for his money, if he is given a bill of exchange by way of security. John Doe may then purchase a 'bill' bearing an *ad valorem* Government stamp from the nearest Post Office. *Ad valorem* means 'according to value', and, in the case of a bill of exchange, the stamp is at the rate of 1s. for every £100 for which the bill is to be drawn. On this bill John Doe will give Robert Brown an unconditional instruction in writing, requiring him to pay the sum of £100 to the order of Richard Roe three months after date. He will do this by writing 'Three months after date pay to the order of Richard Roe the sum of £100'. He will then address it to Robert Brown in the bottom left-hand corner. When he has dated and signed the bill, and has handed it to Richard Roe, Richard Roe has something which is similar to a cheque, except that it is addressed to Robert Brown instead of being addressed to a Bank. The first thing which Richard Roe will want to know is whether or not Robert Brown is prepared to honour the mandate. He therefore takes the bill to Robert Brown and asks him to 'accept' it. If Robert Brown is willing to do so, he will write across the face of the bill 'Accepted payable. Robert Brown'. He may also add the place, usually a Bank, at which it will be paid. If he declines to accept it, he cannot be compelled to do so.

After it has been accepted, Richard Roe has a valid bill of exchange. When it is endorsed by him it is a transferable instrument, and may be negotiated in the same way as a cheque, while the rights of the parties are, generally speaking, analogous to the rights of the parties to a cheque. A bill of exchange may also be 'discounted'. This means that the holder will take it to his Bank, or to a Discount House, who will pay him in cash the amount of the bill less an agreed sum to represent interest which will accrue before the bill reaches 'maturity' – i.e. becomes payable by the acceptor. If the bill is subsequently dishonoured, recourse may, of course, always be had to the holder who has discounted it, for he will be required to endorse it before it is discounted.

When the bill reaches maturity, three days, called the 'days of grace', are allowed to the acceptor for payment, and the bill must be presented for payment on the last of the three days of grace. If the bill is accepted payable only at a Bank, or other specified place, it must be presented at that place. If it is not paid on presentation, it is said to be dishonoured. All parties liable on the bill must then be forthwith notified, for, as in the case of a cheque, the holder will lose his rights against any party not so notified, other than the acceptor, who always remains liable. If the bill is a foreign bill – i.e. if it has not been drawn in this country – and if it is dishonoured, it may be 'noted' for 'protest' within 24 hours, and must then be 'protested' by a Notary Public. 'Noting' and 'protesting' are legal formalities recording the dishonour of a bill. A Notary Public is an official who has power to attest his signature to acts and contracts which have to be evidenced in solemn form. He confers the necessary authenticity on such documents by attaching his seal of office – a procedure called a notarial act – and the noting and protesting of foreign bills of exchange is a matter falling within his province.

A promissory note is another document allied in character to cheques and bills of exchange. It is defined in law as 'an unconditional promise in writing made by one person to another, signed by the maker, engaging to pay on demand, or at a fixed or determinable future time, a sum certain in money to or to the order of a specified person or to bearer'. If John Doe owes Richard Roe £100, and agrees to pay him in three months' time, he may agree to give him a promissory note to secure the payment. In that event, he will sign a note stamped in the same way as a bill of exchange, on which he has written 'Three months after date I promise to pay to the order of Richard Roe the sum of £100'. When Richard Roe has endorsed the note, it becomes a negotiable instrument, and, in general, is subject to the same legal incidents as a bill of exchange or a cheque.

A promissory note is not to be confused with an I.O.U. No particular legal significance attaches to an I.O.U., and the rules applicable to a negotiable instrument do not apply to an I.O.U. nor does it require a stamp. Generally speaking, an I.O.U. is merely a convenient form in which a man who lends money to another obtains an acknowledgement of the debt. The holder of a dishonoured bill of exchange, cheque, or promissory note may commence legal proceedings based on the dishonoured instrument, and, generally speaking, there are very few defences to such an action, short of fraud. No similar action may, however, be brought on an I.O.U. The writ must be issued for the repayment of money lent, and the I.O.U. is useful only as evidence of the debt, if it is disputed.

Criticism of the banking system of this country is frequently due to ignorance of the function of Banks. Until 1945 there was no real Government Bank, other than the Post Office Savings Bank, and its functions are of a different character from those of the other Banks. The Post Office Savings Bank is different because it does not carry on trading operations. It does not lend money, but only receives it, and it pays interest on money which is deposited with it. As its name implies, it is essentially a Savings Bank, and the Government has never made use of it for its financial operations, but has always carried those out through the Bank of England. In 1945, it was argued for nationalization of the Bank of England that the control of Government finance ought to be in the hands of the Government, and not in the hands of a private institution. It was also said that the Government ought not to permit a private Bank to make a profit out of Government business at the expense of the community, and the Bank of England was accordingly nationalized. Under our present economic system it is not clear what advantage the community would receive if control of the other Banks were also in the hands of the Government. They deal in money, which is the recognized token of exchange for buying and selling, and their customers are John Doe and Richard Roe and all the other members of the community. No political party claims the right to dictate how we are individually to use our money. There is no reason why the Government should lend me £500 if I wish to embark upon a speculative venture, and even if I have a sound business proposition, there is no particular reason why I should be financed by the Government – i.e. the community. This is a risk which should be undertaken by a trading concern. It is a business risk which it is the function of a Bank to undertake. Every operation of lending money involves risk, and every Bank loses substantial sums in respect of irrecoverable loans or bad debts every year. A Bank, like every other competently run business, is prepared to take reasonable business risks, but unprejudiced consideration of the matter ought to convince you that if Banks were to 'go haywire' in granting loans, their stability would at once be undermined. A large proportion of the community have banking accounts, and the Bank's customers would not be pleased if they were informed that rash and hazardous speculation by the Bank had resulted in the loss of their money. In fact, the first duty of every Bank is to safeguard its customers' accounts, and there is no reason why *your* money deposited at the Bank should help to finance John Doe when he wishes to set up a speculative business. Rash and hazardous advances for speculative purposes would be equally indefensible if all the Banks were nationalized, and such loans were made by nationalized Banks.

MONEY-LENDERS

'But are they all horrid, are you sure they are all horrid?'

Northanger Abbey

A MONEY-LENDER is the name usually applied to a man who trades in money. It is the legal definition given to a person whose business is that of money-lending. It does not, however, include *bona fide* Banks or insurance companies, registered friendly, loan, or building societies, or pawnbrokers in respect of pawnbroking business. It also excludes every person who carries on a genuine business not having for its primary object the lending of money, even although money-lending may be incidental to the business.

The law has made an attempt to protect the improvident and the inexperienced, but even so, most people will think that an Act of Parliament which recognizes a primary right to lend money at a rate of interest not exceeding 48 per cent per annum is being unduly generous to the money-lender, and is unsocial.

As usual, however, we ought to examine the matter from every angle before we pass judgement. For example, it is obviously fair and proper to consider the point of view of the money-lender. As a member of the community, he is entitled to express his opinions, even if we do not like them. He may contend that prejudice is unfair to him, since the community carries on its business under an economic system which permits the right of exploitation of one individual by another and, indeed, sees nothing unjust or improper in such exploitation. In order to be effective, as well as respected, the law must conform to the state of society in which we live. It would be unrealistic to harness it to social conditions which do not exist, and even at present, the money-lender will argue that the law is putting him into a strait-jacket. Most of us grumble daily at the restrictions which hamper our business activities. Money-lenders may frequently contend that our burdens are but shadows compared with the mass of rules and regulations which must be observed in regard to every shilling they advance.

A money-lender will not, as a rule, claim to be a benefactor of society. He caters for the weak and the improvident, and in many cases the borrower is not a model member of the community. There is also less sentiment on the part of both borrower and lender in a money-lending transaction than there is in other classes of trade or business. When a borrower applies for a loan, there is a reasonable probability that he is either one 'who is generally spoken of as having nothing a year, paid quarterly', or else he will be in fairly desperate straits. Few men of judgement or understanding would ever borrow money from a money-lender, if there was any other method of 'raising the wind'. Therefore Shylock is entitled to claim that, when he lends money, he is running a grave risk of losing it. He contends there is only one way by which he can protect himself and recoup his losses on bad debts, and that is by charging a high rate of interest. When he does this he may gain on the swings what he loses on the roundabouts. In other words, he is compelled to make the 'honest' borrower pay for the bad debt of the 'unscrupulous' borrower. This may be bad ethics, but from his point of view it is prudent business.

When a money-lender asserts that he is hedged in by restrictions he is making a justified claim. He is not entitled to avail himself of the comparatively easy methods open to other litigants who seek to enforce payment of trade debts. Not only does the law require to be satisfied that the money-lender has placed his own house in order, even if the debtor does not defend the proceedings, but it offers a defendant numerous defences of a highly technical character, which may in any particular case be without real merit.

The sheet anchor of the borrower is the Moneylenders Act 1927. It codifies earlier laws, and adds a number of fresh restrictions to the burdens of the money-lender. It does much to make avarice a difficult business, for when the money-lender takes proceedings to recover payment of a debt, any one of the following pleas may be open to a borrower by way of defence, and any single plea, if successfully established, may defeat or modify the claim:

(1) The borrower may plead that the transaction is 'harsh and unconscionable'. This is an old and favourite plea. The right of reopening an 'unconscionable' bargain has been a long-standing privilege, even before any Act of Parliament gave it statutory sanction. The necessity of now proving interest to be both 'harsh' *and* 'unconscionable', a requirement carried forward from the Moneylenders Act 1900, may, *prima facie*, appear to have widened the money-lender's powers of charging excessive interest. In practice this is not the case, for, as a general rule, the phrase is construed liberally in favour of the borrower. This does not mean that the Court is sentimental about the business. Indeed, a sense of justice may sometimes unconsciously compel a Judge to stretch the law in favour of unpopular members of the community, lest it be thought that he is prejudiced in his judgement, for the Courts are equally solicitous for all classes of society.

When the Court has to decide if a particular transaction is harsh and unconscionable, it has to consider not only the risk taken by the lender, but all the circumstances which surrounded the loan. In this connexion, it is important to observe that interest up to 48 per cent per annum is not, *prima facie*, excessive. It is only when interest exceeds 48 per cent per annum that any onus is placed on the money-lender of proving that the interest charged is not excessive. In other words, in every case in which the interest falls short of 48 per cent, the onus is placed upon the borrower to prove it excessive. This does not mean that interest may automatically be charged at such a high rate as 48 per cent. Every case will be considered on its merits, and when adequate security has been accepted by the money-lender, such a rate would frequently be regarded as excessive.

Some of the relevant considerations which the Court might be asked to consider by either party, when a transaction is impeached on this ground, are the age and business experience of the borrower, his social status, the degree of his financial embarrassment, the extent to which he has had previous dealings with money-lenders, the result of such previous dealings, the purpose for which the money was required within the money-lender's knowledge, the probability of the debt being irrecoverable, and the value of any security taken. Particular cases might suggest other considerations. An extreme example might be provided by a borrower seeking relief from an interest charge of 48 per cent, if he satisfied the Court that he required the loan in order to pay his current income tax, and had so informed the money-lender. There is no report of such a case on the records, but if asked to adjudicate in such a quixotic example, the Court might consider the money-lender's risk to be minimal, and not such as to justify a high rate of interest.

Even although the debt has, in fact, been paid, and the transaction has been closed, the Court has power to reopen any money-lending transaction on the ground that it is harsh and unconscionable. A loan brought about by fraud may also always be set aside, and can be dealt with on the same basis as any other contract. For instance, a money-lender might arrange a loan at 15 per cent, but might inform the borrower when he came to complete the transaction that he would have to charge 20 per cent, because of a rise that morning in the Bank Rate. If this statement was untrue the transaction would be fraudulent, and the borrower might be relieved from any obligation to repay the loan.

(2) The borrower may prove that the money-lender was unlicensed at the time when the loan was made. Every money-lender must take out an annual licence under the Act of 1927. Unless he does so he cannot recover payment of money lent.

(3) The borrower may prove that the licence held by the money-lender has not been taken out in his true name. The Act of 1927 does not allow a licence to be taken in an assumed name.

(4) The borrower may prove that the loan was granted at an address other than the registered business address of the money-lender, which has to be specified in the licence.

(5) The borrower may prove that the money-lender did not hold a certificate, which the Act of 1927 requires him to obtain in addition to his licence. The issue of the licence is automatic, if the money-lender supplies the appropriate authority with required information and pays the requisite fees. The issue of the certificate, on the other hand, is a matter of discretion. It is issued by a local magistrate, and may be refused on a number

of grounds – e.g. if the money-lender has been guilty of disreputable trading practices. It may also be suspended by the Court at any time, and suspension or forfeiture of a certificate is automatically followed by suspension of the licence.

(6) The borrower may prove that the money-lender has not registered in accordance with the requirements of the Registration of Business Names Act, referred to in Chapter 7.

(7) The borrower may prove that he was induced to obtain the loan as a result of an advertisement sent through the post or by a traveller or canvasser of the money-lender. Travellers, canvassers, and postal advertising are all forbidden by the Act of 1927, and any loan made as a result of infringement of any of these provisions may bar the money-lender from recovery of his debt.

(8) The borrower may prove that the money-lender failed to supply him at the time when the loan was made with a written statement, specifying the true rate of interest which was being charged for the loan, or that a copy of this statement was not sent to him or signed by him before the money actually passed. The Act of 1927 requires the observance of all these formalities, and the rate of interest must be correctly stated in the document, unless the money-lender has adopted the scale of calculations appended to the Act. In that event the statement must specify this fact.

(9) The borrower may prove that the memorandum which the money-lender must give him with details of the transaction does not disclose all the terms of the bargain. For example, the loan may be made in part to satisfy an old debt; the bargain may include an obligation by the borrower to give post-dated cheques; there may be a collateral guarantee which contains clauses imposing additional obligations on the debtor; a bill of sale (see Chapter 21) which contains a power of seizure and sale may have been given as security for the loan, but a copy of this bill of sale may not have been supplied to the borrower, or may not have been annexed to the memorandum which refers to it; the security may be described as 'a promissory note' when in fact there were two promissory notes.

Each of these circumstances is a term of the bargain which must be fully disclosed in the memorandum. In each instance referred to a borrower has been successful in defeating a claim brought by the money-lender as a result of his omission to set out the necessary facts in the memorandum, or to set them out correctly.

(10) Compound interest is prohibited, and if the borrower proves that it has been charged the amount will be deducted from the claim.

(11) The borrower may prove that the money-lender has failed to supply him with particulars of the loan and interest charged, after a tender of a sum of 1s. has been made for the purpose. This is a further obligation imposed upon the money-lender by the Act of 1927.

(12) Finally, the borrower may prove that the money-lender has failed to commence his action within twelve months of the last instalment of the loan becoming due, and that there has been no written acknowledgement of the debt within that period. In that event the claim is barred.

Usury is the taking of iniquitous or illegal interest on a loan. Since the law sanctions 48 per cent interest on a loan, a money-lender is not a usurer. Accordingly, there is technically no justification for abusing money-lenders. On the other hand, the situation is anomalous and in many respects disturbing. If I want to borrow a piano for a couple of years, it would be fantastic if I had to pay the lender back with two pianos at the end of that time in order to discharge my obligation to him. If interest in excess of, say, 10 per cent was forbidden by law, money-lenders might be worse off, and borrowers in desperate straits would certainly be unable to borrow money. They would perhaps be made bankrupt, instead of being able to continue to prey on the community by 'earning' money by methods which must at times be of a highly suspicious character. Would legislation which restricts interest be beneficial to the community as a whole? We will leave the question unanswered, and you can deliver your own judgement, after you have impartially weighed all the arguments which might be advanced on either side.

GAMING AND WAGERING

'Queen Elizabeth . . . had allwayes about Christmas evens set dice, that threw sixes or five and she knew not they were other, to make her wise and esteame herself fortunate.'

William Drummond

THE law with regard to gaming and wagering is obscure. There is no definition of a lawful game, but an unlawful game is any game in which the element of skill, as distinct from chance or hazard, is virtually absent. In a case in which a jury was asked to decide whether or not the game of poker was a lawful or unlawful game, the only decision reached was that poker as played on the occasion which led to the proceedings was unlawful. The decision does not rank as a precedent since the illegality of any game is a question of fact which has to be determined in every case on the facts. The decision on the occasion in question meant that the jury thought the game was devoid of that particle of skill required to remove it from the realm of illegality into the sphere of legality. The decision does not bar any other person charged with an offence which turns upon the legality of the game of poker from requiring investigation of the facts, and taking a gamble that a different jury would arrive at a different decision.

'Gaming', 'wagering', 'betting', and 'lottery' are the four key words which cause the mischief. These are the Big Four among the lesser sins of the community. What do they each mean?

'Gaming' is the staking of money or money's worth on the result of a game of chance in which there is no appreciable element of skill. 'Wagering' is the term used when money is risked on a contingency in which the wagerer has no active interest, beyond the loss or recovery of his money. 'Betting' is an offshoot of wagering, and is the expression usually, but not invariably, employed in respect of wagers on sports or games. 'Lottery' is a distribution of prizes by lot or chance, and nothing but chance. If real merit or skill plays any part in determining the distribution, there is no lottery.

The year 1388 marks the first legislation passed with the object of suppressing these 'vices'. Labourers were then enjoined, for the purpose of perfecting their military skill, to use bows and arrows on Sundays, and not to play football, quoits, dice, and 'other such importune games'. Over 150 years later, 'bowyers strigers fletchers and arrowhead makers of the realm' persuaded Parliament to pass an Act, which has never been completely repealed, to meet the dangers created by 'divers and many subtil inventive and crafty persons' who had found 'many and sundry new and crafty games and plays as logating in the fields, slide-thrift' (apparently a form of shove-half-penny) whereof 'archery is sore decayed' and 'divers bowyers and fletchers for lack of work had emigrated to Scotland, where they were working and teaching their science to the great comfort of strangers and detriment of this realm'. Penalties were imposed on all persons keeping houses for unlawful games and all persons resorting thereto. Dicing and cards were the principal 'unlawful games' aimed at, but it was further provided that 'no matter of artificer or craftsman of any handicraft or occupation, husbandman, apprentice, labourer, servant at husbandry, journeyman or servant of artificer, mariner, fisherman, waterman or any serving man' should play 'tennis, dice, cards, bowls, coits clash, or logating ... out of Xmas'. They were, however, permitted to play these games during Christmas time, provided they did not do so in their master's house or in his presence. It will be observed that games of skill were included as well as games of chance, and an offence was committed even though the games were not played for money.

The motive prompting this legislation appears to have been the desire to divert the attention of the working man from frivolous pursuits, in order that he might fulfil his military obligations and Sabbath duties. Many statutes passed during the last 500 years have further sought to check these 'sins and iniquities'. They have among other things declared, first, that certain games and lotteries are unlawful; secondly, that it is an offence to keep an establishment for betting, gaming, and lotteries; thirdly, that it is an offence to bet or gamble in streets and public places, and fourthly, that certain claims arising out of betting and wagering are not to be recoverable in Courts of Justice. Offences under the first three of these headings are within the realm of crime. It is to be observed that betting, in itself, is not an offence. There is nothing illegal in receiving or paying a lost bet. 'The law refuses to assist either party in their folly,' remarked one Judge, 'but it is quite another thing to forbid the loser to keep his word.' A bet is, however, a criminal offence if the *manner* and *place* in which it is made are contrary to statute, as explained later in this chapter.

As a result, 'sportsmen' are for ever sparring with the law to avoid being smothered by the blankets laid down for their protection.

Here are some of the operations which free Englishmen are not permitted to perform by virtue of this restrictive legislation.

(1) The Gaming Act 1845 makes it an offence to keep a common gaming house. To prove a house to be a common gaming house it 'shall be sufficient to show that it is kept or used for playing therein at any unlawful game, and that a Bank is kept there by one or more of the players exclusively of the others or that the chances of any game played therein are not alike favourable to all the players, including among the players the banker or other person by whom the game is managed or against whom the other players stake play or bet'. Criminal prosecutions may be brought under this section against persons who organize card parties, and from time to time respectable London clubs, frequented alike by lords and commoners, are raided as a prelude to a prosecution. Premises at which a bridge club is conducted are not regarded as a common gaming house, as bridge is considered to be a game which requires skill, and is accordingly not an unlawful game. Small gaming parties not promoted essentially for private gain are rendered lawful by the Small Lotteries and Gaming Act 1956.

(2) By the Betting Act 1853 it is illegal to keep a house, office, room, or other place for the purpose of any person betting with persons resorting thereto, or for receiving deposits in consideration of bets on contingencies relating to horse races, or other races, fights, games, sports, or exercises.

This Act has given rise to much legal subtlety. The word

E

'place' is not defined, but it has been held to include a public-house, a bar, an archway, a small plot of waste ground, a book-maker's stand, and even the space beneath an umbrella which a bookmaker had opened to attract customers. It has also been held to include club premises, when special telephone lines were installed to connect the club with a bookmaker to facilitate betting by members, and even although no bets were ever taken on the club premises.

(3) By the Betting and Loans (Infants) Act 1892 it is an offence to send a document to anyone known to be an infant inviting him to enter into a betting or wagering transaction, if it is sent with a view to profit.

(4) The Street Betting Act 1906 makes it an offence for any person to frequent or loiter in a street or public place on behalf of himself or any other person for the purpose of bookmaking or betting or wagering or agreeing to bet or wager or paying or receiving or settling bets. A motor driver who passed and re-passed along a street and slowed down to receive betting slips was held to be a 'frequenter', and accordingly to have committed an offence under this Act. Race-courses and land adjacent to race-courses are, however, expressly excluded from the Act on days when racing takes place.

(5) The Betting and Lotteries Act 1934 codified the law relating to lotteries. In addition to this Act the Small Lotteries and Gaming Act 1956 has to be considered. A very wide net is cast to enmesh all those who directly or indirectly take part in the promotion of a lottery. Lotteries which are incidental to bazaars, sales of work, fêtes, and other similar entertainments are not illegal if the whole of the proceeds subject to minor deductions, are devoted to purposes other than private gain, and there are no money prizes. Private lotteries in which tickets are sold exclusively to members of a society, such as a club or institute, or which are promoted at a factory, or other works, or residential premises, where all the participators work or reside on the same premises, are also excluded from the provisions of the Act. They are lawful, provided there is neither advertising of the lottery nor the sale of tickets to anyone outside the group among whom the lottery is being conducted, and if the whole of the proceeds, subject to the deduction of proper

expenses, is used for prize money or club purposes. A third category of lawful lotteries added by the Act of 1956 mentioned above are small lotteries conducted by societies whose main aims are charitable, sporting, cultural, or otherwise non-commercial, and not for private gain. Such lotteries must directly benefit the society's objects. There are restrictions on their magnitude, distribution of takings, advertising, etc., and the society concerned must be registered with the local authority to whom certain information has to be given.

Those who contemplate the promotion of a charity or private lottery would be well advised to make themselves acquainted with the full provisions of the two Acts, as infringement of the law subjects the promoters to criminal proceedings, with the prospect of heavy penalties, and even the possibility of imprisonment after the first conviction.

(6) Football pools conducted through newspapers are unlawful since they contravene the provision in the Betting and Lotteries Act 1934 forbidding a newspaper to conduct a competition in which prizes are offered for forecasts of a result of a future event. However, football pool promoters being well advised, the publicity received by the large national pools in the Press does not make them illegal. The Pool Betting Act 1954 compels the registration of a promoter of pool betting with the local authority. In order that there may be some check, at least theoretically, on the carrying on of his business, a promoter has to supply the local authority with limited statements of accounts. The Act of 1954 gives promoters a concession by removing the ban on ready money pool betting by post.

The agreement between yourself and the football pool promoters is 'binding in honour only', and you would not be able to sue for any prize money if it were not paid to you. On the other hand, the business of the pool promoters, even more than that of the bookmaker, depends upon their ability to retain public confidence, and you, together with the other millions of pool punters, can feel fairly safe in the hope that if your forecast is correct you will not be deprived of your hard-earned windfall.

(7) Totalisators have not been overlooked. As they are, from

their very nature, calculated to infringe the betting laws, a special statute was passed to permit them to be operated on approved horse race-courses and licensed dog-tracks, for pari-mutuel and pool betting transactions. Betting at the dogs has also been the subject of legislation, and betting may take place on licensed dog-tracks, although licences are issued only under stringent conditions.

The betting laws are particularly criticized for permitting credit betting, thereby making an unfair discrimination in favour of the wealthier members of the community, and the Royal Commission, whose report was published in 1951, took this criticism into account in their recommendation that 'off the course' cash betting should be legalized. It is right to observe, however, that a legal authority to bet is not necessarily a boon. In an ordered community, licence to gamble is a doubtful asset, and there is no difference in principle between the get-rich-quick Stock Exchange speculator, and the 'punter' who hopes for unearned increment every time he puts a shilling on a horse. Gambling has brought ruin to many, and will bring ruin to many more. When the present law is criticized, it is fair to remember that restrictions on betting and gambling help to make indulgence more difficult, and the community may benefit, since we are not all inoculated against gambling fever. While, however, the removal of restrictions would have unfortunate results, further limitations on credit betting would undoubtedly be the signal for universal lamentations from rich and poor. Even if the present situation pleases no one, it may still be best fitted to meet the needs of the community, as so often happens when the English exercise their genius for compromise. The Government announced its intention in 1956 to submit to Parliament radical proposals for changing the betting laws along the lines suggested by the Royal Commission.

A person who enters into an agreement to give or receive money or money's worth upon the determination or ascertainment of an uncertain event – i.e. a wager – cannot enforce the agreement in a Court of Law. It is a debt of honour, or 'gentleman's agreement'. The Gaming Act 1845 includes a provision that all agreements, whether verbal or in writing, 'by way of gaming or wagering' shall be null and void and 'no suit shall be brought or maintained in any court of law or equity for re-covery of any sum of money or valuable thing alleged to be won upon any wager or which shall have been deposited in the hands of any person to abide the event on which any wager shall have been made'. The provision expressly excludes any subscription for prize money to be awarded to the winner of 'any lawful game, sport, pastime, or exercise', and there is ac-cordingly nothing to preclude a Court from entertaining a claim for prize money, in a proper case. The Gaming Act 1892 was passed to catch commission agents and to bar their right to recover debts owing to them by their principals, in respect of bets made and paid for them.

Even if a cheque is given in payment of a gaming debt, the drawer may stop payment, and he cannot be sued by the payee, since the consideration is illegal. If the cheque has been passed for value to a third party, the latter can recover payment only if he has taken it in good faith and in ignorance of the illegality which taints the transaction. A third party who has taken a cheque drawn in payment of a betting debt *which does not arise out of gaming* is in a stronger position. In such a case, and by the application of the ordinary rules which govern negotiable in-struments dealt with in Chapter 9, he may recover payment, so long as he has given value for the cheque. The holder of the cheque is favoured in this way, because, as already stated, there is nothing illegal in receiving or paying certain types of lost bet.

The business of a bookmaker might under all these restric-tions appear to be hazardous. Nevertheless, it is conducted with profit by many bookmakers, and most of them naturally know and keep to the rules of the game. It will, of course, be appreciated that they are able, in theory, to carry on their busi-ness only by accepting all bets on credit terms, with the excep-tion of those permitted on days of racing on and adjacent to race-courses, which were referred to above. Any other form of betting is illegal, and would attract the attention of the police in a most undesirable form. Moreover, it must again be em-phasized that even credit bets, if unpaid, cannot be recovered by legal proceedings, and the bookmaker cannot recover payment from his client, if he fails to honour his engagements. The urge to gamble being what it is, bookmakers keep their flags flying.

Whether the community is hypocritical or pharisaical on the subject of betting is a matter of speculation. It is relevant to observe that the bookmaker is under the same obligation as any other trader to pay income tax on the profits of his business, while the law does not refuse to intervene in disputes between partners in a bookmaking business.

Although bookmakers may be unable to recover payment of their debts through the machinery of the Courts, they sometimes have other methods. Defaulting debtors may be ready to come to terms with a bookmaker, if it is suggested by the bookmaker that, if they do not pay, their default will be reported to Tattersall's. After such a report has been made, no reputable bookmaker will accept a bet from the defaulter, and it may mean the end of a gambler's dream.

Wagering includes gambling in stocks and shares, and the law will not enforce a contract to pay monies won or lost in such a case. All transactions carried out through a recognized Stock Exchange are, however, subject to rules and regulations designed to avoid illegality. Speculation, if carried out according to well-settled rules, is not wagering, although the bargain will be unenforceable if it is found to be a simple wager on the price of a particular stock at some future date, and if the real interest of the parties is to gamble in the difference between the price at the date of purchase and the price on the date when the stock would have had to be delivered if the transaction had been *bona fide*.

Stock Exchange transactions are subject to some degree of control, which curtails the wilder aspects of speculation, and many reputable stockbrokers have never been willing to undertake disguised gambling for clients.

Legislation has restricted the activities of a class of stock and share brokers, known as 'outside brokers'. They are not members of any recognized Stock Exchange, and their activities have usually been a veiled form of gambling. Although they took your money, they frequently refused to pay you when you won your bet. Under the Prevention of Fraud (Investments) Act 1939, every dealer in stocks and shares who is not a member of a recognized Stock Exchange must obtain a licence from the Board of Trade before he is permitted to deal. A sum of £500 must be deposited as a preliminary to the grant of any licence, and the Board has power to refuse or revoke a licence when the applicant fails to furnish satisfactory information about his proposed business, or if he appears to the Board not to be a fit and proper person to hold a licence. The regulations are designed for the protection of the unwary, and to save dupes and gulls from scoundrels.

Thus, although our betting and gaming laws are mysterious, inconsistent, and paradoxical, there stands out the predominant desire of the legislature to be a grandmother to those who have insufficient strength of character to resist the potential evils of gambling. Legislation by grandmothers may be undesirable, since 'there is no spectacle so ridiculous as the British public in one of its periodical fits of morality'. On the other hand, let us be honest and admit that some of us run better when we are kept on the straight and narrow path.

FRAUD

> 'I remember when one whole island was shaken with
> an earthquake some years ago, there was an impudent
> mountebank who sold pills which (as he told the
> country people) were very good against an earthquake.'
> Joseph Addison

THE majority of the community are law-abiding and honest,
but there is a minority who wilfully break the law or who are
deliberately dishonest. Some offend from greed – a desire for
wealth and power – others because they have never been
trained in the duties of citizenship, and find crime a stimulat-
ing adventure, and yet others because they have been barred
from participation in the normal life of the community, either
through unadaptability or misfortune.

Imprisonment, i.e. loss of personal liberty, or payment of a
fine is the punishment prescribed by the law for those who are
found guilty of an offence against the rules of the community.

Loss of liberty, however, is no consolation to the individual
who has been physically or financially injured by the offence,
nor is he usually entitled to any benefit from the fine. If you are
assaulted, you are entitled to claim compensation from the
aggressor in the civil courts, although, as an exception to the
general rule, no civil action will lie against the assailant if
criminal proceedings have been taken in respect of the same
assault. If you are the victim of a fraud, you are also entitled to
compensation, and this chapter outlines the nature of the assistance which the *civil* law can give you on such occasions. Very
often, of course, a swindler is impecunious or manages to conceal the proceeds of a fraud. It should be obvious, although the
community do not always appreciate the fact, that the law cannot achieve the impossible. If a man has no money, or if he has
concealed it with sufficient skill and ingenuity to defeat human
efforts to trace it, the law is no more powerful than the individual in effecting its recovery.

There is no precise legal definition of fraud, but it is, in
general terms, any deceit or imposture. Many frauds are action-
able torts. For example, 'share-pushing', or the unloading of

worthless shares on members of the public, by false representation as to their value, is a fraud. Obtaining money by false pretences is a fraud. The sale to an innocent purchaser of property known to the vendor to be stolen is a fraud. Any one of them, irrespective of punishment by the criminal courts, may give rise to an action in the civil courts. You are not entitled to compensation in such circumstances as a matter of course. An allegation of fraud is a serious one, and requires strict proof. An example will illustrate the facts which you must be prepared to prove if you hope to succeed in an action brought to recover damages for fraud.

Let us suppose that you have seen an advertisement in a newspaper advertising for sale for £1,000 a business which is stated to have an average weekly turnover of £100. After some correspondence, and an interview with the advertiser, during the course of which he adds a few 'puffs' to garnish the virtues of the business which he hopes to sell, you foolishly agree to buy the business without seeking any advice, pay out £1,000, and complete the deal.

After a few days you find that the turnover is not £100 a week, or even approximately that amount, but is only about £50 a week. In fact, you realize that you've 'been had'. You then consult a lawyer in order to ascertain your legal position, in the confident belief that the law will rescue you from the bog into which you have innocently, but foolishly, waded. You will be advised that there are five essential ingredients which you must prove to establish your legal right to rescission or cancellation of the contract, or to damages. They are common to all actions for fraud. Each of them requires separate examination.

1. There must have been a representation of fact. The statement in the advertisement that the average turnover was £100 a week was a statement or representation of fact. The first element in the case is thus, in this instance, easily proved. If, however, the advertiser had not made any exact statement of the takings, but had spoken in vague terms of an 'excellent' or a 'first-class' business, you might have no remedy. These are not statements of fact, but are usually regarded as mere expressions of opinion, or puffs, which do not give rise to a legal claim,

for opinions may differ as to when a business is 'excellent' or 'first-class'. Again, the advertiser may have concealed an important fact – e.g. that a rival business was to be opened on adjoining premises. Unless words were used which were deliberately deceitful, you would, however, normally have no remedy merely because you were not informed of this. There would have been no representation of fact unless you had actually been informed that you would not have to contend with any opposition, or words had been used which were deliberately intended to give you that impression.

2. You must next prove that the representation or representations of fact were made without any honest belief in their truth. Of course, if the advertiser had left behind him a set of books, purporting to establish the takings as being £100 per week, and you are able to prove that the entries in the books are false, the Court would be satisfied that he did not believe his statement was true when he inserted his advertisement. Suppose, however, he was just a muddler who kept no books of account. It is possible, in such a case, that he might really have thought his turnover was £100 a week. You may find this difficult to believe, perhaps, but there are many muddlers in the world who are capable of believing anything they wish to believe.

3. The third link in the chain is to prove that the defendant intended you to act upon the representation. When an advertisement offering property for sale is published, the intention is apparent, but the facts are not always so simple. If you meet your friend, John Doe, at the 'local', and he gives you alluring details of the profits of his business, he may, or may not, be merely boasting. You, however, may take his remarks seriously, and decide you would like to buy the business – the remote prospect of acquiring it lending enchantment to your idea of its value. You pluck up courage, and when you meet John Doe a few days later, you ascertain that he is willing to sell, and you enter into negotiations for its purchase which in due course materialize. You may then be in a quandary if you find that the profits suggested by John Doe are illusory, and that the customers are few and far between. If you sue him for damages for fraud, he may plead that he never intended you to act upon his

representations, and you will have to admit that no question of sale had arisen at the date of your original discussion. Even if John Doe had, in fact, lured you into the negotiations, he may have been too cunning to disclose his deceit, and you have no shred of evidence to prove it. You will not, therefore, be able to succeed in your claim for damages, since, although 'the state of a man's mind is as much a question of fact as the state of his digestion', suspicion as to the state of his mind normally proves nothing in a Court of Law.

4. You must prove that you have in fact acted upon the representations made to you. The actual purchase of the business is normally the best evidence that can be given to prove this claim. If you had not purchased the business, because you mistrusted the advertiser, and, in fact, had been astute enough to realize that the advertisement was not *bona fide*, you would have no claim for wasted time. You might, of course, in such circumstances tell your friends, in confidence, that a man like that ought to be prosecuted. You might also think it desirable to report the facts to the police, in order to protect the community from his fraud. Citizens, however, rarely act in this way. They prefer to mind their own business. Moreover, before you make complaints to the police, or suggest to your friends, even in confidence, that some one ought to be prosecuted, you should be very sure of your facts. You may otherwise become involved in an action for slander – a subject dealt with in Chapter 15.

5. You must prove that the representations were, in fact, untrue. This is frequently the most difficult task of all. Suppose, in the example we are considering, that the takings were only £50 during the first week of your ownership instead of the 'average weekly turnover of £100'. If the advertiser has not left behind any books of account, it will not be easy to prove that the takings did not average £100, in accordance with his representation. He may contend that the customers had patronized the business because he was personally popular; and he may say it is not his fault if they refused to transfer their custom to you after the sale. Alternatively, he may say that you are lazy and do not attend to the business properly, or you are inexperienced and do not understand it. He might

even say that you know 'the price of everything and the value of nothing'. If he is very skilful and deceitful, he may also produce a set of books to prove his statements were true. As you purchased the business without any trial period under his ownership, it may be impossible to prove that the entries in the books are false.

However, if you have been able to establish this and the other four points in your favour you may then be able to obtain legal redress.

If you have acted promptly on learning of the fraud, but only if you have acted promptly, the Court may rescind or cancel the contract, and order the defendant to repay the purchase price, and also to pay damages for any loss you have suffered as a result of the fraud. In other cases the Court may order the defendant to pay, as damages, such a sum as will represent the difference between the value of the business, if the facts had been truly stated, and the sum which you paid upon the false representations, together with any expenses which you may properly have incurred. There are some cases of this character when fraud cannot be proved, but the Court is satisfied that there was an innocent, as distinct from a fraudulent, misrepresentation. In these cases the Court may order the contract to be rescinded and the purchase money to be repaid. It will not, however, award damages to reimburse you for the expense which you have incurred in installing yourself in the business.

In any event, you are almost certain to emerge from the affair a wiser but a poorer man, and although we learn every day that we have to pay for our errors, we may sometimes get value for our money if we record the mistakes in our book of experience.

From the foregoing you will have gathered that if you are considering the purchase of a business from a stranger, you should never buy a 'pig in a poke'. If a 'pig' is offered for sale which appears to be attractive, be sure you seek advice before you agree to buy it. There are many members of the get-rich-quick fraternity who are on the look-out for the unwary, and if you have recently inherited money, which you wish to invest in the purchase of a business, it will soon disappear, unless you act with prudence and caution.

Moreover, as a footnote, you should remember that, when you purchase a business, it is always advisable to agree with the vendor, as a term of the sale, that he will not open a competing business within a named radius, and within a fixed period. This is known as a 'restrictive covenant', and is almost invariably included in every properly drawn agreement for the sale of a business. The same principles are to be applied in preparing such a covenant as are referred to in Chapter 5, when the question of 'restraint clauses' in agency agreements was considered. It is, however, essential to remember that the Courts will refuse to enforce the provisions of a restrictive covenant if it falls beyond the limits which are reasonably necessary for your protection on the facts of the case.

13

TRESPASSERS, LICENSEES, AND INVITEES

'Said my mother, "What's all this story about?" –
"A cock and a bull," said Yorick.'
Tristram Shandy

WHEN you walk in the country you may observe a notice-board at the entrance to a meadow marked 'Private. Trespassers will be prosecuted. By Order.' What is the legal significance of such a notice?

A 'trespass' used in this sense is an unauthorized entry on land. If you enter the land of Mr Doe without his authority, express or implied, you are committing the tort of trespass. Hence all squatters are trespassers.

Trespass, formerly regarded as a criminal offence, is not limited to offences relating to land. The term includes a variety of torts committed in respect of land, goods, or persons. Trespass to the person may in certain circumstances be prosecuted as an assault, and trespass to goods may also constitute a conversion, a subject dealt with in Chapter 6.

In this chapter trespass is used in the more restricted sense of an unlawful entry on land, and at the present time it gives rise, generally speaking, only to proceedings in a Civil Court. If John Doe finds you in the act of trespassing on his land, and you refuse to leave when you are asked, he may eject you forcibly. He must not, however, use more force than is necessary for the purpose. If you leave the land quietly, he has, for practical purposes, no remedy, unless you have caused damage to his property, or threaten to repeat the offence. You must not, however, feel encouraged to trespass because of the difficulty which the owner has of enforcing a remedy. The exhibition of the notice may be of little importance in itself, but private property is not public property, and it is a tort to trespass on private land, even if no warning notice is exhibited. You should, in any event, always be careful, when you are walking through a field, to shut every gate and to avoid trampling over growing crops. If you leave a gate open, and cattle stray on to the highway, you may be responsible for any injury which ensues. You may also be liable if you damage growing crops.

Although Mr Doe has so little remedy for a casual trespass, he may obtain an injunction from the Court to restrain a man who persists in the offence. If the trespasser disregards the terms of the injunction, he may then be committed to prison for contempt of Court, for the Court has no sympathy for any member of the community who flouts its orders.

There are many occasions when you will find a footpath leading across a field. Are you committing a trespass if you walk across this path? The answer depends largely on whether or not there is a right of way to the public to use the path. If the path has been open to the public for a period of twenty years, without any interruption or interference from the owner of the land, it becomes a right of way for all time, unless this right is subsequently lost as a result of the abandonment by the public of the right – e.g. acquiescence by the public in a barrier erected by the owner, which bars access to the right of way. However, under the National Parks and Access to the Countryside Act 1949, it became the duty of local authorities to prepare maps showing the existing public footpaths, and these maps are available for inspection by the public.

Mr Doe, who has recently purchased Greengates, with 20 acres of land, may be annoyed to find a right of way across his land. The right once established, however, is attached to the land. It may be either a public or a private right of way, but the sale of the land to a fresh owner cannot destroy the right. If it is a public right, i.e. available to the public at large, it is known as a highway. If it is a private right of way, i.e. for the benefit of an adjoining owner, it is what is called in law an 'easement'. An easement is a peculiar legal privilege or right, and a private right of way is only one of several forms which it may take. It is an essential feature of every easement that it gives a stranger, Richard Roe, the owner of property A, a defined privilege *vis-à-vis* John Doe's property B, and allows things to be done which would otherwise amount to a trespass. For example, there may be easements relating to drains, sewers, or passage of water, which will give Richard Roe the right to the use of specified drains or sewers, or the right to run water across John Doe's land.

When you see a path across a field, you must not assume that it is a right of way. It may be that a public-spirited owner allows the public to use the path. He can do so, and at the same time preserve his rights over it as a private path, by closing it for a single day in each year. Any act performed at intervals, and clearly designed to show that the owner is not dedicating the path to the public, is sufficient to bar any subsequent claim by the public to a right of way.

Apart from your legal authority to use a public right of way across Greengates, you may have occasion to visit the house on the estate for a particular purpose. Your legal rights and obligations will vary according to the circumstances of your visit in each case, and they will depend on whether you are a trespasser, a 'licensee', or an 'invitee'.

A licensee (not, in this instance, to be confused with 'the Voice within the Tavern') is a man who has express or implied permission to do an act which would otherwise be unlawful. If there is no right of way, and you enter the grounds of Greengates without any legal justification, you are a trespasser, but if you enter them in order to visit the premises for a lawful purpose, or if Mr Doe invites you to do so, you are either a licensee or an invitee. You must not confuse 'right of way' with 'licence'. A right of way is, as explained, a right which goes with the land. No permission to use it is given to you by Mr Doe, as he has no say in the matter. A licence, which may be express or implied, is a personal authority, given by an owner, and it can be withdrawn at any time, unless it was given for valuable consideration. If given for valuable consideration it has, generally speaking, the effect of a contract, and your rights will be determined by the conditions under which it was given.

A licence to enter land is not necessarily given by express authority. It may sometimes be implied. For example, you may enter Greengates to fetch your umbrella, which you had inadvertently left behind on your last visit to the house. You then have a licence to visit Greengates, and you will be a licensee and not a trespasser, because fetching an umbrella, in such circumstances, is a lawful act, and when you are entering the land to fetch it, you are doing so for a lawful purpose. The lawful purpose gives you an implied authority to enter the land, even although you have no express invitation to do so.

There is an important distinction between the legal rights of a trespasser and a licensee. Generally speaking, a trespasser has few legal rights. If he is injured when trespassing, and even although the injury results from some neglect or default on Mr Doe's part, he has no legal remedy. He has no business to be there, and he is not entitled to complain if Mr Doe has left a bull in a field, and he takes a toss. Nor has a late-night reveller any legal remedy if, straying accidentally from the roadway, he enters through the gates which give access to Mr Doe's land, and injures himself by falling in a trench dug by Mr Doe for his sweet peas. He has no lawful business on Mr Doe's land, and cannot recover compensation for the injury. On the other hand, Mr Doe is not entitled to set a deliberate trap on the land, in order to catch trespassers as though they were wild beasts. That would be illegal, as it would be taking the law into his own hands, and if a trespasser were injured in such a trap he might be able to claim compensation.

A licensee, however, has a legal status which gives him legal rights. Although he cannot expect Mr Doe to take special precautions for his security, he is entitled to expect the land to be safe from hidden dangers. If he is lawfully on the land, he might claim compensation if he fell during hours of darkness in a trench. It is what is known in law as a 'concealed trap' – although the word 'trap' in this instance does not necessarily mean any deliberate or even any positive act by the owner of the property, and might include, for example, a concealed step in a dark corridor. The liability of the owner for injuries caused by a concealed trap is not an absolute one in every instance. If he can satisfy the Court that he did not know of the concealed trap and could not reasonably be expected to infer any danger, from actual knowledge of the physical situation, he may be able to avoid liability.

The term 'invitee' to which reference has been made is in some respects a misleading one. If you accept Mr Doe's invitation to tea, you might reasonably consider that you are an 'invitee'. This is not the case. You are only a licensee.

Nevertheless, when the milkman calls at your premises and delivers your milk, he is an invitee. You must therefore rid your mind of the mental association between 'invitation' and 'invitee'. The relationship of invitor and invitee arises when there is a mutual interest or common purpose between the owner or occupier of premises – the invitor – and the individual who enters the premises – the invitee. It is not sufficient for this mutual interest or common purpose to be merely social in character, for, as stated in Chapter 2, it does not give rise to a legal claim for damages when a friend who has accepted an invitation to tea fails to arrive. Accordingly, when you visit Greengates in order to accept Mr Doe's invitation to tea, you have not the same legal status as the milkman who has an obligation to deliver the milk. He is, therefore, the invitee, and you are the licensee.

It is not necessary in every case that there should be an express contract in order to create the relationship of invitor and invitee. When a man enters a shop with the intention of making a purchase he is an invitee, because the proprietor has the hope and expectation of selling his goods. This prospective contract creates a mutual interest or common purpose between the parties, even although the customer may not, in fact, make a purchase.

The distinction between licensee and invitee is of importance in considering their respective legal rights. The licensee, as stated, must take the premises as he finds them, provided there is no concealed trap known to the occupier. The invitee, on the other hand, is entitled to protection from 'unusual danger', as distinct from 'hidden danger' or 'concealed trap', and there is a duty imposed on the owner of property to take reasonable care to prevent injury to an invitee from unusual danger of which he knows, or ought to know, by warning notice or otherwise as may be sensible.

If Mr Doe leaves a bull in a field giving access to Greengates, we have seen that a trespasser has no legal ground to complain if he is injured. If, however, a licensee or an invitee is tossed by a bull and injured, Mr Doe might be under some liability, the extent of such liability being dependent on the facts in each case.

If, for example, either a licensee or an invitee is visiting Greengates and sees a bull in the field as he approaches the premises, it would be wise for him to consider his step before he goes forward, particularly if the bull has hay on his horn. It is true that the owner has no business to leave a bull in an open field, but a bull, although perhaps an unusual danger, is not necessarily a concealed trap, or a hidden danger, if he is seen to look aggressive from afar. If a bull bars the way, the visitor must accordingly act with prudence. If he decides to take a chance, although he realizes the risk of an attack, he may not be able to claim compensation if the bull fulfils his expectations. Even an invitee might be without redress in such a case, for it would not be the presence of the bull which is the proximate or immediate cause of the injury, but his own negligence in rashly advancing. The problem would be still more involved, and a fit subject for a legal 'moot', if the visitor thought the bull was a cow. In that event a Judge might be called upon to decide whether a man is legally to blame if he is innocent of the distinction between the bovine sexes. Without giving any assurance on the point, it might be argued that an *invitee*, if a townsman, could plead his ignorance, although a *licensee* would not in any circumstances be able to do so successfully.

Consider these two examples, which further illustrate how difficult it may be to decide in a particular case whether or not compensation is likely to be recovered by a licensee or an invitee when he meets with injury.

1. You are shopping at Mr Roe's stores and you are unfortunate enough to fall and injure yourself on the forecourt, not in the occupation of Mr Roe, which unknown to you has a greasy surface. You are not in Mr Roe's shop so you are not his invitee. You are not on the pavement so you cannot claim damages from the local authority responsible for its condition. The Courts have decided that you are the licensee of the owner of the forecourt, and if he is unaware of the defect in question, you may not meet with success in your court claim.

2. You are visiting your friend Mr Roe in hospital. On your way to his ward you are again unfortunate, and you fall and

injure yourself on highly polished linoleum. The highly-polished linoleum may be a concealed trap, and further, you may be an invitee because your visit is helping the hospital in its treatment of Mr Roe, but the Court may decide in your favour on another ground: namely that the hospital authority has been negligent in carrying out the polishing. The tort of negligence has been referred to previously in Chapter 2.

Yet other difficulties arise in cases involving injury to children.

Children are legally recognized as being playful and mischievous, and as they are not capable of looking after themselves in the same way as adults, the law is more solicitous for their welfare. Owners of property have, in particular, an added burden of responsibility placed upon them in their legal associations with children. If Mr Doe knows that children are in the habit of playing on his land, and he takes no positive step to bar their access, he may be responsible in certain circumstances, if they injure themselves. The law may hold that he has consented to the children coming on his land so that they are not trespassers but licensees. For example, children like to play with farm implements, and if Mr Doe leaves a tractor in a field which he knows is frequented by children, he must take precautions to bar access to the field whilst the tractor is unprotected, and in that state a concealed trap to the average child. If he does not do so, and a child, Fidget, injures himself by interfering with the mechanism of the tractor, Mr Doe may be liable to pay compensation for the injury. It may be no defence to plead that Fidget had been warned not to play round the tractor or that he had not been sufficiently careful while playing.

Mr Doe might, however, be able to escape liability if neither he nor his employee knew that children had ever previously been in the field. In those circumstances the children would very probably be trespassers and would be owed no greater duty than that owed to adult trespassers. He may also have a good defence to a claim if Fidget were accompanied by an adult at the time of the accident. If the child is under supervision, his legal status is that of a trespasser. Finally, Mr Doe might also escape liability if he could prove that an unauthorized person had unexpectedly removed an obstruction which had previously barred access to the field. The law will not hold him responsible for the unpredictable act of an unauthorized person.

As a finish to a difficult subject, here is another 'teaser' of its time.

Fidget was injured by broken glass, left lying in a pond in a public park owned by a Local Council. Was he entitled to compensation? The Judge who tried the case in the first instance arrived at the conclusion that the child was entitled to compensation as an invitee, expressing the view that there was a common interest between the Local Council and the children in its area that the latter should be kept away from the streets, particularly if they were children of ratepayers. The Local Council took the case to the Court of Appeal, who rejected the view that the child was an invitee and came as near to scoffing as was decent at the suggestion of 'common interest' between a Council and the user of one of its parks. They decided that the child was a licensee, and although one Judge observed that he was puzzled by the various decisions as to when the relationship between two parties was to be regarded as invitor and invitee, another Judge accepted the proposition that the true test is that an invitor asks you to enter, i.e. in a business as distinct from a social sense, whilst a licensor permits you to do so. In spite of this decision, however, the injured infant was not deprived of compensation. The Council had exhibited a notice forbidding the deposit in the pond of bottles, tins, and sharp materials, and shortly before the accident had, in fact, swept the surface with a shallow but inadequate rake. This was evidence, said the Court, that the Council knew of the danger which would not be known to the child. Since it was alive to the danger it was its duty to take adequate measures to prevent injury. It had failed to do so, and the Plaintiff was entitled to compensation whether he was an invitee or merely a licensee.

You will observe that this decision met the test laid down earlier in this chapter that the licensor must protect the licensee from a concealed trap or hidden danger.

You will be acting unreasonably if you blame lawyers for the difficulty of ascertaining the law. The law has been moulded by lawyers to meet the incidents of daily life, and is largely based upon the dictates of humanity, reason, and justice with Judge Doe and Judge Roe each having, however, different ideas as to the meaning of these three virtues. It may be that this branch of the law will soon be placed on the basis of an Act of Parliament. If so, it will not mean necessarily that lengthy argument on questions of liability will vanish from the Court. A good or a bad thing? The reader will have to decide which view to take.

14

NEIGHBOURS

'Mr Snoot: "Milord, I rely upon Swale v. The Ecclesiastical Commissioners. Milord, the snails in defendant's garden were not brought there by her, and are
not under her control, being at liberty at any time to
cross the wall into the plaintiff's garden. Milord, I ask
you to rule that the snail is an animal *ferae naturae.*" '

Sir Alan Herbert

MOST of us like to be on friendly terms with our neighbours.
This is more easily accomplished if we understand and appreciate our legal rights and our obligations towards each other,
and the duties imposed on all owners of property.

The first right of an owner and occupier of property is a
right to undisturbed possession. Undisturbed possession
means possession undisturbed by unlawful interference. You
will recall that although it is, for practical purposes, impossible
to obtain redress for a casual trespass, the Courts may grant an
injunction to restrain a deliberate trespass, accompanied by a
threat of repetition. If an ill-mannered neighbour insists upon
encroaching on your property, and refuses to respect your
rights, you are entitled to apply to the Courts for an injunction.

To deal with physical interference of this character is comparatively simple. Difficulty is experienced when you approach
the problem of intrusion of a less personal character. Interference may take a number of different forms. It may be visible –
e.g. a flood of water escaping from your neighbour's garden,
the spread of branches from a neighbour's tree, dust from a
quarry, the drift of smoke from a bonfire or a factory chimney,
or even an aeroplane flying over your house. It may, alternatively, be invisible – e.g. it may consist of noise, vibration,
fumes, or smells. It may consist of something even less easy to
define – viz. a shadow across one of your windows as a result
of a high building newly erected by your neighbour on his
own property. Yet again it may be an intrusion on your
favourite flower-bed by an animal which belongs to your
neighbour.

Which of these incidents constitute an offence against your

legal rights? Which can you restrain? No general answer can be given, as the same legal principles are not applicable in each case, and it is therefore necessary to consider each in turn.

The occupier of property has a positive duty not to permit a dangerous object which he has brought on his land to escape when it may cause injury. The dangerous object may be either animate or inanimate. Water, for example, is classed as dangerous, because it may cause damage if it is allowed to escape. Your neighbour may have built a pond in his garden, and the brickwork which encloses the pond may collapse without any blame attaching to him, or even without his knowledge. He will nevertheless be responsible for any damage done by the escaping water, and he cannot, normally, rid himself of this liability.

Now let us turn to the overhanging tree. What principle is to be applied to this problem?

The owner of property is entitled not only to the soil on which the property stands, but also to all that is above and below it in a perpendicular plane. Subject to an exception which will be noted later, he is therefore entitled to the uninterrupted right of the air above the land. No one may interfere with this, and no one may build a structure on his land in such a way as to cause part of such structure to overhang his neighbour's garden, even although its foundations are on his own soil. On this principle, therefore, the branch of a neighbour's tree which overhangs your garden is an infringement of your legal rights. It is an infringement of your right to the ownership of the air over your land. You are entitled in law to remove the overhanging branch. Even although it is not your tree, you need not first ask your neighbour to cut off the branch, but you may lop it up to the boundary of your land without any notice to him. To lop a branch without notice is, however, not recommended in the interests of good-neighbourly relations. It is preferable to discuss the matter in a friendly way, resolving to exercise your legal rights only if an amicable settlement cannot be reached. If you have to enforce your legal right, you will find that the law in this instance is subtle. You are entitled to lop the overhanging branch, and, if there is a crop of ripe fruit on it, and you are avaricious, you may consider it an advantage to do so. If, however, you are imprudent enough to pick the fruit, either before or after you have lopped the branch, you will lay yourself open to an action for damages for conversion – i.e. appropriation of your neighbour's property. The tree and everything on it belongs to your neighbour. An overhanging branch is not your property. The basis of your right to lop the branch is the infringement of your legal right of ownership over the area which rises perpendicularly from your soil. When the branch is removed it ceases to be an infringement of your legal right, and the branch still belongs to your neighbour. Provided he approaches in an orderly manner, he would be entitled, when you have cut off his branch, to enter your land in order to remove it (with the fruit). You would not be entitled to prevent him from doing so, and he would not be a trespasser.

As you have the same rights to the soil below your land as you have to the atmosphere above it, the same principles apply to roots from your neighbour's trees as apply to overhanging branches. If the roots from your neighbour's tree extend underneath and cause subsidence on your land, you may be entitled to claim damages for the harm done, and an injunction to restrain your neighbour from allowing the roots to intrude in that troublesome manner. It should be noted that your neighbour commits a tort if he carries out excavations on his land which result in a subsidence on your land. A man is entitled to 'lateral support' from his neighbour's land, and, if he is deprived of this, and his land falls, as a result of digging operations carried out by his neighbour, he is, generally speaking, entitled to damages.

There is one exception to your right to the atmosphere over your land. Laws have been made which permit the flight of aeroplanes over property, for without the intervention of Parliament to change the Common Law, the risk of litigation would have been one of the most regular of all flying hazards.

The drift of smoke from a bonfire raises a problem of a different character. Smoke may be what is known in law as a 'nuisance'. Nuisances are classified as either public nuisances or private nuisances.

A public nuisance is, generally speaking, an act not warranted by law or an omission to discharge a legal duty, which obstructs or damages the public in the exercise of their legal rights, or their rights as members of the community.

You will recollect that in Chapter 2 it was explained, broadly speaking, that an act which causes injury to man, his property, or his reputation, is 'an act not warranted by law', and if a failure to 'do one's duty' results in an injury to a third party, it may be an 'omission to discharge a legal duty'.

A public nuisance may be of a quasi-criminal character. It is an offence against the community, as distinct from an offence against the individual, and as such it may usually be prosecuted in a Criminal Court. For example, if you place a barrier across the high road, you are creating a public nuisance. It affects and obstructs everyone who is lawfully using the highway, and you will be laying yourself open to a criminal prosecution.

A private nuisance, on the other hand, is an act or omission which causes inconvenience or damage to a private person. It has been described as unlawful interference with a person's use or enjoyment of land. Such an act is unlawful, but it will be left to the individual to seek his own remedy through the Civil Courts.

The word 'inconvenience' must not be taken in too literal a sense. Not every unlawful act which causes inconvenience is a nuisance. Every occupier of property has a right to certain amenities, but this is no more than a right to occupy it free from interruption, physical or otherwise, which would not be tolerated by a reasonable man adopting reasonable standards. He has not a remedy for every inconvenience.

Bearing these matters in mind, you will appreciate why smoke is not necessarily a nuisance. It is only a nuisance, generally speaking, when it would not be tolerated by a reasonable man adopting reasonable standards. Smoke from an occasional bonfire would not normally constitute a nuisance. Smoke, belching more or less continuously from a factory chimney might, however, be either a public or a private nuisance, according to the extent of the affected area. In an area designated as a smokeless zone under the Clean Air Act, the dissemination of dark smoke or smog or other noxious substances is a statutory criminal offence.

The owner of a factory which emits smoke may, accordingly, have to face legal action at any time. He may have to accept responsibility, not only if he has directly caused the smoke, but also if he has allowed it to arise by neglect of duty, or if he has omitted to remedy the nuisance within a reasonable time after he became, or ought to have become, aware of it. It is immaterial if the smoke is allowed to drift deliberately, negligently, or accidentally. It is his duty to take proper precaution to prevent the nuisance, either by the erection of a chimney of sufficient height to carry smoke at levels where it will not cause inconvenience, or by other methods.

Noise and 'offensive and pestilential smells and vapours' (as they may be legally described) are all to be judged by the same standard. They may all be capable of constituting a nuisance, and in each case the 'reasonable man' test is to be applied – i.e. you must decide whether you would expect the act complained of to be tolerated by a reasonable man adopting reasonable standards. The standards differ with the district. What is a nuisance in Park Lane may not be a nuisance in Pimlico. For instance, the Courts have decided that a speedway race-course would be a nuisance in a quiet residential district.

There is one special case in which you might reasonably describe a nuisance as a 'damned nuisance', but yet it is not a legal nuisance. It applies to building operations. As a nuisance consists essentially of an act not warranted by law, or an unlawful act, and building operations are lawful, the fact that they are at times necessarily of an excessively noisy character does not render the operation unlawful. The law does, however, require a builder to take steps to minimize noise, as far as is reasonably practicable. Moreover, the work must be confined to reasonable working hours, except in the case of an emergency. It must not be a continuous round-the-clock operation which prevents adjoining occupiers from enjoying a night's rest. If a builder fails to comply with these obligations, his operations may cease to be lawful, and he may find he has no defence to proceedings brought against him to restrain the nuisance.

Interference with the light which you enjoy over your property is classified in a different manner from other interference.

As every person theoretically owns the air over his land, he is entitled to build on the land. If the building is erected so that the outer walls rise perpendicular from the boundaries of the land, and is of such a height as to obscure the flow of light to the adjoining occupier, such adjoining occupier is unfortunate. Subject to certain qualifications, he has no remedy, for the owner of the land is making lawful use of his land, and so long as he does not overstep his boundaries, his neighbour has no legal remedy. He is not committing a nuisance. There are, however, two important qualifications to this rule. The first arises if John Doe, the owner of the land on which the offending building is erected, also owns the adjoining property which is occupied by his tenant, Richard Roe. In such circumstances, John Doe may not erect or allow the erection of any building on the adjoining land, if such building would substantially interfere with the light which Richard Roe is already enjoying. Secondly, if John Doe has enjoyed light over his property for an uninterrupted period of twenty years, his property acquires what is called a 'prescriptive' right to light. His property is then entitled to a privilege called 'ancient lights'. This means that there are limits to the building or obstruction which may be erected by an adjoining owner, so far as they may interfere with the amount of light John Doe or his predecessors have enjoyed for the previous twenty years from his building. Emphasis must be laid on the word 'building', as there is no right of light in favour of an open space. The interference must also be substantial. 'Substantial' is in each case a question of fact. A shadow cast across your window is unlikely to be a substantial interference. If you have occasion to complain of the erection of a building on adjoining land, when you are enjoying the privilege of 'ancient lights', you have to consider whether the loss of light is such as to render the occupation of the building uncomfortable, according to the ordinary notions of mankind, and whether it prevents you from carrying on a normal business on the premises as beneficially as you did prior to the obstruction. In each case the Court must take all relevant factors into consideration, and then decide, as a question of fact, whether there has been a substantial interference with the light previously enjoyed for normal business purposes.

The responsibility for damage caused by animals depends to some extent on whether the animal is classified as wild or domestic. A Committee formed to investigate this branch of the law reported in 1953 that the law of negligence should govern liability except in cases of cattle trespass, but their proposal has not as yet been implemented.

Wild animals include all animals which are both untamed *and* not subject to human control. The law does not, generally speaking, recognize any ownership of wild animals, although there are exceptions to this rule, and the subject is complicated. No one, generally speaking, is responsible for any injury caused by a wild animal, but it is necessary to appreciate the importance of the qualifying words in the definition 'not subject to human control'. The owner of a zoo has many animals popularly described as 'wild animals'. As, however, they are under his control, the owner will be responsible if they break loose and cause injury. A wild animal is dangerous, and the owner of a dangerous animal must never allow it to escape, or he will be responsible for the damage which it causes. Other animals, such as cattle, are not wild animals, but they may, nevertheless, be dangerous. If John Doe has any animal which he knows, or ought to know, is dangerous, he must normally keep it under proper control. If, for example, his cattle are allowed to trespass on Richard Roe's property, John Doe will normally be responsible for any damage they cause. He may escape liability only if Richard Roe is under a legal obligation to secure his own boundaries, and the cattle have strayed on his land because he has neglected his duty.

However, if John Doe's cattle stray on to the highway from his adjoining land, and Jane Roe while riding her bicycle comes into collision with them, she has no claim against John Doe for any injury suffered by her, as John Doe is under no duty to keep his domestic animals off the highway. The origin of this rule of law is many hundreds of years old. If John Doe were in charge of a small child carelessly allowed to run into the road and cause an accident he would not be similarly privileged, and would be held to have committed the tort of negligence.

Domestic animals, which include not only all the family pets, but even camels, are, generally speaking, assumed to be harmless. This assumption may, however, be overcome if proof is given that the owner knew that they were not, in fact, harmless. For example, although you may have no remedy if Mr Doe's dog attacks and injures you without provocation, you will be in a position to claim damages if you can bring evidence to prove that the dog had previously attacked a man, and that the owner therefore knew that he was not harmless. This is the origin of the popular theory that every dog is allowed one bite. When he has had his bite, the owner is no longer able to claim that he thought the dog was harmless. He is caught by the legal doctrine called *scienter* – i.e. 'knowingly'. He must thereafter keep the dog under proper restraint, or he will be responsible for the consequences. The same responsibility rests upon the owner of any other domestic animal, if he has knowledge of its being a danger. If he fails in such a case to keep it under proper control, he will be negligent, and will incur the same responsibility as for any other act of negligence.

The owner of bees is not responsible for any sting which one of his disgruntled pets, exasperated by the vagaries of the English summer, may cause. Bees as a class are regarded as wild animals, and there is, generally speaking, no ownership in a swarm of bees. When, however, they have been hived, they are the property of the owner of the hive. If they leave the hive in order to swarm, their owner may follow them so far as he may see and reach them. If, however, they elude him in the chase, he loses his right of ownership, and a stranger may hive and retain them.

You are entitled to stop a man if he wrongfully comes on to your property, and you are also entitled to restrain a trespass by cattle. If, however, the visitor is a dog or a cat, other legal considerations arise. If you wish to safeguard flower-beds from the intrusions of dogs, it is your duty to protect your boundaries in such a way that they are unable to obtain access. If you leave your gate open, and a dog walks in and scratches up your favourite flowers, in his desire to explore every avenue and leave no bone unturned, you have no remedy. Your neighbour has a similar duty to protect his own boundaries. If his dog comes through the boundary fence, however, you will have no right to complain, since you are both at fault. If, however, a hen comes through your fence and lays an egg on your ground, you are not entitled to keep the egg. It is not your property, and you must not count other people's chickens before they are hatched.

If a dog kills your chickens you may claim compensation from the owner of the dog. The Dogs Acts 1906–28 expressly render an owner liable if his dog destroys chickens, irrespective of *scienter*. The owner of a cat has less responsibility, and if your chickens are unfortunate enough to be killed by a cat you will normally have no remedy – at least against the owner of the cat.

The dog-owner is also liable for injury done to livestock, and where a dog is proved to have injured or worried livestock, it may be treated as a dangerous animal, and must in future be kept under proper control, or destroyed. Whether or not it is lawful to shoot a dog which is attacking livestock depends on whether shooting can be considered the only remedy in the circumstances.

Boundary fences or party walls often present problems. If you are able to ascertain, as a fact, from the deeds of the property that a particular boundary fence is your fence, it is your duty to repair it, and you will be liable for damage caused by your failure to repair it. Your neighbour is similarly responsible for the upkeep of his boundary fence. Frequently, however, it is extremely difficult to ascertain the ownership of a boundary fence, and in the absence of definite proof it is better to assume it is a party fence for which each party has, generally speaking, equal liability. It is better to come to a friendly agreement as to its repair than to engage upon aggressive controversy.

When differences arise between your next-door neighbour and yourself, it is no bad thing to start off with an appreciation of the moral duty you owe to render him every kind act which justice may require, and then to act towards him as in similar cases you would wish him to act towards you. If you do this, there should never be any difficulty in adjusting differences which may arise between you, unless your neighbour is determined to give battle. If his 'head is as full of quarrels as an egg is of meat', it is his misfortune and not yours. If you should be driven to sue him in order to obtain redress, and you succeed in your action, he will spend the rest of his life in decrying 'British Justice'. You need not, however, worry over a man who prefers the luxury of an imaginary grievance to the honest pleasure of good fellowship.

15

LIBEL AND SLANDER

'In Silvertop *v.* The Stepney Guardians a man trained a parrot to say three times after meals, "Councillor Ward has not washed today". It was held that this was a libel.'

Sir Alan Herbert

IF you write and publish statements which are defamatory or derogatory of another member of the community, you are said to libel him. Libel as a tort may give rise to an action for damages. In some circumstances it may lead to criminal proceedings. If the defamatory statement is published orally, as distinct from being in writing, it may result in a civil action for slander, but never in criminal proceedings. In order to succeed in an action either for libel or for slander, it is usually essential to prove that the defamatory statement is calculated to bring the person of whom it is written or spoken into 'hatred, ridicule, or contempt', or to damage him by reflecting adversely upon his credit or his business capacity.

Reproduction in a permanent form, as, for example, in a written statement, as opposed to the spoken word, is the great distinction between libel and slander, but to refer to a libel as a written statement is speaking only in very general terms, as it includes any statement which is written, printed, or depicted in some permanent form. It extends to pictures and motion pictures and broadcasting as well as to written words, but although no civil action will lie for damages for libel unless it has been published to a third party, publication is not an essential ingredient in a case of criminal libel. For example, let us suppose that John Doe thinks he has been defrauded by Richard Roe. In an outburst of indignation he writes to Richard Roe, accusing him of being a 'swindler who ought to be in gaol', and adding other equally elegant phrases. He addresses it to Richard Roe, and, knowing a little, but too little, of the law, he marks the envelope 'Private and Confidential' thinking that this will save him from any legal retribution. John Doe is, however, mistaken. If Richard Roe 'sees red' and feels, when he reads the letter, that he would like to take a horse-whip to John Doe for calling him a swindler, Richard Roe is entitled to apply to a magistrate's court for a summons for criminal libel. John Doe's conduct is calculated to provoke a breach of the peace, and it is therefore an offence against the community. It will not avail John Doe to prove as a defence that every word of his letter is true. 'The greater the truth the greater the libel' is a maxim which applies in criminal libel, and a defendant must not only prove truth, but also that the defamatory statement has been written and published in the 'public interest'. Public interest in this sense means a genuine public concern in the matters published, and not mere idle curiosity. It is insufficient to prove that the libel was published to satisfy one's own personal desire for revenge or retaliation. It is only in a civil libel action that justification, or proof of the truth of the defamatory matter, gives a complete defence to the claim, and proof of public interest is immaterial.

There are other defences available in proceedings for criminal libel. The defendant may, if the circumstances so warrant, plead a defence of privilege, or of fair comment on a matter of public interest. These defences, equally available in a civil action, are dealt with later in this chapter. It is also relevant to bear in mind that Richard Roe may be reluctant to set the criminal law in motion. He is sometimes unlikely to enjoy the prospect of publicity, or the risk of a subsequent prosecution for fraud. In some cases John Doe would have the sympathy of the Court, and even if found technically guilty of a criminal libel, he might merely be bound over to keep the peace, without incurring further penalty.

Somewhat akin to criminal libel are the crimes associated with the publication of seditious, blasphemous, or obscene matter. Sedition consists of the speaking or writing of words calculated to excite disaffection against the constitution and to procure the alteration of it other than by lawful means, to incite any person to commit a disturbance of the peace, to raise discontent or disaffection, or to promote ill feeling between different classes of the community. Blasphemy was the offence of challenging the doctrines of the established religion. As may be imagined, prosecutions for sedition and blasphemy are

...pacity are 'privileged statements', made on a privi-
...asion. The privilege does not, of course, extend to
...s made by the official in his private life.

...ar protection is extended to Counsel who conduct
...to witnesses who give evidence. If a witness did not
...eak the truth, because it might involve him in litiga-
...vould be placed in an impossible situation. On the
...ciple, all statements made in Parliament are abso-
...vileged, for it would be contrary to the tenets of
...ic government if a Member of Parliament was un-
...eak freely for fear of legal consequences. Neverthe-
...rtunately, this privilege is sometimes abused.

...regoing are examples of 'absolute privilege'. 'Quali-
...lege' is not so all-embracing. It applies when a de-
...statement is made and received in pursuance of a
...noral duty or obligation. For example, if an employer
...o give a reference for a former employee, he has no
...y to comply with the request. If, however, he feels
...bliged to do so, he is entitled to exercise the right. If
...a letter to the prospective employer, saying he dis-
...e employee for suspected theft, he is making a de-
...statement, but he may have a good defence to pro-
...brought against him for libel, on the ground that the
...was published on a privileged occasion.

...nce of qualified privilege fails, however, if the state-
...made maliciously, or if they extend beyond the neces-
...he case. Malice may be defined in this connexion as
...oper motive, but the word 'improper' does not neces-
...an deliberately improper. For example, a statement
...unfair or unreasonable may be improper, as may also
...hich is reckless or careless.

...occasions when you are entitled to rely upon a plea
...ed privilege, you escape liability if you can rebut the
...tion of malice – e.g. if you are able to satisfy the Court
...had an honest belief in the truth of your allegations.
...e other hand, there had been a quarrel between em-
...d employee before the latter was dismissed, there will
...ds for supposing that a reference given by the em-
...ating that the employee was dismissed for theft, is un-

nowadays exceedingly rare in this country, if not altogether non-existent.

The offence of obscene libel is committed when words or pictures are published which have a tendency to deprave and corrupt those who are likely to be so influenced, and who are likely to encounter the publication in question. This twofold test was authoritatively laid down in Victorian times. Since then the Courts have recognized that good fiction rarely avoids topics once regarded as unmentionable in polite society, but they may also continue to punish severely those who exploit the market for literature by outraging decency, as interpreted by Judge or Jury. In order to help combat the spread of 'horror comics', Parliament in 1955 passed the Children and Young Persons (Harmful Publications) Act, making their distribution a special criminal offence.

When criminal proceedings are not under consideration, a person who has published a defamatory statement may have an action for damages brought against him in the High Court. Proof that the defamatory statement is true 'in substance and in fact' – i.e. that the defamatory matter is substantially true and that anything untrue cannot materially injure the plaintiff's reputation, having regard to the truth of the remaining allegations – is an absolute defence to the claim, and entitles the defendant to ask that the action shall be dismissed.

When a plaintiff succeeds in an action for libel he may be awarded damages, even although he does not prove that he has suffered any pecuniary loss. The law assumes that a written communication published to a third party will cause damage to reputation, if the communication is defamatory. This, however, is not the case in an action for slander. A slander, being a spoken word, does not, in theory, leave the same permanent record as a libel, although Sir Alan Herbert was evidently under the impression that a parrot may provide an exception – and perhaps he is right in so doing. Be that as it may, the law does not, as a general rule, entitle the plaintiff in such an action to recover damages, unless he is able to prove actual pecuniary loss. There are, however, some exceptions, and the following are the excepted cases:

(1) Statements which impute crime punishable by imprisonment.

(2) Statements calculated to disparage a man in any office he may hold or profession, calling, trade, or business carried on by him at the time of publication.

(3) Statements accusing a woman of adultery, or of not being chaste.

(4) Accusations of certain contagious or infectious diseases.

You will observe that the exceptions entitle you to say of a man that he has an illegitimate child, without fear of the consequences, unless he is able to prove pecuniary loss or the exception (2) above applies, but you expose yourself to an action for damages if you accuse a woman of the same offence.

To illustrate one aspect of the law of defamation, let us assume that Joan Doe, the wife of John Doe, is shopping at the local Stores. She purchases and pays for several articles, which she places in her bag. The shop is crowded, and as she is leaving, a man approaches her and asks her to accompany him into the manager's room. She goes with him surprised, but unprotesting, and when she arrives, the house detective – as the man proves to be – tells the manager, in polite terms, that he has seen Joan Doe pick up a pair of stockings from a counter, put them in her bag, and walk away without paying for them. Joan is horrified at the accusation. It is true that she has a pair of stockings among other articles in her bag, but she declares she has paid for them. She admits she is rather careless and muddle-headed about accounts, and she fumbles in her bag, but without success, to find the bill she has received. The manager then insists upon taking her name and address, which she gives him. Later, when she arrives home, she finds the bill. It is unquestionably a properly receipted bill for the pair of stockings which she has purchased. What ought she to do?

We have spoken of 'publication' as an essential feature in all civil proceedings for libel and slander. Publication, in broad terms, means the communication of the defamatory statement to a third party, for John Doe may accuse Richard Roe of every crime in the calendar in the privacy of his own home, without fear of a claim for damages. In the case under con-

sideration, the statement made by manager is sufficient to support the

The next matter to consider is were defamatory. Whatever may h in which the house detective convey ager, and even if the detective had n cusing Joan Doe of having stolen a the implication or 'innuendo', as i plays an important part in the law of of a woman that she is 'a fine examp say it in a context, and with a tone o which means, and conveys to your a she is unchaste, the injured woman ceedings against you. You cannot es that you have not used any defama nuendo, if proved, may be sufficient and the result will be the same as if guage instead of sarcasm. You may c in a frown, and wink a reputation do 'slander' for 'libel', and the sentimer mark from a legal aspect.

As, then, Joan Doe has been accu offence punishable by imprisonment, of the exceptions which entitles a plai of 'special damage'. She will also be against the Stores, since they are res their employee, committed within th ment. She will not, however, necessar She will probably be met with the defe uttered on a 'privileged occasion'.

'Privileged occasions' fall into sev Judge, or other judicial officer, sits in (administering justice, he is frequently famatory statements, either about the p cerned in the case before him, or about to enable him to do his duty, without fe he is, accordingly, absolutely protected of any defamatory statement made by h to be a 'privileged' one, and all stateme

166

official c
leged oc
statemen

A sim
cases, an
dare to s
tion, he
same pr
lutely p
democr
able to
less, un

The
fied pri
famator
legal or
is asked
legal d
morally
he send
missed
famato
ceeding
statem

A de
ments
sities c
any im
sarily
which
be one

On
of qua
presun
that y
If, on
ploye
be gr
ploye

true, and was given maliciously. In that event, the employer will not be able to rely upon the plea of qualified privilege. Even if he suspected the employee of theft, the plea will be of no avail, for suspicion is not always honest belief, and he may be found to have made the accusation recklessly, and without regard to the facts. Beware, also, of the man who prefaces a defamatory remark with the words 'I feel I have a duty to perform'. The term is frequently used by hypocrites to conceal their malice.

If Joan Doe brings an action in respect of the allegation that she has stolen the stockings, she will almost certainly be met with the defence that the accusation was made on a privileged occasion. It will be said that the house detective had a duty to make his report, and the manager had a duty to receive it. There may be a plea that the detective had an honest belief that the stockings had been stolen, and it may be contended that the accusation was made with discretion. If, of course, the detective had made the accusation in the shop, instead of in the manager's room, the plea of privilege would probably be of little avail, since his duty to his employers would not have required him to accuse Joan Doe of theft in presence of the other customers in the Stores, who had no legal interest in the information. The detective had therefore acted correctly when he invited Joan Doe into the manager's room, and the question which the Court would have to decide, on the evidence, would be whether or not malice was established so as to defeat the plea of privilege. If the case comes into Court, the detective may say, when he gives his evidence, that Joan Doe had behaved suspiciously and had loitered on the premises, picking up first one article and then another. He will, however, make matters worse if the Court disbelieves his evidence, and is satisfied that Joan Doe had, in fact, paid for the stockings. Malice can be shown at any time, and if the detective makes an effort, by evidence of this character, to save his own skin at the expense of Joan Doe, he will be acting with an improper motive and will make it easier for Joan Doe to win her action. If, on the other hand, he honestly admits an error, and can satisfy the Court there has been a genuine and reasonable mistake on his part, as a result of the similarity in the appearance of two women, a plea of privilege would stand a better chance of success.

Irrespective of the legal position, however, Joan Doe would, generally speaking, be well advised to accept the gift of a dozen pairs of nylon stockings, which the Stores will probably be pleased to offer her in order to escape the unpleasant exposure of their representative's blunder. She has suffered no injury except to her dignity, and emphasis has already been laid on the uncertainty of litigation.

A further plea open to a defendant in a libel action, in some cases, is that of 'fair comment' – i.e. that the statements amount to no more than fair criticism on a matter of public interest. Everyone has the right to criticize freely his friends, and even his enemies, on matters of public interest, without fear of legal consequences, provided the criticism is a fair comment based on the facts of the case. Such criticism is frequently unpleasant to the person criticized, but he will not have any legal remedy. It is, however, essential that the facts of the case should be correctly stated, for no criticism can be fair if it is not made upon accurate facts, and a defence of fair comment in a libel action must inevitably fail if the author of the libel has allowed his imagination to run riot, and has based his comments on fancies which depart from sober truth. If, for example, a boxer has been booed in the ring, he has no legal remedy if a boxing critic reports the facts, and adds, by way of comment, that it would be better for the sporting world if the boxer were to give up boxing. Both the newspaper and the critic, if identified, would be entitled to plead a defence of fair comment. On the other hand, if a newspaper critic expressed the same opinion, based on the same allegation, but added gratuitously that the boxer was unfit to appear in any ring, because he never took the trouble to train before a fight, a plea of fair comment would fail, unless the newspaper were able to prove the truth of the allegation.

It should be noted that when a newspaper publishes a defamatory article, it is, broadly speaking, in no better and no worse a position than a private individual. The freedom of the Press does not mean that a newspaper, any more than a private individual, is licensed to attack the character of members of the community. As, however, it is essentially the function of the Press to keep the public informed on matters of general interest, the Defamation Act 1952 replacing earlier legislation, contains provisions which entitle newspapers to publish contemporaneous reports of parliamentary and judicial proceedings, and also of public meetings. No action will lie against a newspaper for publishing a report which is defamatory, provided it is a fair and accurate summary of the proceedings, unless the plaintiff is able to prove that the report was published maliciously.

The Defamation Act 1952 authorizes a defence of unintentional defamation. If prior to the Act you had described John Doe in a work of fiction derogatively and in such a way as to enable a real John Doe to bring evidence from reasonable men that they thought your references to John Doe were references to their friend or acquaintance of that name, you might have had damages awarded against you. The Act provides that a disseminator of a libel or slander who did not know and could not reasonably have been expected to know either of the defamed person's existence, or alternatively that the words used were defamatory may make, in accordance with the procedure laid down by the Act, an offer of amends. In the event of the apology and offer to publish a correction, which comprise the offer of amends, being refused and a trial taking place, then provided that it is proved that the original author of the words (if other than the disseminator concerned) wrote them without malice the defence may be established.

A brief reference may here be made to an action analogous to that of libel – viz. an action for damages for malicious prosecution. If John Doe charges Richard Roe with theft, and the latter is brought up in a Magistrate's Court and subsequently acquitted, he is entitled, in certain circumstances, to sue for damages. To succeed in such an action, he must prove: (1) that he has been acquitted, (2) that John Doe has acted without reasonable and probable cause, and (3) that John Doe has acted maliciously.

Actions of libel and slander, and also actions of malicious prosecution, are all heard by a jury in normal times. Juries in civil actions were suspended during the war, but have now been restored. It is the function of the jury to decide questions of fact, and, if the plaintiff has established his case to their satisfaction, they must assess the amount of the damages. There is no scale which will help them to carry out this duty. If they consider there is no merit in the action, and that it ought not to have been brought, although the plaintiff has technically been libelled, they may award him 'contemptuous' damages of one farthing. At the other end of the scale, the jury may award punitive or penal damages – i.e. a sum far in excess of any loss which the plaintiff may have suffered, to mark their sense of disapproval of the defendant's conduct, when the libel is gross or excessive. Normally, however, the amount of damages, which a jury should award after taking every circumstance into consideration, is such a sum as is fair and reasonable to the plaintiff, and higher damages may be awarded if the defendant has relied upon a plea of justification which has failed.

Before the members of a jury reach any decision they will always receive guidance from the Judge in his summing-up of the case as to the issues of fact which they must decide, and the basis upon which damages are to be awarded, if they find the facts to be in favour of the plaintiff. In the absence of a jury issues of fact must be decided by the Judge, as well as questions of law. He must, accordingly, assess the amount of the damages, and he will be less inclined than a jury to award punitive damages, since, in contrast with a jury, he has power to vindicate the plaintiff's character when he delivers his judgement.

The law relating to defamation has the same imperfections as other man-made laws. It has been put forward that no person should be entitled to compensation unless he is able to prove financial loss as a result of a defamatory statement. Nevertheless to some people loss of character is of greater concern than loss of money and if you are avoided by your friends as a result of a false and defamatory report in a newspaper it may not be possible for you to prove financial loss.

Many recommendations of Lord Porter's Committee which reported in 1948 were included in the provisions of the Defamation Bill introduced in Parliament in 1951. The bill was considerably amended by Parliament before reaching the statute book, which may serve as a reminder that the reform of the law is not an easy accomplishment.

16

LANDLORD AND TENANT:
LEASEHOLDS AND LEASES

'A man called at the Town Hall to see the Town Clerk. "Who is my Landlord?" he asked the Town Clerk. "To whom do you pay your rent?" enquired the latter. "I've been in the house since 1939," said the man, "and I haven't paid any rent, but if someone doesn't repair my roof soon, there's going to be a row."'

C. Kent-Wright in *Local Government Service*

THE relation of landlord and tenant is created whenever there is an occupation of property under a lease, or a tenancy agreement, granted by the lessor or landlord, to the occupier – the lessee.

You will want to know the distinction between a lease and a tenancy agreement. The former is a deed and the latter is a document signed under hand, and it has always been the practice to grant a lease for a long-term letting, whilst the tenancy agreement, being less formal, is used for a shorter period.

An agreement to let, being an agreement relating to land, can normally be enforced only if it is in writing. Sometimes, however, a tenant enters into occupation of land under a verbal agreement, and if rent has been accepted by the landlord, the tenant may enforce the verbal agreement as a result of the doctrine of part performance explained in Chapter 3.

Although there is a form of tenancy, called a 'tenancy at will', which may be terminated by either party without notice, land which is demised, i.e. leased or let for any agreed term, must always be so for a period which can be fixed by reference to some certain date or event. For example, a lease granted for a term to continue until such time as the Derby is won by a piebald horse would not be a good lease. It would be void for uncertainty. It would, however, be a good lease if it were for a term of 500 years or until the Derby is won by a piebald horse, whichever period might be the shorter, for in that event its maximum term is fixed.

Rent is the amount of the consideration – usually monetary

– payable to the landlord periodically for the use and occupation of demised premises. It may be either a 'ground rent' or a 'rack rent'. A ground rent is normally equivalent to the annual value of undeveloped land. If, for example, John Doe proposes to grant a building lease to Richard Roe on a piece of land worth £300, he may expect to receive each year, in lieu of interest on his money, a sum of between 5 and 8 per cent of the value of the land, and the ground rent payable under such a lease might, accordingly, be a sum of between £15 and £24 a year. When, however, Richard Roe has erected his house at a cost of £3,000 he may decide to grant an underlease of the premises, and in that case he will either charge a premium and an annual ground rent, or he will require payment of a rack rent – i.e. the full annual value of both the land and the house. The annual amount he may then expect to receive would be a sum in the region of £200 to £330, being 6 to 10 per cent on the £3,000 which he has spent in building the house, together with the ground rent of £15 to £24 which he himself has to pay.

That is the theory. In practice, as a result of the housing shortage, the mathematical calculations of the return which Richard Roe may expect to receive are not applicable. Officially the property market is not described as a black market, but subject to the Rent Acts and recent legislation which applies to the houses referred to in the next chapter, a landlord may let his house or flat to the highest bidder, and as with other things in short supply, he frequently obtains a rent far in excess of the annual value of the property. It is not necessarily reasonable to blame the landlord for acting in this way. The 'ill-used tenant' sometimes becomes the 'grasping landlord', and when he does so he, in his turn, usually accepts the highest rent he is offered. Under our present economic system there is nothing dishonest or immoral in this course. As, however, a roof over every head is a necessity and not a luxury, there is a strong argument in favour of controlled rents for all houses, in the same way as controls are applied to goods in short supply. It is right to add, however, that the ownership of property has not, for many small landlords, been very remunerative since 1914. Restricted rents in the case of controlled properties, have placed heavy burdens particularly on small landlords of private dwellings, and have robbed them of much of their former profit.

When John Doe has granted a ninety-nine-year building lease to Richard Roe, and the latter has built his house, he may prefer an outright disposal of his interest in the lease, instead of granting an under-lease. If he decides to do so, he is not, of course, in a position to *sell* the house. He can only *assign the leasehold* – i.e. the interest which he himself has in the property – for the residue of the ninety-nine years. The purchaser of the premises is then called the 'assignee' of the term.

When you purchase a house, you will, of course, expect to pay less for it if it is leasehold than you would do if it is freehold – i.e. one which will belong to you absolutely. For example, if you purchase in 1958 the residue of the term of a lease for ninety-nine years which John Doe had granted to Richard Roe in 1889 at a ground rent of £5 a year, you will have to base your calculations of a fair purchase price on your obligation to hand back the property to the successor in title of John Doe in the year 1988, when the lease expires – i.e. the property belongs to you for thirty years and no longer. In the meanwhile, you will have to pay the annual ground rent of £5. The price which you will expect to pay for the property in 1958 will therefore be the value of the house, without the land, after taking into consideration the loss of the capital you have invested in the property, which will dwindle each year, until the year 1988, when you will have none left, and by which time, for reasons which will be made clear, the house, instead of an asset, will have become a liability.

When a lease for over twenty-one years of land on which a dwelling-house has been erected is due to expire the Landlord and Tenant Act 1954 may, in some cases, provide continuing security of tenure for the lessee, and protection against indiscriminate rent increases. This Act of Parliament has been already referred to in connexion with business tenancies. Under the Act, the lease of the dwelling-house must be one which would be eligible for protection under the Rent Acts, as amended by the Rent Bill 1956 when law, or which would be so eligible were it not for the rent being under two-thirds of the rateable value. The landlord can only terminate the statutory tenancy, which arises at the end of the lease, by complying with the procedure laid down by the Act for giving not less than six months' notice to the tenant. The tenant has the opportunity, however, to end the arrangement by one month's notice.

If the landlord and tenant cannot agree the terms of a new lease or agreement, the County Court may be approached as the arbiter. The Act provides, among other things, that the rent as fixed by the County Court must be a reasonable rent for that type of property, and that if the long lease which has expired made the tenant liable for repairs, that must be taken into account for the new arrangement. The grounds on which a landlord may successfully apply to the County Court to recover possession of the premises, are approximately those which would enable him to possession under the Rent Acts, and in addition, he may recover possession at the end of the long lease if he has the genuine intention of demolishing or reconstructing the premises. Sub-tenants are also protected by the Act.

The terms and conditions agreed between the landlord and the tenant which are contained in a lease are, for the most part, technically called the 'covenants'. Occasionally a covenant may be implied, but you will recollect from Chapter 2 that this is exceptional, and if any important covenant is omitted, and a dispute is followed by legal proceedings, the Court may not add conditions, however reasonable, which it thinks ought to have been included in the lease.

The first covenant in a lease is usually the covenant by the lessee to pay the rent on the day on which it falls due, and most leases contain a provision which entitles the landlord to forfeit the lease and re-enter the premises on non-payment of rent whether or not a legal demand has been made for payment. Legal demand is a demand made on the premises between sunrise and sunset on the day on which the rent falls due. When no such demand is made, the landlord may not sue for forfeiture of the lease for non-payment of rent unless there is a clause in the lease which expressly exempts him from the obligation of making legal demand.

The express covenant for payment of rent is required by the

landlord, as, in the absence of such a covenant, the letting of premises would only bind the tenant to pay the agreed rent so long as he retained an interest in the lease, and he could rid himself of further liability at any time by 'assigning' or selling his interest in the lease.

The liability of the landlord and the tenant respectively for the payment of 'outgoings' – i.e. general rates, water rates, and other charges which may be levied against the owner or occupier of land – is an obligation which should always be defined. General rates are levied by the local authorities, and water rates by a statutory water company. They are the technical liability of the occupier of the property, but by the terms of a lease the obligations are usually expressly defined. When a house stands on a private road, there may also be a liability to the Local Council for the cost of making up the road, if it is converted into a public highway, and there are a number of other instances when liabilities of a similar character may arise.

Income Tax, technically known as Landlord's Property Tax or Schedule A Tax, is an outgoing which falls into a different category. The Inland Revenue assesses a figure which is calculated to be the gross annual income which the owner may expect to receive from the letting of his property when he remains liable for repairs. After deduction of a sum assumed to be the reasonable amount which a landlord may expect to have to spend each year on repairs, insurance, and management, the balance is called the 'net annual value', and the landlord is obliged to pay income tax on the net annual value at the standard rate of tax in force from year to year. At present this is 8s. 6d. in the £. The demand note for this tax is served on the person in actual occupation of the land, whether he is the owner or the tenant. If it is, in fact, paid by the tenant, the landlord is bound to allow the amount of the tax so paid as a deduction from the next payment of rent, on production by the tenant of the tax receipt. When a tenant agrees to pay 'outgoings', this does not include landlord's property tax, as the law compels the landlord to accept responsibility for payment of what is, in effect, his own income tax, and he is subject to the imposition of heavy penalties for any attempt at evasion. When, however, the tenant has paid an instalment of this tax, he must deduct the amount of the tax instalment from the ensuing payment of rent, or he may forfeit the right to do so at a later date.

Important covenants in a lease are those which relate to repairs. The lease should always define the responsibility for repairs of the landlord and the tenant respectively. If the lease has no reference to the subject, the Court may only order the landlord to carry out repairs if the house is what is legally termed a 'small house' – i.e. if it is let at a rent not exceeding £40 a year in London and £26 a year outside of London, and if, at the same time, the letting is for a period of less than three years. In such a case the landlord must keep the premises reasonably fit for habitation. In other cases, and in the absence of express agreement, the tenant is deemed to undertake to use the property in a tenant-like manner, as a reasonable tenant would use it, according to the purpose and length of the letting, and he must do reasonable repairs. Other than in these respects, the Court has no power to assist either party if they have not recorded their agreement as to repairs in the lease.

For example, neither you nor your landlord may be under any obligation to repair a defective roof if there is no covenant in your lease which has reference to roof repairs. It is true that in such a case water may damage the property. On the other hand, it may also damage your furniture. Which of you will suffer a greater loss from a leaking roof? You and your landlord will have to consider this question, and come to your own decision, for the law will not be able to assist you. Moreover, the landlord is not responsible for rats, mice, or beetles, except in the case of a furnished letting, and then only if the invasion is sufficiently severe to interfere seriously with the tenant's comfort.

Repairing covenants assume a number of different forms, according to the character of the lease or tenancy agreement. The times are now abnormal, but under ordinary conditions they may be roughly classified in four divisions:

(1) In long leases – i.e. those for a term exceeding twenty-one years – one would expect to find full repairing covenants. These are very onerous, as under such covenants the tenant must not only be prepared to carry out all repairs necessary to

keep the premises in a state of good and substantial repair, even although they are in a state of bad repair at the time of the letting, but he must also be prepared to carry out all work necessary to hand the premises over to the landlord in a good and substantial condition of repair at the end of the term.

(2) In leases for a term of from seven to twenty-one years you may sometimes find covenants under which the tenant agrees to carry out all interior repairs, whilst the landlord will agree to carry out external and structural repairs.

(3) In leases for a term of from three to seven years, it is reasonable either for the tenant to agree to keep the interior of the premises in a good state of repair or else in the same state of repair as they are at the time of the letting. The landlord will on his side undertake external and structural repairs as in the previous case. In order that the tenant's covenant should be effective in this case it is necessary for a schedule of the condition of the premises to be taken at the commencement of the term, and this can then be checked when the lease comes to an end.

(4) In short tenancies it is unusual for the tenant to assume any serious responsibility, and the covenant usually requires him to keep the premises in a good state of repair, 'fair wear and tear excepted'. This means what it says, and a careful tenant will seldom be called upon to pay anything for want of repair, although it does not, of course, relieve a tenant of responsibility if his children scribble over the walls. In such a case he must expect to be called upon to pay for any damage caused.

It is necessary to emphasize that these four categories are not 'cut and dried'. There may be a number of variations, and the exact covenant in any particular case is one for bargaining between landlord and tenant when the negotiations for the lease are under discussion. It is also essential to remember that, when houses are scarce, landlords are more exorbitant in their demands than when there is an abundant supply of houses. During the war years legislation provided that all covenants in a lease which required the lessee to carry out repairs were of no effect, in so far as the repairs were required by reason of war damage.

Another usual covenant is that which deals with assigning

and under-letting. A prudent landlord will always ask for references to establish the character and financial status of the proposed tenant. As, moreover, he will want to exclude undesirable occupiers in the future, he will usually require the tenant to agree not to 'assign, under-let, or part with possession of the premises or any part thereof' at any time during the term without his written consent. Until 1927, demand for compensation could be made by a landlord when he was asked under such a clause to consent to an assignment or sub-letting, but the Landlord and Tenant Act 1927 normally no longer permits the consent to be unreasonably withheld by the landlord in the case of a responsible and respectable assignee or under-tenant, although it is still permissible for a landlord to prohibit all assignment and under-letting by express covenant.

Assigning, i.e. selling, and *under-letting* are two totally different transactions. If you assign or sell your interest in a lease which you hold from John Doe, you transfer it to the purchaser, and you yourself retain no further interest in the lease, subject to certain contingent obligations which are referred to hereafter. If, on the other hand, you under-let it, you remain a tenant of John Doe, and the under-lessee becomes your tenant. If you under-let it to Richard Roe, he will hold the property from you on whatever conditions you stipulate in your lease or tenancy agreement with him. Care must, of course, be taken not to include any conditions in the tenancy agreement which might lead to a breach of the terms in your own lease from John Doe. Unless caution is exercised in this respect, you may find yourself involved in legal complications. You may under-let the property to Richard Roe, and include a covenant which allows him to use the premises for a billiard saloon. If John Doe has let you the property on condition that you may use it for a private dwelling-house only, he might then obtain an injunction against you and against Richard Roe for an infringement of the covenant. Richard Roe might, in his turn, claim damages against you for breach of the covenant which allowed him to use the premises as a billiard saloon. A covenant as to user – i.e. as to the purposes for which the premises may be used – is usually inserted in every lease.

A lease should define the liability of the parties in the event of destruction of the premises by fire. When a lease contains full repairing covenants it is usual for the lessee to undertake the liability to insure against fire risks.

Most of the obligations in a lease are obligations by the tenant. The landlord is letting property which belongs to him, and he lays down the conditions on which he will do so. There is one obligation which is, however, always imposed on the landlord. He must covenant to give his tenant a legal right called 'quiet enjoyment' of the property. 'Quiet' enjoyment means undisturbed possession. It is not an antithesis to 'noisy'. It means that the tenant must not be disturbed in his occupation by the landlord, or anyone claiming through the landlord, so long as he observes all the conditions of the lease. It is no guarantee against disturbance by a superior landlord, if the landlord should fail to carry out his obligations under the head lease. Although the tenant may, in such a case, have a claim for damages, for what it is worth, against his landlord, he will have no remedy against the superior landlord. Moreover, the convenant will not give a tenant a claim against the landlord if there is interference by a stranger, over whom the landlord has no control, as he is only responsible for all acts which he is in a position to control. The landlord is not, however, entitled to 'derogate from his grant', and if he owns adjoining houses separated by a partition, and he lets one to John Doe for residential purposes and later lets the other to Richard Roe for use as a factory for processing hides, John Doe might have a legal cause of action against his landlord if the hides were to emit unpleasant odours. This right against the landlord would be additional to any remedy which the tenant might have against the factory owner for nuisance, a subject dealt with in Chapter 14.

When a lessee, under a lease for a term of years, remains in occupation of the premises, with the lessor's consent, after the lease has expired, the law will usually deem the continued tenancy to be an annual tenancy. The significance of this is that an annual tenancy, without provision as to notice, can only be terminated by six months' notice to quit given to expire on the anniversary of the date when the term commenced. In the case of a monthly or weekly tenancy, however, the law usually regards the tenancy as running from month to month or from week to week as the case may be. In such circumstances, a month's or a week's notice to quit is necessary. There are special rules which relate to agricultural tenancies designed to prevent a farmer from being evicted after he has his crops in the ground, and before they are ready to harvest. Twelve months' notice is usually the minimum notice in such a case, and the tenant is generally entitled to insist on the landlord's obtaining the consent of the Minister of Agriculture before giving the notice. A notice to quit is a very technical document, and it is null and void if it does not give the tenant the proper notice required by the law or by the agreement between the parties, as the case may be. If, however, a landlord wants possession of his premises on the date when the lease or tenancy agreement expires, no notice to quit is normally necessary, although the landlord must be careful, in such a case, not to accept rent for a further period. Except when the premises are controlled under the provisions of the Rent or Landlord and Tenant Act, a fresh tenancy is usually created if rent is accepted for a period after the term has expired.

'Fixtures and fittings' are dealt with in Chapter 18. It should be observed here, however, that if a fixture is brought on to the premises by a tenant, or if an improvement is made by him during the course of the tenancy, it may become part of the property and cannot be removed by the tenant at the end of the tenancy. The landlord is entitled to receive back his property with all additions and improvements. To this rule, trade, ornamental, domestic, and agricultural fixtures are an exception, the latter by statute. In the case of trade and agricultural fixtures and improvements which add to the letting value of the premises, the tenant is entitled to compensation. If he wishes to claim compensation he must comply with the provisions of the Landlord and Tenant Act 1954, when giving notice to the landlord.

A lease of premises is usually executed in duplicate. One copy, executed by the landlord, is delivered to the tenant, and the other copy, called the counterpart, is executed by the tenant and retained by the landlord, as evidence of the obligations which the tenant has undertaken to observe. The lease must be stamped with an *ad valorem* impressed stamp of 2 per cent of the annual rent, but the counterpart requires only a 5*s.* impressed stamp. In addition to the lessee's liability for his own legal costs, there is a custom in London and many parts of the country under which the lessee has to pay the landlord's legal costs and stamp duty as well as his own. A specimen scale of charges is set out at the end of Chapter 32.

When a landlord alleges there has been a breach by the tenant of any covenant, and there is a 'forefeiture' clause in the lease – i.e. a clause which gives the landlord the right to forfeit the lease for a breach of covenant – the landlord is not entitled to exercise this right arbitrarily. Unless the breach is a failure to pay rent he must first serve the tenant with a written notice specifying the breach and requiring it to be remedied, and he is also entitled to require payment of reasonable compensation. If the tenant fails to comply with the terms of the notice within a reasonable period, the landlord may then take proceedings to forfeit the lease, and also for payment of compensation. If, however, the covenant which has been broken is the covenant to repair, the law refuses to allow compensation to the landlord in excess of what is called the damage to the 'reversion', meaning, in effect, the actual damage which the landlord will suffer by reason of the failure to repair. If it is proved by the tenant that the premises are to be demolished or reconstructed at the end of the term, and the landlord has no intention of reinstating them to their original condition, the landlord will not be able to recover, as compensation, the imaginary sum which he might have spent on imaginary repairs.

The Court has extensive powers of granting 'relief' to a tenant when forfeiture proceedings are taken. For example, if proceedings are taken in respect of a default in payment of rent, and the tenant asks for 'relief', it is the practice of the Court to make an order relieving the tenant from the penalty of forfeiting the lease upon payment by him of the arrears of rent and all costs incurred by the landlord. Similar relief may be given in the case of the breach of other covenants. A subtenant may be able to obtain protection when proceedings have been commenced against his immediate landlord by the superior landlord. An exception is the breach of a covenant against assignment or under-letting.

The landlord has additional remedies available to him for non-payment of rent. He may levy a distress or 'put in the brokers', as it is usually called. The brokers may seize everything on the premises except the instruments of a man's trade, or his or his family's wearing apparel to a value of £5. If the effects of a lodger or under-tenant are seized, they may, however, be reclaimed under certain conditions. For example, if you are Richard Roe's lodger and your goods are seized to satisfy rent due from Richard Roe to his landlord John Doe, you may serve a notice on John Doe giving him particulars of your claim, and thereupon, upon payment by you to John Doe of any rent owing from you to Richard Roe, your effects must be released. Articles seized under a distress may be sold at the expiration of fifteen days, unless the arrears of rent are discharged within that period.

If you take a lease of premises, you can never rid yourself of your liability to the landlord for the breach of any condition or covenant in the lease unless you are expressly released by deed. You still remain liable under your covenant even after you have assigned your interest in the lease. Assume, for example, that in 1939 John Doe took a full repairing lease of certain premises for a term of fourteen years, and in 1946 he assigned the residue of the term, with the consent of his lessor, to Richard Roe. In 1950 Richard Roe became insolvent and disappeared. When the lease expired in 1953, John Doe received notice from the lessor that the rent was three years in arrears, and the premises were in a state of dilapidation, and he required John Doe to carry out his obligation to pay the rent, and also to pay as damages the sum required to put the premises in repair in accordance with the covenant in the lease. In such a case the licence or consent which John Doe received permitting him to assign the premises does not relieve him of his obligations. Such a licence or consent is merely a permission given to him to assign his term to Richard Roe. There will be nothing in the document to suggest that he is himself to be released from any past or future liability. Indeed, the licence may even include an express condition that it is granted without prejudice to the lessee's continuing obligations under his covenants.

A tenant's only safeguard against a contingent risk of this character is to assign his interest in the lease to a man of undoubted financial status. As the assignment carries with it a legal obligation by the assignee to be responsible for the covenants in the lease, and to indemnify the assignor against all claims made by the lessor, the original lessee is able to pursue his claim for indemnity against the assignee, so long as the latter is solvent.

Richard Roe, the assignee, may, of course, himself re-assign the premises to a second assignee, subject to his landlord's consent, when required. If he does so, Richard Roe normally ceases to be under any further obligation to the lessor. He has never entered into any agreement with him and has never had a direct covenant with him. The only document Richard Roe has signed is the deed by which John Doe assigned the lease to him. Richard Roe's obligations to the lessor, by virtue of that assignment, are to observe the covenants of the lease so long, and only so long, as he himself retains an interest in the land. On the other hand, he remains liable to John Doe because the assignment imposes the obligation to indemnify him for the full term of the lease.

The practical effect of these rather complicated transactions is that: (1) the lessor may always sue for a breach of covenant in the lease either (a) the original lessee, or (b) the person in actual occupation of the land at the time of the breach; (2) the original lessee may sue the first assignee for damages for breach of his covenant to indemnify, and (3) the first assignee may sue the second assignee in respect of the latter's covenant to indemnify. If the second assignee, in his turn, has re-assigned the lease to a third assignee, he may similarly pass on to the latter any claim which is made against him, and so on, however long the chain of assignees. As a general rule, even the death of a lessee or an assignee will not affect the liability, which will fall on the estate of the dead man. At the end of a term of ninety-nine years, however, it may be impossible to trace some assignee, where indemnity has become enforceable by a prior assignee (or the original lessee) and the chain will then be broken.

It follows in such an event that someone may be 'stung' for the cost of repairing a property with which he has parted many years earlier.

You should, accordingly, never accept a lease without consideration of your potential liability, and unless you feel sure you are justified in accepting a responsibility which will continue for the full term of the lease.

17

LANDLORD AND TENANT:
THE RENT ACTS

' "And I think, my dear brother," said Nicholas' first friend, "that if we were to let them that little cottage at Bow which is empty, at something under the usual rent, now? Eh, brother Ned?" "For nothing at all," said brother Ned. "We are rich, and should be ashamed to touch the rent under such circumstances as these." '
Nicholas Nickleby

IT is not easy to grasp the complicated provisions of the Rent and Mortgage Interest Restriction Acts 1920–39, the Housing Repairs and Rent Act 1954, and the Rent Bill 1956 (known for short as the Rent Acts), and if it were not a contradiction in terms, I would say that this chapter is merely an attempt to give a bird's-eye view of legislation which, in R.A.F. slang, is shrouded in 10/10 clouds. The pattern of the Acts is, however, perhaps not so difficult to understand. Their general scheme is to control profiteering in the letting of dwelling-houses by limiting the rent which landlords may demand in respect of certain houses rated below a certain figure, and also by restricting the rights of the landlord to possession of those houses. The first Rent Act was introduced in 1915. This laid down a maximum rent for the smaller type of house, and prohibited the eviction of any tenant who was paying his rent and observing the obligations of his tenancy, unless the landlord found alternative accommodation for him. Controlled houses to which the Acts apply under the Rent Bill 1956, assuming this legislation becomes law, are those which had a rateable value on 7 November 1956 not exceeding £40 in London (the City and Metropolitan Police District) and £30 elsewhere, but tenancies where the rent is less than two-thirds of the rateable value and fresh tenancies arising after the Bill comes into effect are excluded from control. The rateable value of a house is the annual value assessed by the Inland Revenue, and is based upon its postulated letting value. Where a part of a house which is let by itself has no rateable value of its own recorded in the valuation list, a special apportionment of the rateable value of the whole unit either by agreement between landlord and tenant, or by the County Court, may be required to determine the position.

The Acts have never had any application to the sale and purchase of houses – a market in which there is no price control. They have also had only very limited application to furnished premises, but an attempt has been made to stop profiteering in respect of furnished premises, by the Furnished Houses (Rent Control) Act 1946 and the Landlord and Tenant (Rent Control) Act 1949. If a tenant considers he is being charged an excessive amount for furnished premises, he may apply to a Rent Tribunal to fix a fair rent. And in order to protect the tenant from retaliation by his landlord, the Acts prevent a landlord from taking proceedings for possession for a period of three months after an application has been heard. The Tribunal is also entitled to grant protection for further periods of three months at a time. Under the provisions of the Rent Bill 1956 furnished premises which would be controlled premises were they let unfurnished, are the only ones with which Rent Tribunals have the power to deal. They also have power to fix the amount for services provided for a tenant of such furnished premises.

To return to the Rent Acts proper, it should be noted that they have no application to business premises, unless such premises are also used for residential purposes. They apply solely to unfurnished 'dwelling houses', and this expression includes flats, parts of a house, or even a single room in a house, when occupied as a separate dwelling. (It is not known whether cave-dwellings are included.) Houses and Flats let by local authorities, Development Corporations, Housing Trusts and Associations, or completed or substantially converted on or after 30 August 1954 are outside the scope of the Acts altogether.

Premises to which all the provisions of the Acts apply are colloquially said to be 'controlled', and the word 'premises' is used throughout this chapter for any unfurnished dwelling-house, flat, rooms, or room controlled by the Acts.

The premises which are within the ambit of the Acts were divided into two classes before the coming into force of the Rent Bill 1956: (1) those which were controlled before the

Second World War, (2) those which came under control through the Rent Act hurriedly passed on the outbreak of the Second World War. Assuming the Rent Bill becomes law, the rent which may be charged will generally be twice the gross rateable value of the dwelling, together with an amount covering the rates if the tenant does not pay these himself. There may also be added a sum for any services provided by the landlord, furniture or shared accommodation, as may be agreed between the landlord and tenant or determined by the County Court. Further, any improvement to the dwelling effected after the Bill becomes law may lead to 8 per cent of the expense borne by the landlord being added to the yearly rent. The tenant may apply to the County Court if he considers the improvement is unnecessary or unreasonably expensive.

The factor of twice the gross rateable value which has been referred to in the preceding paragraph, becomes 'two and a third times' if the landlord is responsible for all repairs, 'one and a third times' if the tenant is responsible for all repairs, and 'one and two-thirds times' if the landlord is responsible only for internal decorative repairs.

If the condition of the premises is below a standard set by their 'age, character, and locality', as this may be understood by the local authority or ultimately by the County Court, it may be possible for the tenant to obtain a certificate of disrepair from the local authority so that he may withhold a proportion of the rent so long as the necessary repairs are outstanding. However, the Rent Bill will allow the landlord to give an undertaking to do such repairs within six months, and rent may only be withheld if the undertaking is not complied with after the six months have passed.

The rent increases which the Rent Bill will permit for rent-controlled premises may take effect up to 7s. 6d. a week after three months' notice, and as to the remainder of the increases (if any) not before a further six months have elapsed, but any increase in rent on account of the rates may be imposed so as to be retrospective for not more than six weeks.

If the payment of rent includes bona-fide payments in respect of board, attendance, or use of furniture, the property is *not* controlled. These payments must, however, be really genuine and substantial. A landlord cannot escape the provisions of the Acts by including two wooden chairs in the letting and calling it a furnished letting. Where a tenant shares essential living accommodation with his landlord by agreement, the tenancy is treated as a furnished tenancy for the purpose of the Rent Acts.

Under the Rent Acts, before the coming into effect of the Rent Bill 1956, the dwellings to which the Acts applied were those, subject to certain general exceptions which have been mentioned, which had a rateable value in 1939 not exceeding in London £100 and elsewhere £75. The Rent Bill provides for a very considerable measure of complete decontrol, but only after a waiting period of fifteen months will landlords of premises of over £40 rateable value in London and over £30 elsewhere on 7 November 1956 or the first available date thereafter, be free to raise rents and evict tenants at their unfettered discretion, subject one may presume to the forces of supply and demand. With the intention of avoiding an excessive abuse of a power which the landlord may not have enjoyed since 1939, no premium or key-money may be charged in connexion with such decontrolled premises until a further one year and nine months has elapsed. At any time during the initial fifteen months period the landlord and tenant may agree a new lease or tenancy agreement at any rental, provided the tenant obtains at least three years security of tenure from its commencement.

No new tenancy commencing after the Rent Bill 1956 becomes effective will be subject to Rent control, whatever the rateable value of the premises concerned. The Bill contains provisions which may prevent a landlord who is unscrupulous from tricking an existing tenant into accepting a 'new tenancy'. An innovation introduced by the Bill into the law, which will be of assistance to tenants in general, is that no notice to quit may take effect in less than four weeks.

When you enter into occupation of property under a tenancy agreement, the agreement defines the terms of the bargain made between the landlord and yourself. When your agreement expires, you are normally expected to vacate the property in accordance with your covenant, and if you fail to do so you may be liable to pay double rent, whilst the landlord may speedily obtain an order from the Court for possession of the property. When, however, the tenancy agreement relates to controlled premises, a different situation arises. A tenant of controlled premises may refuse to vacate premises at the end of his term, and if he remains in occupation after he has been given notice to quit he is known as a 'statutory tenant' holding under a 'statutory tenancy'. A statutory tenancy, however, never comes into existence until *after* the tenancy agreement has expired. If a tenant is in occupation of premises under a written or verbal agreement, the Acts, even as to the maximum rent which may be charged, have no application, so long as the agreement remains in force. However, the landlord is not entitled to break the agreement in order to raise the rent. Any increase may be imposed only *after* the agreement has been terminated either by a proper notice to quit or by expiration of the term, and then only by the permitted sums mentioned on p. 187.

If a tenant remains in occupation of premises, as a statutory tenant, after his agreement has expired, the obligations of the tenancy agreement remain binding both on the landlord and tenant, but the Acts protect the tenant from his obligation to vacate the premises, and the landlord, generally speaking, cannot obtain possession. This protection normally extends after the death of the tenant to his widow if residing with him at the time of death, and alternatively to other members of his family, provided they have lived with him for six months prior to his decease. This kind of succession may only apply once. The suppression of the landlord's right to possession of his property on the termination of a tenancy agreement was a unique feature when the first Rent Act was passed in 1915. Statutory tenancies which have arisen as a result of an agreement between the landlord and the local authority which originally requisitioned the premises, will not be decontrolled before 31 March 1965, and rent increases in respect of them must be brought to the notice of the local authority.

There are some occasions on which a landlord may obtain an order from the Court for possession of controlled premises.

Where proceedings are taken by a landlord against his tenant, and the Court is asked to make an order for possession, the first question it must consider is whether or not it is reasonable to make the order. To enable him to decide this question, the Judge must take into consideration every relevant factor. He must listen to every point argued both by the landlord and by the tenant, and he must then decide the question without being influenced by prejudice, or sentiment, for or against either party. Even, however, if the Judge considers it reasonable to make an order, he is not entitled to do so unless he is also satisfied, either that suitable alternative accommodation is available for the tenant, or, alternatively, that one of a number of other conditions is applicable. Suitable alternative accommodation cannot be defined in a word, but the following points have to be considered: (1) it must consist of premises of similar character which will, in the opinion of the Court, give the tenant security of occupation reasonably equivalent to that which he already enjoys – a council house will probably not be good enough for this purpose, because a Council tenant has no similar protection against a notice to quit; (2) it must be reasonably suitable to the needs of the tenant and his family, as regards proximity to place of work; (3) it must be either similar, as regards rental and accommodation, in comparison with other premises in the neighbourhood, occupied by those whose needs are similar to those of the tenant and his family, or otherwise be reasonably suitable to the means and needs of the tenant and his family, as regards extent and character. These provisions mean, in effect, that the Court must take every factor into consideration and apply the key word of 'common sense'.

If no suitable alternative accommodation is available, the circumstances in which the Court may make an order for possession include the following: (1) if the rent is in arrear, or if the tenant has broken some other obligation imposed on him by the tenancy. For example, an order for possession might be made under this heading if the tenant had agreed, by the terms of his tenancy, not to keep animals on the premises, but nevertheless insisted upon doing so. (2) If the tenant has been guilty of conduct which is a nuisance or annoyance to adjoining occupiers, or if he has been convicted for allowing the premises to be used for illegal or immoral purposes, or if he has allowed the condition of the premises to deteriorate by his neglect. If, however, the deterioration is due to the act of a lodger, or sub-tenant, the Court must be satisfied, before making an order for possession, that the tenant is in some measure responsible for the default, by his personal failure to take steps to dispossess the lodger or sub-tenant. (3) If the tenant, after giving notice to quit, has refused to leave, and in consequence of the notice the landlord has either agreed to sell or let the premises with vacant possession, or has undertaken an obligation which he will be unable to carry out unless he obtains possession. (4) If there has been either a sub-letting, or, in certain circumstances, an assignment, without the landlord's consent, and, in this con-nexion, the Court may also make an order for possession, if it considers it reasonable to do so, when the tenant has sub-let part of the premises at an excessive rent. (5) If the premises are reasonably required by the landlord for occupation as a resi-dence for one of his employees under certain specified condi-tions. (6) If the premises, being premises purchased by the landlord on or before 7 November 1956 (when the Rent Bill was mentioned in the Queen's speech on the opening of a new session of Parliament), are reasonably required by the land-lord for occupation by himself, or for specified members of his family. In this last instance the tenant must satisfy the Judge that he will suffer greater hardship if the Judge makes an order for possession so that he has to vacate the premises, than the hardship suffered by the landlord if the order is refused.

If you consider these points you will appreciate that, while there are many cases in which the Courts have power to order possession, a tenant of *controlled* property has many privileges. If he pays his rent punctually, and is exemplary in his be-haviour as a tenant, and if the Court is satisfied that no suitable alternative accommodation is available, he will be able, in a large number of cases, to remain in occupation. If the Court refuses to make an order for possession after giving proper consideration to the facts, the landlord, generally speaking, has no remedy.

The landlord is not entitled to include terms in a tenancy

agreement which exclude the provisions of the Rent Acts, and evasion or attempted evasion of the Acts either by landlord or tenant may be punished by penalties. For example, a landlord cannot get round the Acts by asking for a payment of a premium as a condition for granting or continuing a tenancy. A demand for an exorbitant sum for furniture may be regarded, under the Acts, as a demand for a prohibited premium. Nor can a tenant demand a premium as a condition of an assignment or sub-letting. Assignment or under-letting of a statutory tenancy, without the consent of the landlord, is a ground for making an order for possession, since the statutory tenancy is designed for the personal protection of the tenant, but an authorized assignment or under-letting by the tenant, *during* the currency of his tenancy agreement, and *before* the statutory tenancy arises, will protect the assignee or sub-tenant when the tenancy expires, and, generally speaking, he will be entitled to the same protection as a tenant.

If a tenant is in doubt as to whether or not he is paying an excessive rent, he should take steps to ascertain the standard rent. This should appear in his rent book, and if it is not there, he is entitled to demand the information from his landlord. If it is not supplied within fourteen days, the landlord commits an offence punishable by a fine. If rent in excess of the permitted rent has been paid, excess payments made over a maximum period of two years may normally be recovered, either by legal proceedings or by deduction from current rent as it falls due.

In the next chapter we shall be dealing with the subject of mortgages. It may be observed here that the Rent Acts also contain provisions to protect a certain class of mortgagor – i.e. a person who has borrowed money on the security of property. These provisions restrict the right of the mortgagee – i.e. the person who has lent the money – to take possession of controlled premises, and also restrict the rate of interest which the mortgagee is entitled to charge.

The Rent Acts until the coming of the Rent Bill 1956 undoubtedly have given the large majority of tenants of private house property, both security of tenure and protection against most rent increases above the 1939 level. Consequently, the

Rent Bill 1956 with its massive decontrol and provision for
further decontrol at the discretion of the Government, has
aroused much criticism. Will rents be stable, will repairs be
done, will there be many evictions? On the one hand, it is
contended that most private landlords are so acquisitive and
shortsighted that part of the solution to the nation's housing
problem is for local authorities to municipalize, with compensation, nearly all private rented housing. On the other hand it
is contended that good landlords keep their property in good
repair so long as they can obtain sufficient rent, that landlords
as a class ought not to be penalized by rents being pegged at
more or less the 1939 level, when the value of money has fallen
so much, and that the Rent Bill will result in much under-
occupied property being placed on the market for tenants. The
argument has in fact become a political controversy in a big
way, and that is where we shall leave it.

G

18

SALE AND PURCHASE OF PROPERTY AND MORTGAGES

'O Lord, thou knowest that I have nine houses in the City of London, and that I have lately purchased an Estate in fee simple in Essex. I beseech Thee to preserve the two counties of Middlesex and Essex from fires and earthquakes.'

Prayer of John Ward, M.P., 1727,
quoted in Hine's *Uncommon Attorney*

SOME of the essential features of a contract for the sale and purchase of 'property', the term used in this chapter for land with the house which stands on it, were considered in Chapter 2. In such a transaction you do not, from the legal aspect, primarily purchase a house. You purchase the land, either as your absolute property, when you call it a 'freehold' (sometimes described as an Estate in Fee Simple), or you acquire it for a limited number of years, as described in Chapter 16, when it is known as a 'leasehold'.

When you buy or sell property, it is not the same thing as when you buy or sell a piano. You identify the piano, you pay or are paid the purchase price, and it is then delivered. This completes the transaction. On the other hand, when you buy or sell property you cannot hand it over in the same way as a piano. The ownership of the property is identified, not by the bricks and mortar with which the house has been built, but by the title-deeds or documents which legally constitute the right of ownership or title to the land. Without possession of such deeds you have, generally speaking, no legal title to the property.

Even if you are absolute owner of the property you will not necessarily be entitled to use it exactly as you wish. An attempt to prevent the uncontrolled development of property is constituted by the Town and Country Planning Act 1947. If you wish to change the existing use, i.e. the use on the 1 July 1948 when the Act came into force, you will have to obtain the permission of the planning authority which will normally be the County Borough or County Council. Jane Doe can no longer turn her house into a nursery school for her neighbours' children without its being regarded as a change in the existing use. Planning permission will also be needed before you can carry out any substantial structural alterations. However, the Town and Country Planning Act 1953 abolished development charges for developments commenced on or after 18 November 1952, and the Town and Country Planning Act 1954 provides in a highly elaborate manner for compensation to be paid to persons who are prevented from enhancing the value of their land, because of planning restrictions.

Planning authorities have a duty to submit to the Minister of Housing and Local Government their development plans for their respective areas, and, notwithstanding the Act of 1954 last mentioned, you should make sure before you purchase a house that the development plan does not contain any proposals which would affect you adversely.

Apart from restrictions on use or development under the Town and Country Planning Act 1947, there may be other restrictions which would make you think twice before binding yourself to buy. A house on a residential housing estate may be sold with a restriction, for the mutual benefit of all the owners of houses on the estate, that no business is to be carried out on the premises and that it is to be used for private purposes only. The owner of property held subject to a restrictive covenant may be restrained by the High Court if he commits an infringement. The owner of house property, still requisitioned by the local authority, is to have his property restored to him with vacant possession by 31 March 1960 at the latest.

It is clearly in your interest if you are purchasing a house that the preliminary inquiries should be made before you enter into a binding contract. It is equally important that you should have the property surveyed on your behalf by a qualified surveyor. You must take the house as you find it, and only your surveyor will be able to tell you if the drains are in a good or bad state or if there is any sign of dry rot on the premises. It will be too late to make these investigations after you have signed a binding contract to purchase, for although the reports may prove unsatisfactory, you are not entitled to rescind this agreement.

The vendor should also be careful not to enter into a binding contract until the terms have been settled by his solicitor. Otherwise he may find that he has entered into what is described as an 'open contract' and that he has undertaken certain legal obligations with which he may not be able to comply. For example, it is an implied term of an open contract that there are no restrictions apart from planning restrictions affecting the use of the property. If in fact there is a restrictive covenant which is not disclosed to the purchaser before the contract, the vendor may be sued by the purchaser for damages, or the purchaser may have the right to rescind the contract.

The prospective vendor and purchaser should both avoid binding themselves to a bargain before they know all that it involves, by making sure that their preliminary agreement is made 'subject to contract'. The purchaser will normally be required at an early stage to pay a deposit, but if these protective words are inserted on the receipt, neither party will be bound to proceed with the transaction, for they will have done no more than record an agreement to agree. If the purchaser wishes to back out he will be entitled to have his deposit returned to him; if the vendor refuses to sell, the purchaser cannot compel him to do so and is entitled only to the return of his deposit. If you have set your mind on a house, it may be a disappointment not to be able to clinch the deal when you pay the deposit, but the risk that the vendor will go back on his bargain will usually be less than the danger of buying a property which may be a liability to you.

Fixtures and fittings may also be conveniently dealt with in the contract. It is sometimes necessary to distinguish between landlords' fixtures and tenants' (or trade) fixtures. Generally speaking, anything which is affixed to the premises, and cannot be removed without damaging the structure, such as a mantelpiece or a bath, is a fixture, and anything of a movable character, such as an electric-light bulb or a pendant, is a fitting. A fixture, being part of the structure of the premises, is usually deemed to be included in the purchase. Fittings, however, are excluded from a sale unless expressly included in the contract, although the contract frequently provides for the sale of the fittings at a valuation.

When you have entered into a binding agreement to purchase property – i.e. as soon as the contracts are exchanged between yourself and the vendor – the property is said to belong to you 'in equity'. This means, in effect, that it is your responsibility. If it is destroyed by fire before the sale is completed, the loss usually falls on your shoulders, and it does not relieve you from your liability to pay the balance of the purchase money on the agreed date. In practice, property is usually insured against loss by fire, and it is necessary for the purchaser to notify the insurance company of his equitable right to the property, or to insure independently, as soon as the contracts have been exchanged.

There has been considerable simplification in the transfer or conveyance of property since the passing of the Land Transfer Act 1897, which provided for the compulsory registration of land titles in London and certain other parts of the country. When property has a registered title, it is recorded in the official registers at the Land Registry in London. The entry of a particular property on the Register may involve little difficulty when the title is free of complication, but, unfortunately, the history of English land law is of a most involved character. It would be useless to attempt to embark upon any explanation in a work of this kind, and it would be unreasonable to expect a layman to evince any interest in the subject. The procedure has been substantially simplified since a series of Acts, shortly called the Law of Property Acts 1925, were passed, and we must content ourselves with observing that 'hangovers' of the past have left great obstacles to registration in country areas, where the land has not been split up into the comparatively simple 'parcels' which now characterize properties in built-up areas.

After the exchange of contracts there are certain formalities which are incidental to every sale and purchase. The vendor's solicitors must prepare a document called an 'abstract of title', which consists of a précis of the deeds and events which are relevant to the vendor's title to the property. This abstract must be examined by the purchaser's solicitors, and they must check its contents with the original title-deeds. The purchaser's solicitors will also be required to raise queries called 'Requisitions on Title', which examination of the deeds and documents necessitate, and these requisitions must be answered by the vendor's solicitors. These matters are bound to take time, but when the formalities have been settled, the purchase of the property can be completed – i.e. the title-deeds are handed over, with a formal deed of conveyance or transfer to the purchaser, in exchange for the purchase price. It is not the practice to pay the purchase money by cheque, but always in cash or by banker's draft. A banker's draft is a cheque drawn by a banker, and is therefore regarded as being the equivalent of cash, since it will never be dishonoured on presentation. Apart from the risk of dishonour of a cheque, there is always the possibility of the death of the drawer before the cheque has been paid by the Bank. Death revokes the authority of a Bank to pay a customer's cheque, and the vendor might, therefore, be deprived of his money for weeks, or even months, until the legal formalities described in Chapter 27 give the deceased purchaser's personal representatives the right to deal with his affairs.

In the absence of a stipulation to the contrary, the purchaser is generally bound to complete the purchase unless there is a defect in the title or a substantial misdescription of the property. The time for completion is usually fixed by the contract. A delay in completion, for which the purchaser is responsible, will probably result in his having to add interest to the purchase money, but except where 'time is of the essence of the contract', delay will not cause the transaction to be avoided. 'Time is of the essence' means that completion within a certain period is of fundamental importance, either because the nature of the transaction demands it, the contract expressly contains a clause to that effect, or one party to the contract has served a notice to the other to complete within a reasonable time.

When you buy property, you may not always have available the whole of the money necessary to pay for it. You may raise part of the money on mortgage, or borrow it from a Building Society. It is their business to lend money, on the security of the title-deeds of property, at a rate of interest generally maintained at 1 per cent, or more, above Bank rate. As security for the advance the society will hold the title-deeds, and the borrower, or 'mortgagor' as he is called, will execute a deed, called a 'mortgage', which binds him to repay the debt to the society, called the 'mortgagee', by monthly or quarterly instalments over a period of years. The amount of each instalment is calculated to include a certain proportion in respect of capital and a certain proportion in respect of interest. It is frequently a convenient way in which to pay for a house, and it results in every payment made being a payment towards the purchase price. Unlike rent, which is expended without return, every payment made is a form of saving. It has, however, its disadvantages. It may well be satisfactory so long as the mortgagor is in employment, and is able to keep up his instalments, but if he becomes unemployed his prospects may become grim.

Although, as a general rule, a Building Society mortgage contains provisions which do not allow the society to require repayment of the total debt so long as the instalments are paid punctually, it will also contain other provisions which give the society extensive powers to enable it to obtain repayment of the advance, and also a right to possession of the property, if the instalments are not kept up to date. Most Building Societies are reasonably sympathetic with misfortune, but they are in business to make a profit, and are not charitable institutions. If a mortgagor does not pay his instalments, the society will sooner or later apply to the Court for leave to enforce its rights. The society may, for example, sue for possession of the property free of any obligation to account to the borrower, or for repayment of its money, or it may take proceedings, called 'foreclosure proceedings', the effect of which is to dispossess the borrower of any further interest in the property. Alternatively, if the property has been let by the borrower, the society may appoint a receiver who will receive the rents and profits of the letting. These are only some of the powers, but the exercise of any of them is bound to be unfortunate for the mortgagor.

As an alternative to borrowing money from a Building Society, it is usually possible (in the case of a freehold or long leasehold property) to obtain a mortgage of a sum equivalent to one-half to two-thirds of the normal value, but not necessarily of the inflated value, of the property. The mortgagee will probably be a private investor who requires a long-term investment. He may expect interest of up to 8 per cent on the amount which he advances, but, unlike a Building Society mortgage, he will not ordinarily require repayment of his capital by small instalments each month or each quarter. He will, however, retain the right to ask for repayment of the entire advance at any time at three months' notice, and the mortgagor, on his part, will have the right to repay the loan at any time on six months' notice. When a mortgagee requires repayment of his money, it is usually possible to arrange for a transfer of the mortgage, although this may involve substantial expense.

If the mortgagor fails to repay a mortgage after he has received due notice, the mortgagee may take steps to enforce his rights in the same manner as a Building Society. In every instance, however, the mortgagor has the right to redeem the mortgage – i.e. to repay his indebtedness – at any time before a sale or foreclosure. American films may portray the villain foreclosing on the innocent mortgagor at twenty-four hours' notice, but enforcement of legal rights under a mortgage in England cannot be effected overnight, and it frequently involves protracted Court proceedings.

A mortgage debt is a personal debt. The property is security for the debt, and is not a substitute for it. If the property is destroyed by fire the mortgage debt must still be repaid. It also remains a liability on the death of a mortgagor, and if you have mortgaged the house in which you are living, and you wish your wife to enjoy the property after your death, free of the mortgage liability, you should take out a life-insurance policy for a sum which will be sufficient to discharge the mortgage.

The provisions of the Rent Acts, so far as they relate to mortgages, mitigate certain hardships which arise when a mortgagor of small property cannot pay the principal or interest, and the Court has extensive powers of protecting him in proper cases. They are analogous in character to those given to the tenant by the Rent Acts.

A word of caution is required for the benefit of any would-be house purchaser who is offered the bait of a 'Free Conveyance'. Between the wars a number of purchasers were unfortunately caught in this trap. In some instances builders had mortgaged the land on which the houses had been built, and when they handed out the 'Free Conveyance' they did not arrange for the land which had been purchased to be released from the mortgage. In cases in which the builders subsequently failed in their enterprise, and were made bankrupt, the house-owner then learnt that his property was subject to a mortgage, and he had no redress against the bankrupt vendor. No purchaser of a house should be so imprudent as to dispense with legal assistance. If he does so, he must blame himself, and not the law, if he is had for a 'mug'.

Some of the possible consequences of borrowing money on mortgage may appear harsh. When, however, John Doe has borrowed money from Richard Roe, the latter has always been entitled to stipulate the conditions of the loan. In the course of years, many of these conditions have become stereotyped. John Doe will now have to accept them or go without the money. If you feel disposed to criticize this practice you should consider if you yourself would be willing to lend money to a stranger, unless you were permitted to dictate the terms of the loan. Moreover, if the borrower defaulted, you should ask yourself if you would not expect the law to assist you in recovering payment of your money. The law has, in fact, done much to temper justice with mercy by the enactment of legislation designed for the protection of the 'small man', and it is a mistake to think that in its day-to-day operations the law is uninterested in the poor, and will work its machine only for the benefit of the wealthy. Poor men used formerly to tremble before the Majesty of the Law. It is now no longer necessary for them to do so, for even lawyers sometimes have democratic instincts. It is, however, unrealistic to pretend that the community would benefit from a system which permitted a borrower to dictate the terms on which he was to obtain his loan. There are still too many rogues in circulation to render such a scheme workable. It is not only capitalists who are greedy, and even capitalists are not always greedy.

19

COMPANIES

> 'Did you ever expect a Corporation to have a con-
> science, when it has no soul to be damned, and no body
> to be kicked?'
>
> Wilberforce: *Life of Thurlow*

WHEN an association of persons is formed for the purpose of sharing profits it usually carries on its business either as a partnership or a Limited Liability Company. A Limited Liability Company, unlike a Partnership (which was dealt with in Chapter 7), is a legal entity constituted by laws which define and limit its rights. It has a life cycle starting with incorporation, or birth, and ending in dissolution, which is equivalent to death. Unless it is dissolved, however, it continues its existence indefinitely, subject to the power to remove a Company from the register of 'live' Companies if it has become moribund. There is also a process called 'winding-up' or 'liquidation', which precedes dissolution and is a kind of death-bed affair.

The Limited Liability Company is not the only type of Company; indeed, it is a commercial upstart by comparison with Companies constituted by Royal Charter such as the Royal Academy or the Law Society, or with Companies such as public-utility Companies established by special private Acts of Parliament. There are even cases of ancient Companies which have operated as Corporations for so long that no one can say with certainty how or by what authority they were formed, and they are known as 'prescriptive Companies'. Some of these prescriptive Companies (which are extremely rare) operate certain rights of fisheries.

The vast majority of Companies are, however, Limited Liability Companies, and the word 'Company' as used throughout this and the next chapter means a Company formed under the Companies Acts 1862 to 1948, in which the shareholders have limited their liability to the nominal or face value of their shares.

You will recall that the owner or owners of a business organized and operated by a firm or partnership are individually responsible for the debts of the firm. There is, in general, no limit whatever to their liability. If the firm is insolvent the owner or each of the partners may be made personally liable for the debts, and if they are not paid in full, each partner may be made bankrupt. From the commercial point of view, perhaps, the most essential distinction between a firm and a Company is the immunity enjoyed by the owners of a Company to pay debts incurred by the Company. If a Company fails to meet its liabilities, the owners of the Company – namely, the shareholders who own the capital employed in the Company – are only liable to pay to the Company the nominal value of the shares held by them, in so far as such shares have not already been paid up. They are not liable for the debts of the Company. Those in charge of its affairs, called its directors, also incur no legal liability for any of the debts, unless they have committed some breach of their duty in their conduct of the business.

The Companies with which we are concerned in this chapter are divided into two main classes – viz. Public Companies and Private Companies. A Public Company has the right, under certain conditions, to invite the public to subscribe for its shares. Public Companies often apply to a Stock Exchange to allow dealings in their shares, but permission is given only to Companies which can satisfy the Stock Exchange Regulations designed to secure certain safeguards for investors. The great majority of Companies, however, are Private Companies. A Private Company, as is implied by the name, is not entitled to invite the public either to subscribe for its shares or to grant it a loan, and the number of shareholders in a Private Company (other than employees of the Company) is limited to fifty.

The right to nominate the directors – i.e. the persons who direct the policy of a Company – is usually vested in the persons who have subscribed to the Company's capital by purchasing shares. A business with assets valued at £1,000 might be owned by a Company incorporated or formed with a capital of £1,000. This capital is usually subscribed by two or three shareholders. They decide to undertake and operate a specific business, and they promote a Company for the purpose. When the signatory or original shareholders have incorporated the

Company, they meet together and appoint the directors who will conduct the Company's business operations.

Individually a shareholder has few powers beyond the power to vote. The conduct of the business of the Company rests entirely in the hands of the directors, and when the term of office of any director has expired, the shareholders may either re-elect him or appoint another director in his place. Shareholders have the privilege of attending at general meetings of the Company, and an annual meeting must be held at least once in each calendar year. Their participation in the affairs of the Company usually begins and ends with these meetings, but it is not possible to particularize their rights with any exactness. They vary with each particular Company, for they are contained in the contract made between the Company and each of its shareholders. This contract is contained in a document, considered later in this chapter, called the Articles of Association of the Company. The generalizations in this chapter on the rights of shareholders are, accordingly, based on the rights which are, *in general practice*, given to them by the Articles of Association of the Company. It must not be assumed that they apply in any particular case, for the only way in which you are able to ascertain the rights of the individual shareholder in any particular Company is to examine the Articles of Association of that Company.

When you hold shares in a Company, you are not entitled, as a rule, to demand repayment of your money. You are not a creditor of the Company. You are one of its members, and if you wish to dispose of your shares, and obtain repayment of your money, you are able to do so only if you can find someone who is willing to purchase your shares, and, also, in the case of many private companies, if the directors are willing to accept the purchaser of the shares as a member of the Company in your place.

The promotion of a Private Company to operate a business is an everyday occurrence, for to own a business and at the same time to limit your liability is often a convenient procedure for regulating your affairs. You may decide to risk a certain amount of money, and no more, in the venture. If you fail to achieve your object, you may cut your loss and start with a fresh venture. If John Doe wishes to start a business, he may promote a Company, hold all but one of the shares, and arrange for his wife, or an employee, to hold the remaining share. His wife, or his employee, will usually be his nominee. When the nominee takes his share, he may, at the same time, execute a transfer of the share in blank, and hand it with his share certificate to John Doe. If at a later date John Doe wishes to part company with his nominee he may make use of the transfer to vest the nominee share in a new shareholder. In this way John Doe retains a 100 per cent control of the Company. This type of business is called a 'one-man Company', but it is important to realize that John Doe as an individual is quite distinct in law from the corporate person the John Doe Company Ltd. Although such a Company is both lawful and common, suppliers should not be too ready to give it more credit than they would give to the individual behind it.

While the law allows a man to limit his business risks in this way, it also gives some measure of protection to those who have business dealings with him. Every Company which is incorporated with a view to carrying on business for profit must have the word 'Limited' or 'Ltd' as the last word of its title. When it is not formed for the purposes of gain, the word 'limited' may be omitted from the title, if sanction is obtained from the Board of Trade. If John Doe is using his own name for trading purposes, but his business is, in fact, owned by 'John Doe Limited', he must make this fact clear to the world. The name, with the addition of the word 'Limited' or 'Ltd', must appear on all documents which relate to the business. If this is not done, it renders John Doe liable to penalties as well as making him personally responsible to anyone who has given credit without notice of the business being owned by a Company. Conversely, it is an offence to describe a business as being 'limited' when it is not, in fact, registered as a Limited Liability Company.

The addition of the word 'limited' to the title of the Company is not the only protection given to the public. Every Company formed or incorporated since the Registration of Business Names Act 1916 must also disclose the names and former names of its directors, and also their nationality and former nationality (if they are not natural born British subjects), on all business letters and all notices and other publications of the Company. Disclosure of the names enables you to identify those in control of the Company. You are able to ascertain before you give credit to the Company whether the directors are men of good repute or men of straw. You must not forget, however, that, even if the directors are men of substance, they are not under any personal liability for the debts of the Company. If, however, they are men of integrity, they are less likely to be engaged upon an enterprise of doubtful financial character. Incidentally, a director is usually required by the Articles of Association to acquire a specified number of shares to qualify him for his office, and if he fails to acquire this stake in the Company's fortunes within a certain time after his appointment, he may automatically cease to be a director.

As a further safeguard to creditors, there is a statutory obligation placed upon every Company to make an annual return to the Companies Registration Office at Bush House, Kingsway, London, giving certain information regarding its constitution and financial structure. Every Company has its own file, and every file is open to inspection by any member of the public upon payment of a fee of 1s.

Every Company must have an office, known as a Registered Office, at which it may be served with all legal documents. There is no need to institute a search to trace the office of a Company which has ceased to carry on business. Notice of the situation of its Registered Office must be filed at Bush House, and documents served at the Registered Office are validly served for all purposes.

There is no limit to the objects which a Company may set out to achieve when it is first promoted. The only legal obligation is to define these objects clearly and specifically in a document, called its Memorandum of Association, which has to be filed with the Registrar of Companies, before a certificate of incorporation is issued. The usual practice is first to define the principal objects of the Company, and then to take extensive powers to carry on business of an ancillary nature, or upon which the promoters may later wish to embark. If, however, a Company carries on a business which is beyond its defined powers, it is said to act '*ultra vires*' (beyond its powers), for when the objects of its existence have been so defined, it may never do any act beyond the scope of those defined powers, unless it has first carried through the formalities necessary to alter its objects. Moreover, as a Company cannot bind itself by an act which is *ultra vires*, those who propose to enter into a contract with a Company should satisfy themselves that it has power to complete its side of the bargain. As the Memorandum is open to inspection, a plea of ignorance will not avail if a contract entered into by the Company is later found to be *ultra vires*. There are, however, some cases in which one or more directors of the Company may be personally liable for *ultra vires* acts, in the same way as an agent may sometimes be personally liable when he has acted without authority, a matter which was considered in Chapter 5.

The Memorandum must also specify the amount of the nominal capital of the Company. This enables everyone to obtain an indication of its financial structure before trading with it on credit terms. A Company may be formed with a nominal capital of £1 or even less, or with a nominal capital of a million pounds or more. The expression 'nominal capital' must be distinguished from 'issued capital' and from so-called 'loan capital'. The nominal capital is the maximum sum which the Company takes power to issue in the form of shares. The issued capital represents the actual sum which has been subscribed for shares, issued either for cash or for some other valid consideration. Loan capital, or 'debentures', represents money borrowed by the Company, usually on the security of a mortgage or charge on some one or more or all of its assets. It is not strictly *capital* of the Company. Those who lend are creditors, not members, as such, of the Company.

The share capital of a Company need not necessarily be subscribed for in cash. For instance, if a Company purchases a business as a going concern, the vendors of the business may accept payment of the purchase price in shares, instead of in cash. When these shares have been issued, or allotted, to the vendors they will be part of the issued share capital. If, however, the business acquired by the Company is purchased for the sum of, say, £1,000, the Company is not entitled to allot shares in excess of a nominal value of £1,000 in payment. A Company may, if its 'Articles' permit, pay a commission, called an underwriting commission. Apart from this, no new shares may be issued by the Company at a discount, or for less than their face or par value, although if shares are issued but not taken up the Court may sanction their reissue at a discount.

Shares may be of different classes. The three principal categories are preferred shares, ordinary shares, and deferred shares. Provision is usually made for the preferred shares to receive a dividend – i.e. a proportion of the profits which are available for distribution – in priority to the other shareholders. Their dividend each year will usually be limited by the terms of issue to, say, 5 or 6 per cent of the nominal value of each share. In addition, they may have priority rights to the return of capital, over other classes of shareholders, when the Company is liquidated. Ordinary shares usually take a larger percentage of the profits, but are not normally entitled to receive any of the distributed profits until the preference shareholders have received their dividend in full. Deferred shares usually come last, but may take, by way of dividend, all profits which are lawfully decided to be distributed and which are not distributed to the preference and ordinary shareholders. A 'cumulative preference', or 'Cum. Pref.' share is a share which entitles the holder to carry forward arrears of dividends when there is insufficient profit in any year to pay the shareholder his priority dividend for that year. Shareholders are not entitled to receive any dividend in any year in which the Company has earned insufficient profit to provide for a distribution, for dividends may be paid only out of profits. When a Company which has been running at a loss is again earning sufficient profit to declare dividends, the holder of 'Cum. Pref.' shares receives payment of arrears before the other shareholders receive a dividend.

As the nominal capital may not give a true indication of the financial structure of a Company, it is also necessary for every Company to include in its annual return a statement which shows the amount of the issued share capital. If, upon inspection of a Company's file, it is found that the annual returns are not up to date, it is some guide that its business affairs are not conducted with the regularity demanded by the law.

The Memorandum must be filed prior to the incorporation of a Company, and revenue fees or duties are payable at the rate of 10*s*. per cent on the nominal capital of the Company.

In addition to its Memorandum, every Company must file with the Registrar its Articles of Association, which are the rules and regulations which govern the internal management of the Company, and constitute a contract between each shareholder and the Company. The Articles must not be confused with the Memorandum. The Memorandum defines the objects of the Company. The Articles define the administrative procedure to be adopted by the Company. There is annexed to the Companies Act 1948 a schedule of specimen articles for a Company called 'Table A'. Many Companies adopt 'Table A' as their Articles, with such modifications as appear in each case to be desirable to the Company's professional advisers.

Among the matters dealt with by the Articles are the rules relating to the issue and transfer of the shares in the Company, the rights of the shareholders as to dividends and voting, the procedure to be adopted at meetings of the Company, the appointment and retirement of directors, and their powers and duties.

The Memorandum and the Articles of a Private Company must each be subscribed by two signatories, and of a Public Company by seven signatories. Each signatory must subscribe for at least one share in the Company.

Company law is one of the most complicated branches of our legal system. It cannot reasonably be simplified, since one is dealing with the rules and regulations under which an artificial body is to conduct its business. These rules and regulations have to be designed to meet every situation, but alterations both in the Memorandum and in the Articles may be effected by a resolution of the shareholders, called a Special Resolution. A Special Resolution is a resolution which is passed at a meeting of shareholders, properly convened, after at least twenty-one days' notice, by a majority of 75 per cent in value of the shareholders who take part in the voting. There are, however, safeguards to enable holders of shares of not less than 15 per cent in the aggregate to apply to the Court in proper cases to refuse its sanction to the proposed alterations in the Memorandum.

When all the formalities relating to the formation of the Company have been completed, and the necessary fees have been paid, the Certificate of Incorporation will be issued. Every Company must exhibit its Certificate at the registered office of the Company, and must also affix a notice outside the door to indicate the office as being the Registered Office.

As soon as the Certificate of Incorporation is received, the subscribers should appoint the directors, if they have not been appointed by the Articles. Among the first duties of the directors will be the issue of the shares to the original signatories to the Memorandum, and this is done by formally impressing the Seal of the Company on each share certificate in accordance with the provisions of the articles, and pursuant to the resolution of the Board of Directors. The Seal of a Company is always affixed 'pursuant to a resolution of the Board of Directors'. It is the talisman of the Company, and is a necessary adjunct to its business, as although a Board of Directors may empower one or more individual directors or managers to enter into contracts on behalf of the Company, most contracts of importance made by the Company are executed under seal.

20

COMPANIES *(Continued)*

> 'All the speeches put together did what they were in-
> tended to do, and established in the hearers' minds
> that there was no speculation so promising, or at the
> same time so praiseworthy, as the United Metropoli-
> tan Improved Hot Muffin and Crumpet Baking and
> Punctual Delivery Company.'
>
> *Nicholas Nickleby*

SOME of the obligations of the directors, who are the persons
who operate a Company, were given in the preceding chapter.
The Articles define many of their powers and duties. The law
imposes a number of further obligations. If you wish to promote a Company to operate your business, you should acquire
some knowledge of the duties of a director before you embark
upon the adventure. Many Companies are operated in an irregular manner, and most of these have a short life. It is a privilege to be permitted by the law to undertake a commercial risk
under the cloak of limited liability. You abuse the privilege if
you are not willing to accept the corresponding responsibility.

It is not easy to define the exact status of a director. In some
respects he is the servant of the Company. Sometimes he is its
agent. On other occasions he is the trustee for the Company. It
is always his duty to act with integrity. If he acts fraudulently,
or with negligence, or *ultra vires*, he may be dismissed by the
shareholders. He may also be sued in respect of any fraud or
breach of duty which he has committed.

A director may be appointed only in accordance with the
powers contained in the Articles, and his remuneration may
be fixed only in the manner laid down in the Articles. The
Companies Act 1948 contains provisions intended to bar anyone entering the twilight of life from taking control of the des-
tinies of a Public Company, as distinct from a Private Company, and, subject to certain exceptions, every director is now
required to retire from office shortly after his seventieth birthday. However, a brisk trade in bath chairs has not followed the
operation of this enactment, as the exceptions have proved
more popular than the rule.

Directors may usually agree among themselves for the appointment of one or more of their number to carry out specific duties, and for this purpose they may be allowed a remuneration additional to their directors' fees. A director is never entitled to act individually, unless he has received authority to do so from the Board, or unless the Articles give him this power. Subject to any such authority, the affairs of a Company are conducted by the Board of Directors collectively. Each director must normally carry out such duties as are imposed upon him by the Board as a whole. If he exceeds his authority, he may make himself personally liable for any unauthorized act.

If a director has a dispute with his co-directors, they may pass a resolution which will limit his powers to the bare statutory rights of a director. This means he will be entitled, at all reasonable times, to inspect the books and the accounts of the business, and to satisfy himself that its affairs are being lawfully conducted. He will be entitled to be duly notified of meetings of the directors, and to attend and express his opinion. He will not, however, be entitled to take any active part in the management, and he will not be entitled to give instructions to individual employees of the Company.

A Private Company may have one or more directors. The minimum and maximum number will be prescribed by the Articles. If there is more than one director, it will be necessary to hold directors' meetings from time to time, in order to decide upon the policy of the Company, unless the Articles authorize resolutions of the directors to be passed without the formality of a Board meeting. Minutes of the business transacted at directors' meetings should be carefully and accurately kept. If you promote a Company, but have no experience of office routine, you should appoint a competent and knowledgeable person to act as Secretary. It will be part of his duty to keep minutes, and to observe generally the statutory requirements relating to Companies.

Once each year, the directors must lay before the annual general meeting of the Company accounts which will show the financial results of the business transacted by the Company during the previous twelve months. The normal business transacted at the annual general meeting of shareholders will include the question of dividends and the election of directors, as well as the approval of the accounts. Shareholders may accept or reject any recommendation made by directors as to the declaration of a dividend. They also have power to re-elect retiring directors, and to appoint new directors. Other business, transacted at the annual meeting is usually formal. The shareholders are, however, always entitled, and frequently expected, to show their appreciation of the services rendered to the Company by the directors by passing a resolution to provide for payment of directors' fees, and at the conclusion of the meeting it is traditional to pass a vote of thanks to the Chairman of the meeting.

No meeting of shareholders can be effective unless there is a 'quorum' present in person. A quorum is the minimum number of shareholders, prescribed by the Articles, required for the purpose of transacting business at any meeting of the Company. Any shareholder who does not intend to attend the meeting may give a 'proxy' to any other person to vote for him. A proxy is a document by which one shareholder appoints another person to vote in his place, and it is valid for one meeting. The Articles will prescribe the form which the proxy is to take, and it will be used only when a 'poll' is taken on a resolution placed before the meeting. A resolution is first put to a meeting for a decision on a show of hands, given by those present and entitled to vote. If no poll is demanded, the result of the show of hands decides the fate of the resolution. If, however, a poll is demanded in proper form, a shareholder is often entitled to one vote for each share which he holds, so that if he holds 100 shares he may be entitled to 100 votes. The Articles will, however, in each case, prescribe the exact voting rights of shareholders, both on a show of hands and when a poll is taken, and they will also prescribe the circumstances in which a poll may be demanded. It is not unusual to preclude preferential shareholders from voting.

In addition to the annual general meeting, the Company has power to hold 'extraordinary' general meetings for the transaction of special business – special business being any business outside of normal routine, e.g. a proposal for alteration of the Articles would be special business.

The dividends which a Company may decide to pay are the sums which the shareholders decide, upon the recommendation of the directors, to distribute among the shareholders, out of the profits of the Company, the rights of the different classes of shareholders being regulated by the Articles. Income tax at the full standard rate must be deducted by the Company before payment of the dividend to each individual shareholder, but if the total income of the shareholder for the year is a sum less than that upon which he would be liable to pay tax at the full standard rate, he will be able to obtain a refund of overpaid tax from the Inland Revenue. The subject of income tax is dealt with in Chapter 28.

A trading Company is entitled to borrow money, unless its Memorandum expressly precludes it from doing so. Other Companies may borrow if the Memorandum contains the necessary power, and within the limit of such power. If a Company proposes to charge all or any of its assets as security for a loan, it will usually seal a document, called a debenture or charge, which is a mortgage, recording the terms and conditions of the loan. Notice of a debenture or a charge in a required form must be lodged with the Registrar of Companies within twenty-one days. Particulars of the charge are added by the Registrar to the file of the Company, and are available for inspection by any member of the public. If, however, the notice is not lodged within twenty-one days, the debenture-holder will lose the benefit of his security, unless he obtains an order from the Court which extends his time for filing the notice. The object of registration is to protect creditors. If there were no register of debentures or charges, a creditor would have no means of knowing that the Company had charged its assets, even although he had inspected the file of the Company. The Register of Charges should accordingly be inspected in order to obtain a supplementary and essential picture of the financial position of a Company.

If default is made by a Company in complying with the conditions of issue of any debenture, the debenture-holder usually has power (given under the debenture) to appoint a Receiver and Manager over the property which has been charged. The Court also has power to appoint a Receiver and Manager at any time after the principal money secured by the debenture has become due, if the debenture-holder is able to satisfy the Court that this security is in jeopardy. The Receiver and Manager takes control of the property charged by the debenture, and when the Company has charged its entire undertaking the effect is to give him the control of the Company. His primary duty is then to protect the debenture-holder, whose debt must be paid before all other debts due from the Company, with the exception of certain claims which rank for preferential treatment. Preferential debts include rates and taxes, within certain limits, and also wages and salaries for a specified maximum period. A Receiver and Manager is frequently faced with difficult problems, and he must act strictly within his powers, or he may make himself personally liable for debts. For this reason, it is usual to appoint a qualified accountant or other person of experience as a Receiver and Manager.

A Receiver is not under a personal obligation to discharge debts, even although contracted after the date of his appointment, unless he has exceeded his powers or expressly agreed to accept personal liability. Although the Receiver is usually nominated by the debenture-holder, the debenture normally provides that he shall be the agent of the Company, and you will remember from Chapter 5 that an agent is not, normally, personally liable for debts incurred by him on behalf of his principal.

If a Company has been formed for a specific purpose, and that purpose has been fulfilled, the Company may be put into liquidation. That is to say, its life may be brought to a peaceful end. When an individual dies, his personal representative must pay his debts, and then realize and distribute his assets. In the same way, when a Company is liquidated, it is necessary for an appointed person to liquidate its affairs before the Company is dissolved. He is called the liquidator.

If the Company is solvent when the proposal for liquidation is made – i.e. if it is able to pay its creditors in full – the directors may file a 'declaration of solvency', embodying a statement of the Company's assets and liabilities, and the shareholders may within five weeks thereafter resolve upon a form of liquidation known as a 'members' voluntary winding-up'. A declaration of solvency is a solemn declaration made by a director declaring that the Company is solvent and able to pay all its debts within a period of twelve months. The shareholders may then appoint a liquidator to proceed with the liquidation. If, at a subsequent date, it appears that a director has made the declaration of solvency without reasonable grounds for his opinion as to the Company's solvency, he may be liable to imprisonment not exceeding six months or a fine not exceeding £500 or both. A clause to this effect was inserted in the Companies Act 1948 to remedy the scandalous abuse of the old law, as there were many occasions when declarations of solvency were recklessly made without any real hope of realization of the assets at their paper values.

When a Company is not able to pay its debts, the shareholders may pass a resolution for liquidation, and invite the creditors to nominate the liquidator. This is called a 'creditors' voluntary winding-up'. When a liquidator is appointed, he must, normally, dispose of the business of the Company and all its assets to the best advantage, and out of the money which he receives he must pay the debts due from the Company. Preferential debts, which have been referred to earlier, must be paid in priority to other debts.

Many Companies end their activities in voluntary liquidation or winding-up. The appointment of a liquidator terminates the activities of the directors, and they have no power to act after his appointment. Although the Court has extensive powers of investigation in the course of a voluntary liquidation, these powers are seldom invoked. There is a general tendency among shareholders and creditors to cut a loss when a Company is in liquidation. They do not desire time and money to be wasted on investigations which will be difficult and costly to pursue. Occasionally directors are able to avoid awkward questions as to their activities by persuading shareholders and creditors to agree to voluntary liquidation.

A liquidator does not always act upon his own responsibility in liquidating the affairs of a Company. The creditors have power to appoint a committee, called a 'Committee of Inspection', to act with the liquidator. If the members of the Committee are energetic, they may frequently insist upon investigations which might not otherwise be undertaken.

Compulsory liquidation, as distinct from voluntary liquidation, may be procured when a creditor or a shareholder (or the Board of Trade after investigation) presents a petition to the Court asking for a winding-up order. Instances when a petition will be appropriate include cases in which a Company is unable to pay its debts, or fails to pay a debt within twenty-one days of demand, or fails to discharge a judgement obtained against it. If the relevant facts are duly proved by the petitioner the Court may order the Company to be liquidated, and the management of its affairs will then come under the control (pending the appointment of a liquidator) of an official of the Board of Trade called the Official Receiver.

There are many grounds upon which the Court may make a winding-up order, and without specifying them in detail, it may be said, broadly speaking, that the Court has power to make a winding-up order in every case in which it is 'just and equitable' for it to do so. This phrase must be interpreted reasonably. The Court will not act arbitrarily. It will take every factor into consideration. The power to make the order is a discretion vested in the Judge who hears the petition. For example, a winding-up order may be made in a case in which deadlock is reached between two shareholders holding between them in equal shares all the issued capital of the Company, and where there is no other person who has any power to intervene in the management of the business. Again, a winding-up order may be made if the 'substratum' or the foundation of the business of the Company has ceased to exist, or if there is no reasonable hope of carrying on the business of the Company at a profit.

When a Company is in liquidation every creditor and shareholder of the Company will receive a notice which invites him to attend a meeting. At this meeting the financial history of the Company will be outlined by the Official Receiver. If you are a creditor, and you complete the form which you receive, called the 'proof of debt', you will be entitled to vote at the meeting upon the question as to whether the conduct of the liquidation is to remain in the hands of the Official Receiver, or whether another liquidator should be appointed. It is common practice to appoint a qualified accountant on these occasions. The

Official Receiver does not regard it as a reflexion on his office if he is not maintained in office as liquidator, for when an accountant is appointed as liquidator, the Board of Trade still has the conduct of the liquidation under its control, and the Official Receiver must make a report to the Court. As in the case of a voluntary liquidation, a committee of inspection may also be appointed to act with the liquidator, and an order may be obtained in proper cases for an examination under oath of one or more of the directors suspected of irregular practice. In the case of fraud criminal charges may be laid against any director responsible, and civil proceedings may also be brought, resulting in his being ordered to reimburse the Company or to pay personally the whole or some part of the Company's debts. In addition, any such directors may be restrained for a period not exceeding five years from acting as a director or managing the affairs of any other Company.

The death of a Company is seldom followed by floral tributes. The conduct of the directors which has led it into the abyss is frequently criticized, but criticism will not repay the creditors their lost money. It may be hard for a man in a small way of trade to refuse an apparently profitable order, but success in business is not achieved merely by obtaining orders. The 'profitable' order is a snare if the debt is never paid, and you are caught in the trap.

This and the previous chapter have dealt almost entirely with Private Companies. The principal feature of a Public Company which you are likely to encounter is the 'Prospectus'. This is an invitation to the public to subscribe for shares. A prospectus gives the public particulars of the business of the Company with details of any results already achieved, and a forecast of future prospects. You will frequently see a prospectus published in the financial columns of a newspaper. Generally a prospectus is an honest document, but in some cases expectations of a most extravagant character are suggested, although there is nothing tangible to justify them, or to inspire confidence. Promoters of Companies who advertise in this way are anxious for one thing – to make as much money as they can out of those members of the public who are inveigled by a reference to prospects of great profits.

e to make concrete proposals for settlement of *all*
e Registrar will usually make a receiving order, for
onsiders the interests of all the creditors, and,
, does not permit its machinery to be used as a
ng agency.

ceiving order has been made, the debtor is still not
but there are no longer any natural obstacles which
n from bankruptcy, and he must forthwith attend
ial Receiver and disclose all his financial affairs.
Receiver is, moreover, entitled to take immediate
of all the debtor's valuables, including even any
watch which he may have on him at the time of
w. So soon as practicable, it is the duty of the Offi-
r to convene a meeting, called the 'first meeting of
There is a general belief that it is necessary for a
lodge his claim, or 'proof of debt', as it is called,
meeting takes place, and that he will otherwise be
his right to share in the distribution of the bank-
rty. This idea is erroneous. If, in fact, a completed
e debt is lodged before the first meeting of credi-
ditor is entitled to vote at the meeting, but there is
vantage gained from proving the debt at an early
bankruptcy. It may be proved at any time before a
paid, and this is unlikely to occur for many months,
creditor receives advance notice of any intended

rst meeting of creditors, the creditors present and
vote will decide by a formal resolution whether or
ntor is to be adjudicated bankrupt, and, if they so
ey may also decide to appoint a Trustee in Bank-
ractice, it is usual to pass the resolution for adjudi-
ess the debtor puts forward a scheme for meeting
es which the creditors are willing to consider. He
xample, offer a 'composition' – i.e. a proposal to
ortion of his debts for a sum of not less than 5s. in
l if such an offer is deemed worthy of consideration,
g may be adjourned to enable the scheme to be car-
gh, with the approval of the Court, after which the
y proceedings may be annulled. The Court's appro-

In order to satisfy the law, a prospectus must comply with a number of regulations. In the past these regulations were not sufficiently stringent to afford an effective safeguard to the more credulous members of the public, but a number of additional obligations as to disclosure of material and relevant facts were imposed on every promoter of a Company under the provisions of the Act of 1948. Dishonest concealment of material facts or reckless statements, promises, or forecasts had already been made offences under the Prevention of Fraud (Investments) Act 1939, but although it is necessary for every statement purporting to be a statement of fact to be true, it is impossible to exclude every form of prophecy or wishful thinking on the part of the promoters. These may be included under the heading 'prospects' or 'estimates', and will usually be 'subject to unforeseen circumstances'. You may frequently read that the directors 'confidently expect further important and successful developments'. Other phrases in a prospectus may be ambiguous, although it may not be possible to describe them as untrue or reckless.

Untrue statements may render a promoter liable to a criminal prosecution. In addition, if it can be proved that these untrue statements have misled an investor who has purchased shares in the belief that the statements were true, he has a legal right of action for damages against every person who has taken part in the promotion of the Company. Success in an action of this character is, however, unfortunately never easy to achieve. The burden of proof is a heavy one to establish, and a 'prospectus action' is one of the most costly forms of litigation.

'Take-over bids', by which expression is meant the attempt of one company to purchase the shares of another company from its shareholders, usually over the heads of the directors, have come increasingly to hit the headlines. The Companies Act 1948 legalizes the making of these bids so that a minority of shareholders with not more than a tenth of the share capital concerned may find themselves being forced to sell against their will. It is not to be supposed, however, that the Court is never solicitous for an oppressed minority of shareholders.

21

BANKRUPTCY

'Poverty is no disgrace to a man, but it is confound-
edly inconvenient.'

Sydney Smith

THE law relating to bankruptcy is principally governed by the Bankruptcy Act 1914. When a debtor is insolvent and unable to pay his debts, he may, after a number of legal formalities, which will be referred to in this chapter, be adjudicated a bankrupt. The conduct of his affairs will then be taken away from him and placed in the hands of a trustee, called the 'Trustee in Bankruptcy'. It will be the duty of the trustee to realize the bankrupt's property, and to distribute it among the creditors.

The first step towards bankruptcy is called an 'act of bankruptcy'. Unless and until an act of bankruptcy has been committed, bankruptcy proceedings cannot be initiated. An act of bankruptcy may be committed by a debtor in several ways. Frequently, if a debtor does not meet his liability under a judgement, his creditor may serve him with a document called a 'bankruptcy notice'. This requires him either to meet the judgement liability within eight days or to compound it to the satisfaction of the creditor, and if this is not done, an act of bankruptcy is committed.

There are a number of other acts of bankruptcy. They include the following:

(1) The seizure and sale by a creditor of the property of a debtor under an 'execution'. Execution against a firm, described in Chapter 7, may be similarly effected against an individual who fails to pay a judgement debt.

(2) The execution by a debtor of a deed by which he voluntarily assigns all his property to a trustee for the benefit of his creditors generally. Such a deed must be registered, and if not impeached, the trustee may in due course realize the property and divide the proceeds of realization among the creditors. Any creditor, however, is entitled to ignore the deed and to 'treat the trustee as a ghost and see through him', if he does

---

not wish to recognize the deed. If
bound by the deed within one mo
in bankruptcy at any time within
the deed.

(3) The act of a debtor in absco
yond the reach of his creditors wi
them. If a debtor is insolvent and
it may, for example, be an act of
land on a world cruise or otherw

(4) Notice of suspension or inte
debts, or filing a declaration of
notification by the debtor to one
owing to his insolvency, he is no
The latter is a formal document,
advice.

(5) A 'fraudulent preference',
a deliberate act of showing prefe
ment of his debt, after the debto
he is insolvent and unable to pay
is adjudicated bankrupt after he
ence, the preference may be set
creditor who has been paid his d
the money to the Trustee in B
then share equally with the othe
subsequently made of the bankru

A bankruptcy petition may b
Court within three months afte
ruptcy by any creditor who is
who are owed, a specified sum i
gate. The petition asks for the
'receiving order' – i.e. an order
Receiver', a Board of Trade off
deals with the affairs of a Comp
the debtor's property, and to ta
his affairs. If the debtor applies,
ing of the petition, for further
bilities, the Registrar dealing wi
one or more adjournments. Ot

---

debtor
his deb
the Co
theoret
debt-co

Whe
a bankr
separat
on the
The Of
possess
jeweller
the inte
cial Re
creditor
creditor
before t
deprivec
rupt's p
proof o
tors, the
no othe
stage of
dividend
while ev
dividenc

At the
entitled
not the
resolve,
ruptcy. I
cation, u
his liabil
may, for
pay a pro
the £ – a
the meeti
ried thro
bankrupt

val is not, however, automatic. It will consider all the circumstances, and if it is of the opinion that the debtor's conduct requires investigation, it may refuse to sanction the scheme.

If the creditors resolve upon adjudication, they may also decide to appoint a Trustee in Bankruptcy. If they do not do so, the administration of the bankrupt's affairs will remain in the hands of the Official Receiver.

Bankruptcy was at one time regarded as little short of a crime. This view was modified when a Court of Bankruptcy, expressly declared to be a Court for the Relief of Insolvent Debtors, was established in 1831, and after that date debtors who had been confined in prison until their debts had been paid in full were able to obtain their release as soon as they surrendered all their property. Even so, a bankrupt was not able to start life afresh, for any property which subsequently came into his hands had to be made available for his creditors. He remained, in fact, bankrupt until his debts had been paid.

The present procedure enables the Bankruptcy Court to grant relief to the honest debtor who has met with misfortune. It may also be used at times by a dishonest debtor to escape payment of his liabilities. The Court, however, has a number of powers for punishing dishonest debtors, and it will use them in proper cases.

When a debtor is adjudicated bankrupt, the resolution of the creditors at their first meeting will, as stated, decide whether his affairs are to be left for administration in the hands of the Official Receiver, acting as the Trustee in Bankruptcy, or in the hands of an accountant or other person qualified to act as trustee. The duties of a trustee are analogous to the duties of the liquidator of a Company dealt with in the previous chapter, although his powers are more extensive. Moreover, as in the case of the liquidation of a Company, the creditors have power to appoint a committee, called a 'committee of inspection', to act with the trustee. It is the duty of this committee, which consists of not fewer than three and not more than five of the creditors, to consider questions which arise in the bankruptcy, as, for example, whether the trustee is to compromise a claim or to take or defend proceedings.

When a debtor has been adjudicated bankrupt, the bankruptcy dates back, generally speaking, to the act of bankruptcy on which it was founded. All financial transactions entered into by the bankrupt after that date are liable to be set aside. Anyone who has received money from the bankrupt, with knowledge of the act of bankruptcy, may accordingly be called upon to repay the money to the trustee. A creditor is never safe in accepting a payment from a debtor when bankruptcy proceedings are pending, unless the money has been provided by a third party.

A bankrupt is under a number of obligations to his trustee. Primarily he must make full disclosure and supply full information about his affairs. From the moment of his appointment, the trustee becomes, in effect, the owner of the bankrupt's property. It is said to 'vest' in him, and the bankrupt no longer has any rights over it.

The expression 'property' is a comprehensive one. It is sufficiently wide to include all property which the bankrupt has in his possession, or under his control, in the way of his trade or business, with the consent of the true owner, and of which he is the apparent owner. Even 'after-acquired property' – i.e. property which comes into the hands of the bankrupt after the commencement of the bankruptcy – may pass to the Trustee in Bankruptcy. This includes both legacies and gifts. Property which the bankrupt holds in trust for a third party under the terms of a bona-fide trust, and also the actual tools of his trade, together with his bedding and wearing apparel up to £20 in value, are, however, all excluded.

It frequently happens that a debtor is hard pressed, and in order to raise cash he sells or mortgages his furniture, but by arrangement with the lender he retains it in his possession and continues to use it. If he is subsequently made bankrupt, the lender may then lose the furniture, as it may be the 'property' of the bankrupt within the scope of the definition. To meet this difficulty, the lender may avail himself of the facilities offered by the Bills of Sales Act 1878 and 1882. A 'bill of sale' is a legal document executed when personal chattels are to remain in the possession of the vendor after their sale or after they have been charged as security for a loan. A bill which records an actual sale is called an 'absolute bill of sale'. In other cases it is called a 'bill of sale by way of security'.

Bills of sale are highly technical documents. A number of formalities must be strictly observed both before and after signature. Unless there is compliance with every detail, the bill of sale may be declared void and the protection which it was intended to secure will be lost. Among the formalities required are the registration of the bill at the Registry called the Bills of Sale Registry, which is open to inspection by every member of the public. Registration must be effected within seven days after execution, and thereafter every five years. Notice of all such registrations is given in the publications of the Trade Protection Societies, and many traders subscribe to one or other of such societies to enable them to ascertain something of the financial status of a new customer before extending credit. From a practical point of view, a bill of sale is sometimes the last resource available to a harassed debtor, for it frequently destroys such credit as he still enjoys. In many cases it therefore merely postpones the inevitable financial crash.

Although a bankrupt is compelled to surrender all his property, he is entitled to continue to earn his living, subject to certain restrictions. He is not, for instance, fettered as to the work which he chooses. If, however, he obtains employment which yields him more than an adequate wage or a reasonable standard of living, the Court has power to order part of his earnings to be set aside for the benefit of his creditors. Moreover, the law protects the community from unfair trading activities during bankruptcy, for if the bankrupt continues to trade, he is not entitled to incur credit in excess of £10 without informing the proposed creditor that he is an undischarged bankrupt. He is also not entitled to act as a director of a limited company, or to take part in the active management of the company, unless he first obtains the consent of the Court. A breach of any of these obligations renders him liable to a criminal charge.

A trader may have a bona-fide wish to protect his wife or family if he is unfortunate in his business affairs. In order to achieve this aim he may settle or place his property in his wife's name. If he complies with the necessary formalities and is

H

subsequently adjudicated bankrupt, the creditors, as a general rule, will have no claim to the settled property. There are, however, two cases in which the trustee may claim the settled property for the benefit of the creditors. The first arises if a man is made bankrupt within two years of making a voluntary settlement, and as the expression 'settlement' includes gifts it means that if the bankrupt has presented his wife, within two years prior to his bankruptcy, with £1,000 or a pearl necklace, she will be ordered by the Court to hand it back to the Trustee in Bankruptcy. A voluntary settlement, however, does not, generally speaking, include a settlement made by a man in favour of his wife on his marriage. Marriage is a good consideration in law for an agreement to settle property, and property so settled will not revert to a trustee in the event of subsequent bankruptcy. The second case arises if the bankrupt has made a settlement within ten years prior to his bankruptcy. In such an event, however, the settlement will not be set aside as a matter of course. The trustee will have a claim to the settled property only if the bankrupt is unable to prove that he was solvent when he executed the settlement – i.e. that he was able to pay all his debts without the aid of the settled property.

These exceptions do not mean that a wife may claim the stock in trade of her husband's business on the ground that he had given it to her five years before his bankruptcy, and that he was solvent at that time. The trustee may normally always claim the stock in trade of the business of a bankrupt. On the other hand, if husband and wife are living together, she is not barred from claiming that the household effects are her property. Such effects are not the property of the bankrupt in his possession in the way of his trade or business.

In every bankruptcy a date is fixed for the examination of the affairs of the bankrupt in open Court. This is called the 'public examination'. At this examination the bankrupt must answer upon oath any questions asked of him either by the Official Receiver, the trustee, or any creditor. If he refuses to do so, it is a contempt of Court punishable by imprisonment. The examination is designed to throw light upon the causes of the bankruptcy and the affairs of the bankrupt. Any conduct which suggests fraud will be closely scrutinized.

When a Trustee in Bankruptcy administers an estate there are certain debts due from the bankrupt which have to be met in priority to the general claims of the creditors. They are said to be 'preferential debts'. They include certain wages and salaries due to employees, and also certain rates and taxes and National Insurance contributions due to the Crown. Although a landlord is not a preferential creditor for rent, he is in a favourable position if he has levied a distress, for in order to save the debtor's assets from sale under the levy, the trustee may agree to treat the landlord's claim for rent up to a maximum period of six months as being preferential.

When the trustee has paid the preferential debts, and has realized sufficient assets to enable him to make a distribution to creditors, he will give notice of his intention to pay a dividend. Irrespective of the payment of a dividend, however, and at any time after the conclusion of the public examination, the bankrupt is entitled to apply to the Court for his discharge from the bankruptcy. Every creditor receives notice of this application, and is entitled to oppose it. Opposition is not usually necessary, for before deciding whether to grant or refuse such an application the Court will always examine the circumstances of the bankruptcy, which are detailed in a report prepared by the Official Receiver. Facts in this report may be disputed by the bankrupt, and if the Court is satisfied that the bankruptcy was the result of misfortune, it has power, in certain cases, to order the immediate discharge of the bankrupt. On the other hand, if the Court considers the bankruptcy to have been brought about by fraud, or by rash and hazardous trading, or extravagance, the discharge may be 'suspended', or even refused. In some instances the Court has no power to grant a discharge without a period of suspension. These include bankruptcies in which: (1) the assets are insufficient to provide a dividend of 10s. in the £ to the creditors (except in the case of misfortune); (2) proper books of account have not been kept; (3) the bankrupt has traded after knowledge of his insolvency; (4) the bankrupt has contracted debts without reasonable probability of being able to pay them; (5) the bankrupt has failed to give a satisfactory account of the deficiency in his assets; (6) the bankrupt has contributed to his bankruptcy by rash and hazardous speculation, gambling, or extravagance; (7) the bankrupt has been guilty of a fraudulent preference; (8) the bankrupt has been adjudicated bankrupt on a previous occasion; (9) the bankrupt has been guilty of fraud.

If the Court decides to grant the discharge, subject to a suspension or otherwise, it may also require the bankrupt, as a condition of the discharge, to submit to a judgement for a specified sum, and it may either order that this sum shall be paid forthwith, or direct payment by instalments, out of future earnings of the debtor.

As soon as the discharge becomes effective, the bankrupt is again a free man. He may then carry on any trade or business without restriction. There are, however, some obligations which he must still meet. They include any claim arising out of a judgement for fraud, or for damages for seduction, and also the claims of a former wife for maintenance. No husband can rid himself of his liability to support his wife. The Crown also has powers to claim arrears of Income Tax, but in practice it does not do so.

There are occasions when a trader realizes that his financial position is desperate and he is anxious to rid himself of his burdens as easily and as quickly as possible. There are alternative courses which he may pursue in such a case. First, an insolvent trader is always at liberty to present or file his own petition in bankruptcy, instead of waiting for a creditor to make the initial move. As an alternative, he may execute a 'deed of assignment' of his property to a trustee, one of the acts of bankruptcy referred to earlier in the chapter, and a third alternative is to effect a composition with his creditors. If he wishes to adopt this method, he may inform them that he has debts which amount to £1,000 but assets of a value of only £500, and he may then offer each creditor a composition of 10s. in the £. Normally, if you offer a creditor £50 cash in settlement of a debt for £100 he may take your money and still lawfully claim payment of the balance. Unless the acceptance of a lesser sum for a larger amount is accompanied by the legal consideration which is essential to every contract, it is not an enforceable agreement. On the other hand, if a debt is genuinely disputed and you contend that you owe the creditor £25, when he claims that you owe him £100, you are entitled to agree to settle the claim for £50. In such a case the mutual agreement to compromise the dispute, as an alternative to litigation, affords a valid legal consideration. After such an agreement has been concluded, the creditor is not entitled to pursue his claim to the balance. When you offer your creditors a composition you do not dispute the debts which you owe, but a valid and enforceable agreement may always be made in such a case. The mutual agreement by the creditors not to sue, but to accept the composition, is a valid legal consideration, and the debtor would therefore be able to resist any subsequent claim made against him by any creditor to enforce payment of the balance of the debt.

Any composition by a debtor with his creditors must always be recorded in a deed registered in the same way as a deed of assignment, and if it is not so registered, it is void. Any creditor who refuses to agree to the composition is at liberty to start bankruptcy proceedings, but unless the proceedings are commenced within three months after the date of the deed, it becomes valid and binding on all the creditors. Every creditor is thereafter, by operation of the law, deemed to have accepted the composition and is bound by its terms.

An insolvent debtor has yet a fourth method by which he may rid himself of his liabilities. If his friend, Flush, wishes to assist him financially, Flush may make a cash offer to each of the creditors in turn to buy up his debt for less than its full amount. Arrangements of this character may be informal, for there is nothing in law to prevent one creditor from making an agreement with a third party to sell his debt of £100 for £25, while another creditor, either more hard-hearted or more shrewd, who is owed a similar amount, may require payment of £75. Unless the debtor makes a false representation and contends, for example, that every creditor has agreed to settle on the same *pro rata* basis, the creditor who sells his debt for 5s. in the £ has no remedy, if he subsequently ascertains that another creditor has received better terms.

Any one of these alternatives may be preferred to bankruptcy both by creditor and by debtor. Any one of them may result in a more speedy settlement of claims than the tortuous procedure of bankruptcy. On the other hand, a creditor will be wise to scrutinize any such proposals with vigilance. He should not accept the first offer made to him, unless he is satisfied, either that the debtor has been the victim of genuine misfortune or that he is a man of undoubted integrity who would not be guilty of sharp practice. An unscrupulous debtor who avails himself of any of these methods successfully will not only avoid exposure in the Bankruptcy Court, and rid himself cheaply of his creditors, but will also be able to retain funds for fresh business trickery. It may not always be desirable to adopt caution in a world which is in need of courage and initiative. In travelling along the high road of life, however, we all meet rogues and scoundrels. Accordingly, when we deal with strangers, 'Forever amber' might well be our watchword.

22

PATENTS, DESIGNS, TRADE-MARKS, AND COPYRIGHT

'A fortune is being made by a man of 99, who after 16 years of self-imposed poverty, living on £2 a week, invented and patented a method of turning old bibles into gun-cotton, artificial silk cellulose, and expensive note-paper. His machinery has already been installed at a Cardiff factory, and at eight others in various parts of the country, where armaments are being made from ancient testaments.'

Daily Express – quoted in 'This England'

THIS chapter deals with special rights, first, in what may be termed industrial property, and, secondly, in artistic property, which is capable of a proprietary right – i.e. right of owner-ship, legally called 'copyright'.

Industrial property may be classified under three headings: Patents, Designs, and Trade-marks. Patents are governed by the provisions of the Patents Act 1949, Designs by the Regis-tered Designs Act 1949, Registered Trade-marks by the Trade Mark Acts 1938, and unregistered trade-marks by the Com-mon Law.

A patent gives the owner a monopoly right to use, exercise, and vend a novel invention for which Letters Patent have been granted. The words 'patent applied for' are frequently seen on manufactured articles or in advertisements. The phrase means that the manufacturer, or the advertiser, claims that there is some novelty in the article in question, or the process by which it is produced, and that application has been made to the Patent Office in Chancery Lane, London, for a grant of Letters Patent in respect of the invention. It does not, however, mean that the patent will necessarily be granted.

A patent may be granted to the true and first inventor of an invention which possesses utility and novelty or to his assignee. Although the degree of utility need not be great, a substantial degree of novelty is essential, and a patent will not be granted unless the Comptroller-General of Patents is satisfied that the invention is novel, in the sense that it has never previously been published or publicly used in this country, either by the inventor himself or by anyone else. When two inventors make the same invention independently, and at about the same time, the first to file his patent application at the Patent Office obtains precedence, and the other gets no patent rights at all in the invention.

Invention must be something of a tangible or concrete character which has not previously been projected. You cannot patent an abstract idea or some fanciful notion designed for the improvement of the human race. If you had been 'eight years upon a project for extracting sunbeams out of cucumbers, which were to be put into vials hermetically sealed, and let out to warm the air in raw inclement summers' you would not be able to patent the idea. An application for a patent could be entertained only after you had worked out the details of the process by which the sunbeams were to be extracted. If, however, you had prepared plans for the type of machine, or the process by which you hoped to obtain your results, you could apply for a patent. Your results, whatever form they might take, would have to be phrased in a document called a 'specification' which may be either 'provisional' or 'complete', usually accompanied in the case of a complete specification by one or more drawings or blue-prints. Inventors usually avail themselves of the services of a patent agent if they propose to apply for a patent. It is not simple for an amateur to deal with the technical requirements of a specification, and a patent agent is a skilled expert, trained for the job.

When an application for a patent is filed, it does not give the applicant any immediate monopoly. Anyone may, in the meantime, copy the invention without risk of legal proceedings, but if the patent is subsequently granted the patentee may apply to the Court for an injunction to restrain its infringement.

If a provisional specification is filed with the application the applicant has a period of twelve months during which he may work the invention publicly before filing a further or complete specification embodying the results of his experiments. This complete specification must include a full description of at least one practical way of carrying out the invention.

One of the duties of the Patent Comptroller, when a complete specification is lodged, is to investigate the files of earlier specifications, and other relevant publications, in order to ascertain whether the invention can satisfy the test of novelty, and he may require amendment of the complete specification so as to give protection only to such part of the invention as is novel. He may also refuse a patent in any case in which there has been prior publication of the whole invention. Before the patent is granted, the specification is laid open to public inspection for two months, to enable any aggrieved person who has proper grounds for the belief that the patent ought not to be granted to oppose the grant. Any such opposition is adjudicated upon by the Comptroller, after considering all the evidence. Before the Act of 1949, the Comptroller had no power to consider the question whether or not an invention had inventive merit, but now he may refuse to grant a patent if an opponent satisfies him that the invention is clearly obvious.

When two or more people have jointly evolved the invention, the names of all the inventors must be mentioned in the application for the patent. This frequently occurs when a company finances the development of an invention. A workman who carries out the instructions of the inventor in working out practical details of the invention is not a joint inventor, unless he has personally added to or shared in the actual process of invention, as distinct from following the instructions given to him. The inventor himself may not be the owner if the invention is made in the course of and as part of his employment with the company.

When a patent is granted, the owner has a monopoly or sole right of exploitation for sixteen years, provided that he pays the annual renewal fees necessary to keep his patent alive. Apart from limited extensions of time allowed under special war legislation, when a patentee was unable, owing to the war, to exploit his patent, this period may be extended by the Court, in cases where the patentee has been inadequately remunerated for the patent, for five years, and in exceptional cases for ten years. When application is made for an extension, the Court must in coming to a decision consider all the relevant circumstances, including not only the profits made by the patentee, but also the public interest in the invention it-self.

The owner of a patent need not necessarily manufacture it himself. He may sell the right, or lease, or license it, on such terms, within limits, as he chooses to dictate. He is not, how-ever, allowed to include in a licence any condition which pur-ports to prohibit or restrict the use of articles supplied by a third party or to compel the licensee to use other articles not protected by the patent. The Acts declare any such conditions to be null and void, since they are in restraint of trade and con-trary to public policy.

Moreover, if a patentee abuses his monopoly rights by fail-ing to exploit his patent and refusing to grant licences to others to do so, as a result of which the interests of the com-munity are prejudiced, the Comptroller of Patents has power – although it is rarely exercised – to compel him to grant licences for its exploitation, or, in extreme circumstances, even to re-voke the patent upon the application, made more than three years after the date of sealing the patent, by any person inter-ested or by any Government Department. It is a common be-lief that abuse of monopoly rights is widespread, especially among powerful companies. The fact that these provisions of the Patent Act are extremely rarely invoked may be regarded as evidence that the belief is not well founded.

When a patentee brings an action to restrain infringement of his rights, he will usually ask for an injunction and for dam-ages. The defendant may resist the claim on the grounds that he has not in fact infringed the patent, or that the patent is in-valid, or both. If he alleges invalidity he may also counter-claim for revocation. The validity of a patent may be attacked on the grounds that the invention is not novel, or is obvious, or lacks utility, or that the specification is inadequate. These and other technical defences are all of a complex character.

If, however, you are the owner of a patent, and you think that it is being infringed, you must act warily before you for-mulate your complaint. There is a unique form of action, ap-plicable only to patents, called a 'threats action'.

In the normal way, if you write a letter to complain of an infringement of your legal rights – e.g. a nuisance by noise or a trespass to your land – and you hint at possible legal proceedings, your opponent does not retaliate by issuing a writ against you. In the case of a patent, however, any letter, or other threat, by a patentee, complaining that his patent is being infringed, may be immediately countered by the issue of a writ by the alleged infringer, asking for an injunction to restrain a repetition of the threat, and for damages. The onus is then placed on the patentee to establish the validity of his complaints.

A patentee is in a highly privileged position during the life of his patent. When, however, it has expired, his invention is open to exploitation by all, and it must be remembered that the specification of every granted patent is available for inspection. If an inventor shuns disclosure of his invention, he should not apply for a patent. He can then only rely upon a secret process. In that event, however, the inventor will not have any legal protection for his process if the secret is solved by another manufacturer.

A registered design gives the owner a monopoly right (analogous to that possessed by the owner of a patent) in respect of an industrial design, the novelty of which resides wholly in shape or in appearance. No proprietary rights exist in any industrial design unless it has been registered under the provisions of the Registered Designs Act 1949 or the earlier Patents and Designs Acts, and an artistic production protected by the Copyright Act 1956 (to be considered later) may be registered, if eligible, under the Acts mentioned, in which case the Copyright Act 1956 will no longer spread its wings over it for most purposes. Broadly speaking, in order to be capable of registration, a design must be one which is capable of being or intended to be produced in quantity for industrial purposes. Although the law as to registered design is closely akin to the Patent Law, and it is advisable to invoke the services of a patent agent if you wish to register a design, an essential difference between a registrable design and a patentable invention is that the test of novelty in a design (and likewise also the test of infringement in a registered design) lies wholly in the appeal of the article to the eye, as contrasted with its practical utility. Novel patterns on wallpaper, curtains, upholstery, and dress materials, and also many varieties of mass-produced simple articles of attractive and novel shape or appearance are frequently registered as designs.

Trade-marks are marks by which merchants and manufacturers brand their goods for the purpose of distinction. The sole right to use a particular mark may be acquired, without registration, by long exclusive use of the mark, but it is safer to register a trade-mark in order to establish the right satisfactorily. You may defend any commercial advantage you gain from the exclusive right to use a mark, whether registered or not, by bringing an action against any person who brands his goods with the same or similar mark in such a way as to make it likely that his goods will be 'passed off' as yours. You will probably be granted an injunction, and may also be awarded substantial damages, if your commercial reputation has suffered.

Traders may also acquire rights, similar to those in unregistered trade-marks, in the names or trading titles of their businesses where these have become distinctive in their particular fields, but it is important to note that a man who trades honestly under his own name is immune from attack by another trader of the same name, however extensive the reputation of the latter may be. However, if a Mr Woolworth were to set up a shop with a distinctive 'Woolworth' frontage, and to sell similar articles, the Courts would not find it difficult to conclude that he intended to mislead the public, and would restrain him by injunction if Messrs Woolworths brought a 'passing-off' action against him.

By the terms of the Trade Marks Act 1938, a trade-mark is capable of registration only if it contains one of a number of alternative essential features. These include: (1) the name of a company, individual, or firm represented in a special or particular manner; (2) the signature of the applicant or a predecessor in his business; (3) an invented word or words; (4) a word or words not having direct reference to the quality of the goods, and not, according to its ordinary signification, a geographical name or a surname; (5) any other distinctive mark, subject to certain limitations. These are general indications only of the character which a trade-mark must assume. There are a number of qualifications and restrictions on registration, and anyone contemplating registration should seek advice from a patent agent. Application to register a trade-mark may be made in one or more of thirty-four classes, ranging from 'chemical products', which fall within Class 1, to 'tobacco, raw or manufactured', which comes within Class 34. The application must be made on special forms, and must be lodged with four representations of the mark, prepared in exact compliance with the rules, and a filing fee of £1. After the application has been made a certificate of registration does not follow as a matter of course. The Comptroller of Patents (in his capacity as Registrar of Trade-marks) must be satisfied that the proposed mark does not resemble any existing mark to such an extent as to be likely to cause confusion, and not only must search be made, but the proposed mark must be published in the official *Trade Mark Journal*, to enable opposition to be lodged by an objector who considers that the mark may injure his existing legal rights. When such an objection is lodged, the Comptroller has power to adjudicate upon the dispute, in accordance with prescribed procedure.

The right given by registration is expressed in the Act to be the exclusive right to use the mark registered, but this is subject to the limitation that the registration must be valid and to the further limitation that nothing in the Act shall be deemed to affect rights of action against any person for passing off goods as the goods of another person or the remedies in respect thereof. Hence an infringer of a registered mark, if he is sued, may contend that the mark should never have been registered and seek to have it expunged, and a person who has, by long use, acquired the exclusive right to use a mark may restrain the use of that mark by another person, even if the latter has subsequently succeeded in registering it.

Commercial use of a trade-mark prior to an application for registration (unlike corresponding prior use of a patentable invention or a registrable design) is not in any way a bar to registration, provided that the prior use has been confined exclusively to the applicant for registration. Indeed, if a trader has exclusively used a trade-mark for many years and has established a 'goodwill' in the mark, so that it is widely recognized in his particular trade as indicating goods obtainable from him alone, he can obtain registration of the mark because it has become distinctive of his goods, even although the mark would not otherwise have been capable of registration.

While a patentee is an inventor of a machine or process or of an article of industrial usefulness, an author is a man who 'invents' artistic property, and subject to certain limitations, the author of any literary, dramatic, musical, or artistic work has an ownership in his work, termed *copyright*, which gives him the sole right of publication, performance, and production. Copyright, governed now by the Copyright Act 1956, endures, as a general rule, for the life of the author and for fifty whole calendar years after his death. In the case of photographs, cinema films, and sound recordings the period is for the fifty whole calendar years *following publication*. There are other special cases. Although there is no copyright in a mere idea, copyright does extend protection to almost everything which is committed to permanent form, provided it has involved skill and labour and is in some sense original. For example, the compilation of a time-table is the subject-matter of copyright, since it is not only original, but also involves skill and labour. On the other hand, the House of Lords has held that the selection of commonplace memoranda in the forefront of an ordinary pocket diary is not a copyright work. This decision would seem not to apply to a special diary, compiled for a particular purpose, which had involved the preparation and selection of particular data. Copyright extends to paintings, drawings, charts, plans, photographs, sculpture, architecture, in fact to every work of artistic craftsmanship or performance, but, as stated, there is no copyright in an idea.

There is, normally, no copyright in the title of a book or other work. On the other hand, if a work has obtained, or established, a goodwill under a particular title, application may be made to the Court to restrain a plagiarist, if he is seeking to exploit its goodwill by the use of a similar title, or a title so nearly resembling it as to cause confusion in the minds of the public. An action in such a case is not based upon copyright, but upon 'passing off', and the essence of a passing-off action is the appropriation of another man's goodwill involving him in financial loss. For example, if John Doe publishes a monthly journal called *Gloom and Misery*, he might be able to restrain publication of another journal called *Gloomy Misery* if he could satisfy the Court that his journal had established a goodwill under the title of *Gloom and Misery*, and that *Gloomy Misery* was first published after he had established his goodwill, and provided also that the Court was satisfied, by evidence, that the similarity was likely to cause confusion in the minds of the public, and would involve John Doe in financial loss.

The author of every original literary work is entitled to copyright in the work, and it is not necessary to secure the right by registration.

Although the author of a work is normally the first owner of the copyright, this is not the case if he produces the work under a contract of service, and as part of and in the course of his duty to his employer. In that event, the employer is entitled to copyright in the work, in so far as its publication is material to his business. The position may be otherwise regulated by the term of the service agreement. A *contract of service* — i.e. an agreement between an employer and an employee — must be distinguished from a *contract for services* — i.e. an agreement by which one person undertakes to carry out certain specified services in the capacity of an independent contractor. For example, if you write a book at the request of a publisher, you will not be his employee, but your work will be carried out under a contract for services. The ownership of the copyright should be a matter dealt with in the contract. The same problem may arise in regard to photographs. If a photographer gives a 'complimentary' sitting, he usually retains the copyright in his work, and may publish it as he thinks fit. If, on the other hand, payment is made by the sitter, the latter retains the copyright, and the photographer is not then entitled to reproduce the photograph. As regards letters, the copyright remains in the writer, and the recipient of a letter is not entitled to publish it.

As a general rule, copyright is infringed by any person who produces or reproduces a substantial part of the copyright work, or any colourable imitation of it, in any material form without authority from the owner. It is, in each case, a question of fact as to whether the infringing material is a substantial part of the work. For example, four lines extracted from a long poem might in some circumstances be regarded as sufficiently substantial to constitute a legal infringement. It is not, however, an infringement of copyright to make use of extracts from a copyright work for the purpose of review, or fair criticism, or for the purpose of a newspaper summary, or as part of a course of education, provided there is a sufficient acknowledgement.

If copyright has been infringed, the owner has a number of remedies. Foremost among them is his right to apply for an injunction to restrain further infringement, an account of all infringing copies sold, and damages for the infringement. Moreover, copyright being a species of property, both the original and the infringing work are deemed to be the property of the owner of the copyright, and he is therefore entitled to ask for delivery up of all copies of the infringing work and damages for the conversion. This does not mean that a single article in an encyclopedia which infringed copyright would entitle the owner to delivery up of the entire encyclopedia. He would, however, be entitled to ask the Court to order the offending article to be excised, and for delivery up of such excised part.

In the assessment of damages for the infringement, the Court will consider the financial loss and the loss of reputation, if any, which the plaintiff has suffered. Damages for conversion are assessed upon the same basis as in any other case in which property is wrongfully converted. This means that the plaintiff is entitled to recover, as damages for the conversion, such sums as the infringer has himself received in respect of the infringing matter. Sometimes it is very difficult to assess the amount of this damage. The Court will make the calculation as best it can, after it has taken all relevant factors into consideration. This remedy may sometimes result in a penalty on the infringer which is out of proportion to the damage which the owner has suffered, and if the infringer did not know that he was infringing the author's copyright it may cause considerable hardship. An innocent infringer is relieved from any liability for damages but he may still have to account to the plaintiff for any profits he receives. The Courts have held, however, that 'innocent' does not mean ignorant of the identity of the true owner of the copyright. It means that the infringer did not know, and could not have been expected to know, that the work was the subject of copyright. For example, if a writer submits a story to a publisher as his original work, and the publisher publishes it in good faith, the publisher is not entitled to plead 'innocent infringement' if it transpires that the writer had filched another man's work. The work, having been submitted to him as an original work, would automatically be the subject of copyright. The publisher's 'innocent' error consists in thinking that the copyright was vested in the contributor, and his ignorance as to the identity of the original author will not save him from having to pay damages. The Court is empowered to award exemplary damages in scandalous cases.

An action for infringement must be brought within six years after the date of the publication complained of, and this means six years from the date when the infringing work was last performed or sold, since every separate performance or sale is an infringement of copyright.

When an author writes a book and is able to find a publisher willing to publish it, he does not usually sell or assign the copyright in the work, although he is entitled to do so. It is the usual practice for an author to license it for publication on agreed terms, and whilst most publishers will offer fair terms, there are a few who will seek to exploit the author. In these circumstances, it is desirable for an inexperienced author to obtain expert advice from a reputable literary agent before he signs a contract for publication, or he may join the Incorporated Society of Authors, which was formed expressly to protect the rights of authors.

If an author writes a book, no one is entitled to write a play or produce a film based on the book without his consent. Although publication is in a different medium, the author is nevertheless entitled to restrain the production. Dramatic rights and film rights in a literary work have great potential value, and an author who signs a contract for publication of his work should see that these rights are taken into consideration and that he does not part with them for a 'song'. 'Serial rights' may be another equally valuable source of income.

Copyright is infringed not only by copying, but also by performance of a work in public. This is called infringement of the performing right in the work, and it frequently occurs when plays are produced by amateur dramatic societies in village halls. No copyright play or other copyright work may be performed in public without a licence from the author; record playing for rather limited recreational or charitable purposes is one exception to this rule, for example in a hostel or institution, and the making public of wireless and television programmes in slightly different circumstances, another. 'In public' has been held to extend to a performance given by a Society to its own members, even if no charge is made for admission to see the performance. The decisive test is whether or not the audience is really of a domestic character, and performances in the home, and among the family, or those given by schools from which members of the public are excluded, are usually the only ones exempt from the obligation of obtaining a licence.

At one time it proved extremely difficult to ascertain when a particular work, and more especially a musical work, had been performed in public. A composer would not know every time one of his songs had been sung at a concert. Accordingly, a number of authors, composers, and publishers formed a Society called the Performing Right Society, and they now vest the control of all their performing rights in this Society, who make it part of their business to track down infringements. Most authors, composers, and publishers of repute are members of the P.R.S., as the Performing Right Society is called, and it controls performing rights by granting licences, which permit the performance in public of the compositions of any of its members or of its affiliated Societies on payment of an annual fee. These fees are then divided among the members of the Society and the affiliated Societies. Broadcasting and television rights are included in performing rights. The P.R.S. maintain a staff of inspectors who visit theatres, music-halls, concert-halls, hotels, restaurants, public-houses, village halls, institutes, hostels, canteens, and other places in which musical performances are given, either by individuals or by mechanical reproduction such as gramophone records. The Society will require application to be made for a licence in all these cases, and if the occupier proves recalcitrant and unresponsive, proceedings may be brought against him to restrain infringement of copyright. Since the public performing rights in most musical works are controlled by the Society, infringements are almost inevitable in such circumstances, unless the performances are confined to music published before about 100 years ago, in which case the copyright may have expired. The Performing Rights Tribunal, a statutory body, has jurisdiction to settle disputes which may arise over the granting or withholding of licences.

The P.R.S. has reciprocal agreements of affiliation with all the Performing Right Societies which operate in the British Dominions and foreign countries where copyright is the subject of protection by law. Under these agreements, the English P.R.S. controls in its territory the performing rights in the works comprised in the repertoires of all such Dominion and foreign Societies, and *vice versa*.

From time to time attempts have been made to argue in the Courts that it is wrong for artists and performers through their promoters to be compelled to pay licence fees when they perform copyright work. It is said that the author or composer ought to be grateful for the benefit conferred on him by the publicity which he receives. These arguments have always failed. Publicity does not buy provisions, and there is no valid reason why an artist should refuse to pay for the privilege of making money out of the labour which an author or composer has to expend before his work is brought to fruition and is ready for public performance.

The Copyright Act 1956 has brought English Copyright law into a position, where adherence to the International Copyright Convention has at last been made possible. The copyright laws of this country may now by order of Council extend protection to rights arising under foreign laws, where protection of rights arising under English Copyright law is reciprocally granted in the foreign countries concerned. Another advantage of the new Copyright Act is that the old Copyright law inevitably ignored the commercial future of the gramophone record, the cinema film, wireless, and television with all the effects of these new media of publication on the artist's claim to be reimbursed and the public's claim to be entertained.

23

CHILDREN

She was not really bad at heart,
But only rather rude and wild,
She was an aggravating child.'
Hilaire Belloc

THE birth of every child must be registered with the local Registrar of Births within forty-two days of the birth. The registration should be effected by the father or the mother. Birth certificates contain the names of the child's father and mother, but since January 1948 it has been possible to obtain on payment now of ninepence a shorter form of certificate which omits any reference to parentage. This form is accepted for most purposes, for example, by school authorities and employers, so that an illegitimate or adopted child is spared the embarrassment of discovering or disclosing that his supposed parents are not in fact his real father and mother.

Infants enjoy certain legal privileges, and are also subject to a number of legal disabilities. A child under eight years of age cannot be charged with any criminal offence. If it is over eight and under fourteen, it can be convicted of an offence only if it is proved to be capable of understanding and appreciating the effect of its actions. A child between the ages of eight and seventeen is legally described as a 'young person', and is not subject to the normal legal penalties for a criminal offence. Moreover, when a child under the age of seventeen is charged with a crime, other than homicide – i.e. murder or manslaughter – it will be brought before a special Court, set up under the Children and Young Persons Act 1933, and known as a Juvenile Court. The atmosphere of a Juvenile Court is intended to be different from that of a Magistrate's Court. Although a child ought to learn to appreciate the gravity of breaking the rules of the community – i.e. of committing an offence against the law – it ought to be neither terrified nor encouraged to despise its social obligations.

If the Court considers that the home conditions of the child are unsatisfactory, and the child is in need of care or protection, it may make an order which deprives the parents of custody. The child will then be placed under the care and protection of selected foster-parents, or officers, called probation officers, who may be directed to supervise its welfare.

For the more serious offences and for the constant offender there are Approved Schools and Borstal Institutions. It has, however, been recognized that although these institutions are suitable where long periods of detention and corrective training are necessary, they cannot cater adequately for the first offender or the person who needs a sharp lesson rather than a long course of training. The Criminal Justice Act 1948 attempted to fill the gap between probation and the Approved School by a series of centres and schools, ranging from attendance centres where the offender, while living at home, would be required to report or to spend some time each day, to remand homes and detention centres for short periods of detention. Society cannot afford to allow its young offenders to grow into hardened criminals.

Juvenile Courts are always conducted 'in camera' – i.e. in private – and the name of any child brought before the Court must not be disclosed. In this way children are protected from the publicity which usually attends crime. It may be hard even for an innocent person to resume his occupation after the spotlight of the Press has scorched him. It is infinitely more difficult for a convicted person to make a fresh start in life.

Since the beginning of the century the law has become extremely solicitous for the welfare of children, and the passing of the Children Act 1908 paved the way for later reforms. The law not only safeguards children from physical cruelty, by imposing severe penalties for ill-treatment, but also displays great regard for their mental and moral welfare. Children are not permitted to beg, bet, gamble, or smoke. The law will not allow them to be unduly chastised, for the country has long since decided that 'perpetual flogging is not the best method of imparting knowledge and maintaining discipline'. Reasonable physical punishment may, however, be administered by a parent, guardian, or a schoolmaster to whose care the child is temporarily committed, and in considering whether or not physical punishment has been reasonable, regard must be given to the severity of the offence, and the age and mental capacity of the child. If excessive physical punishment is administered, the child has the same remedy for assault as an adult.

The negative protection given by the earlier Children Acts has since the Second World War been superseded by a more positive approach to the whole problem of child care. The Curtis Committee, which was set up by the Home Office to consider the particular problem of the child who is deprived of a normal home life by the loss of parents or from any other cause, reported in 1946 that there were 124,000 children in this country who did not have a normal home life. Many of them were living in institutions run on lines which would have been antiquated at the beginning of the century. The Committee's major recommendations for dealing with this situation received parliamentary approval mainly in the Children Act 1948. All homes in which children are boarded voluntarily must now be registered and inspected regularly by specially trained visitors. Local authorities have been given the responsibility of looking after all the children in their area who are homeless or whose parents or guardians are unable or unfit to maintain them properly, and they must not be slow in acting when a case of child neglect is brought to their attention.

It is not easy to deal adequately with 'hard-boiled young devils', and regulations are lacking to fix sufficient responsibility for juvenile delinquency on parents, who are normally the guardians of the children. Lack of parental control, and the indifference of parents, are so frequently the origin of the trouble that the community might benefit if parents were compelled to accept greater responsibility for the criminal activities of their children.

By common law, but now of little relevance, the father is the legal guardian of a child under the age of twenty-one, and technically has the right of custody. The father has no legal rights over an illegitimate child, although he may be under an obligation to make payments to the mother for its support, and this liability may be enforced even when the mother is a woman living apart from her husband. Since the Legitimacy Act 1926, an illegitimate child is legitimized by the subsequent marriage of its parents, if the father is domiciled in England or Wales, and if, at the date of the birth of the child, both parents were free to marry.

The mother of an illegitimate child will usually require financial support from the father. Within time limits she may apply for an affiliation or bastardy order, and on proof of paternity she may obtain an order against the father for a sum not exceeding 30*s.* a week, payable until the child is sixteen years of age. Provided the child is engaged in a course of education or training, such an order may be extended for not more than two years at a time until the child reaches the age of twenty-one years. If the mother does not know the whereabouts of the father, or if she is unable to satisfy the Court, by her evidence, that he is, in fact, the father, she will not be able to obtain any legal redress, and will have to support the child out of her own resources. The National Assistance Board may also bring proceedings for the purpose of being reimbursed by the father of an illegitimate child.

If the mother wishes to be rid of the responsibility for the child's upkeep, she may find someone who is willing to adopt it, either directly or through the offices of an adoption society. If Mr and Mrs John Doe are anxious to adopt a child, and think Fidget a 'little dear', they are not permitted to adopt him until a number of legal formalities have been completed. They are all designed to prevent Fidget from falling into the hands of unsuitable adoptors, and the Adoption of Children Act 1950 gives still greater protection to the Fidgets of this world and extends their rights. An application for adoption may be made in a Court of Summary Jurisdiction, in a County Court, or in the High Court. It was formerly common to reproach an illegitimate child for permitting itself to be born. An illegitimate child is now no longer kept under the counterpane. The law is as solicitous for its welfare as it is for a baby born in honest wedlock, and a Court will never make an order for adoption until stringent inquiries have been made by one of its own officers into the antecedents and living conditions of the proposed adoptors. The order may, in particular, be refused if the proposal is based upon a financial bargain, by which the adoptors are to be paid for accepting the burden of the child.

To protect the interests of the child to be adopted, the child's mother will normally have to sign a consent to the adoption, and agree to renounce absolutely and unconditionally any control or rights over the child. The consent is not extracted as a punishment, but because it might be disastrous to Fidget's interests if his parent sought to reclaim him after many years. He may then have come to regard John and Jane Doe as his parents, and their home as his home, for if the order is made, the child loses his original identity, and becomes Fidget Doe for all practical purposes, even for the purpose of inheritance on the death of his adoptors. If John or Jane Doe dies intestate, Fidget would be entitled to a share in their estate as one of the next-of-kin.

The question of a child's custody is bound to arise if the parents quarrel and separate. Although, generally speaking, the father has the technical right of custody, it does not always work out this way in practice. As a general rule a mother commits no offence if she retains possession of the child contrary to the father's wishes, and if, as sometimes happens, one parent takes possession of the child from the other parent by a trick, there is no effective remedy except by an application to the Court. There is a general jurisdiction given to the Magistrates' Courts to deal with questions which concern the custody, welfare, and maintenance of children. However, if proceedings for divorce are pending between the parties, and the child is under sixteen, an application for custody may be made to the Divorce Court. The paramount consideration for the Court is the welfare of the child, and it will often allow the mother to retain the custody, even although she is the guilty party in divorce proceedings, more particularly when the child is very young. Each case is considered on its merits, but the Court is less likely to be induced to make an order in favour of a woman who is living with a co-respondent. If the mother has married the co-respondent, after the conclusion of divorce proceedings, an order for the custody of a young child may be made in her favour, particularly when the father is unable to provide suitable home conditions. The Divorce Court will not, as a general rule, make any order for custody of a child over sixteen years of age. It is often not realized that when an order is made in divorce proceedings for the custody of a child, the child cannot leave England without the consent of the Court. This consent is, however, normally given to allow the child to go abroad for short visits or holidays unless the parent who has not got the custody of the child raises valid objections. The parent with the custody will generally be required to give an undertaking that the child will be returned to this country.

The welfare of a 'pretty young Ward in Chancery' is a matter of concern to the Court, and a child may be made a Ward of Court if the High Court so orders. An application for such an order automatically gives a short period of temporary Wardship which is continued until the Court hears the case, which may be some time later. The Court will make the Order if it is satisfied that the existing situation with regard to the custody or general upbringing of the child is unsatisfactory, and that it is in the interest of the child (the solitary matter for consideration) that it should enjoy the general surveillance of the Court which is brought into operation by an order of Wardship. The Court may decide that neither parent shall have the actual 'care and control' of the child, and may make an order for care and control in favour of a suitable relative or other person. The Wardship will continue until the child becomes twenty-one, unless the Court sees fit to discharge the order, which it will do, for instance, if John and Joan Doe, having resolved their difficulties which caused a separation, become truly reconciled and are regarded thereby as fitted to discharge parental duties. Disobedience to any order made by the Court is a contempt of Court, which may be punished by imprisonment.

When a child reaches school age, he must attend school until he reaches the leaving age, which is at present fifteen.

After leaving school, a child is protected by legislation from entering any employment which would subject him to 'sweated labour'. Until he reaches the age of eighteen, a child may not normally be employed for an aggregate of over forty-eight hours in the week, exclusive of intervals for meals and rest. There are many regulations dealing with overtime, meal intervals, half-holidays, night work, Sunday work, and welfare, and an employer who infringes any of these regulations may be penalized. The sense of communal responsibility has travelled a long way since a child of five spent its days in the factory, and might be deported for life for stealing a pocket-handkerchief.

After a child has left school and has entered employment, there are many restrictions which continue to affect him as a minor, and, subject to certain exceptions, contracts made by an infant are not enforceable against him. When, however, an infant receives, by agreement, goods or services necessary to his station in life it would be inequitable to refuse proper reward to the man who has rendered them. The law will then impose an obligation to pay, because every man is entitled to be paid proper compensation for a genuine service. A child, for example, may enter into a valid and binding contract if it is for the purchase of necessaries, or, in certain cases, if it is for its benefit. Necessaries are goods suitable to the condition in life of the infant, and to his actual requirements at the time of the sale and delivery. If an infant enters into such a contract, he may be sued for the purchase price of the goods. The purchase price is not necessarily the price he has agreed to pay. Price limitations and controls in this instance were enacted by the Sale of Goods Act 1893. By the relevant section, an infant is only required to pay a reasonable price for necessaries, and if the trader seeks to recover an excessive price, he will not be able to enforce his claim. By the terms of the Infants Relief Act 1874, contracts made with an infant for the sale of goods, other than necessaries, or for the loan of money, are void and unenforceable. The vendor or money-lender has not rendered a service to the infant, as occurs when necessaries are supplied. Indeed, it may be that the trader, or the money-lender, has done the child an injury by indulging his extravagance. An infant is neither legally nor morally required to recognize any obligation in such a case, and the purchase price, or the money lent, cannot be recovered. Moreover, neither the mother nor the father of an infant is normally liable for any debt which the child may contract, even if it is for necessaries.

A certain class of service agreement, such as a contract of apprenticeship, may be enforceable and binding on an infant if it is for his benefit and he derives special advantage from it. The validity of such a contract is dependent upon the facts in each case, and the Court will investigate all the circumstances, declaring the contract unenforceable if it bears evidence of being for the advantage of the employer without corresponding benefit to the infant. Fidget may have musical talent, and an impresario, or concert manager, may think the child will develop into a brilliant pianist. Naturally, he will not wish to spend time and incur expense training Fidget, if he is not to have any return for his outlay. He may, therefore, ask the child to appoint him as his manager for a stated period of years. If the contract between them requires the manager to give the child proper training, and to find engagements for him, it may well be to the child's advantage. It will then be fair for the manager to receive remuneration out of the earnings, as compensation for his trouble. If, on the other hand, the object of the impresario is to exploit Fidget as an infant prodigy, or if the contract entitles the impresario to a percentage of the child's earnings, although there is no obligation to train him or obtain engagements for him, the contract may be unenforceable. It would not be to Fidget's advantage, for it would be an attempt by the manager to exploit the child's youth and ignorance, and the law will not permit this to be done.

There are some contracts made with an infant which are not necessarily good and not necessarily bad. They are called 'voidable contracts', and relate, generally speaking, to those which involve continuing rights and obligations. Voidable contracts were referred to in Chapter 3.

If a boy of nineteen enters into a contract to serve an employer in business for a period of five years, without any obligation on the part of the employer to train him in the business, similar to that contained in an agreement for apprenticeship, he may not ordinarily be sued for breach of the contract if he breaks it before he becomes twenty-one. If, however, he continues to give his services under the contract after he is twenty-one years of age, he may then be sued for any subsequent breach. The contract, made during infancy, is voidable on his attaining his majority, and he is then entitled to repudiate it. It is, however, a case of then or never! If he continues to treat it as a valid contract, it becomes binding upon him and he may not later reject it.

When a contract is unenforceable, it cannot be made legally effective, even though the infant promises, at the time of making of the contract, to fulfil his part of the bargain when he attains the age of twenty-one. A shopkeeper may not, therefore, take advantage of a child of eighteen by selling him a gold watch, on condition that he agrees to pay for it on his attaining his majority. The contract will be void, since it is a contract for the sale of goods, and the child may keep the watch without having to pay for it, unless the shopkeeper is able to satisfy the Court that a gold watch was suitable to the infant's condition in life and his actual requirements at the time of the sale and delivery. After the age of twenty-one, a child is, of course, free to make any bargain he chooses, but even then he will not be under any legal obligation if he promises to pay a debt resulting from a void contract made by him during infancy. He will not be liable, because the promise, unsupported by consideration, involves no legal obligation.

It follows from these restrictions that, although not inherently illegal, it is not easy for an infant to set up an effective business on his own account. Business involves contracts, and anyone under the age of twenty-one will find it difficult to find business men willing to trade with him, when his contracts may be unenforceable. Another disadvantage from which he would suffer would be his difficulty in operating a banking account. The relation between a banker and his customer, as we have seen in Chapter 9, is based upon contract. A banker does not like to open an account for a customer who is not responsible for his contracts. The banker will therefore usually refuse to keep an account for an infant.

Fidget may consider it a hardship not to be able to set up his own business, but there is no remedy for these legal disabilities. He probably will not appreciate that it is to his advantage that restraint should be imposed on his commercial operations. It is not easy to master the elements of any trade without experience, and operating a business successfully is not child's play. It usually requires knowledge of the particular trade, and of markets, together with experience of organization, office routine, and accounts. A child will not often be skilled in these subjects before he is twenty-one, and most greenhorns come to grief early in their business career. A man will be able to organize his business with better prospects if he is backed by knowledge and experience after repeated trials and errors. These are more certain keys to success than intuition.

Although a child has this freedom from liability in respect of contracts, he is not absolved from responsibility if he commits a tort. He may be sued for damages arising from any negligent act which he commits at any time after he is old enough to understand and appreciate the reasonable and probable result of his actions. This is a question of fact in each case, but as boys and girls under twenty-one are seldom wealthy enough to meet claims for compensation based on negligence, it may often not be profitable to sue them. If a youth, aged eighteen, is cycling and he negligently knocks down and injures a pedestrian, the pedestrian must hope that the cyclist is insured. Otherwise it is improbable that the child's financial resources will justify the expense of litigation. On the other hand, if John Doe, Jr, aged eighteen, induces a jeweller to sell him a gold watch by fraudulently representing to him that he is over twenty-one, there might be a criminal charge against him for obtaining goods by false pretences, but the jeweller could not sue for damages for the tort of fraud, as this would be an indirect method of trying to enforce the contract.

A further disability suffered by an infant is his inability to make a will, for no will made by an infant is valid, unless it is made when he is in one of the Armed Forces on active service, or a seaman at sea. Otherwise his fortune, if any, on his death, will revert to his next-of-kin – a subject dealt with in Chapter 26.

Finally, John Doe, Jr, may seek to enlist sympathy for his inability, until he attains his majority, on the day before his twenty-first birthday, to qualify as a Member of Parliament, to fill any public office, to have his name entered on the Register of Electors, or to enter any of the learned professions – not excepting the law!

24

BREACH OF PROMISE, MARRIAGE,
AND ALIMONY

' "Come, come," said Tom's father, "at your time of life,
There's no longer excuse for thus playing the rake.
It is time you should think, boy, of taking a wife –"
"Why, so it is, father – whose wife shall I take?" '

Thomas Moore

IT is unromantic to record that the breach of an agreement to
marry has the same legal consequences as every other broken
contract. An arrangement which should be emblazoned with
chivalry does not differ in its effects from a cold bargain between two hard-headed business men. Judges must administer
the law, but they do not, as a rule, like the flavour of an action
for breach of promise of marriage. It does not reflect twentieth-
century ideas of citizenship. When time brings a change to
sentiment, it seems harsh for a young man, or a young woman,
to be faced with the alternatives of a wrecked life or an action
for damages.

The essential legal features of an engagement to marry are
an unconditional offer and acceptance of the offer of marriage.
Consideration is implied by the mutual agreement to enter into
the married state. When the contract is broken, the injured
party may sue in respect of the breach, provided there is corro-
borative evidence of the engagement, and the damages will be
the financial expense incurred in contemplation of the marriage, together with a sum reasonably calculated to be the
value of the lost marriage. If the engagement has been a long
one, and the girl claims to have devoted what are described as
'the best years of her life' to the proper contemplation of
matrimony, the damages may be substantial. Similarly, if the
man is wealthy, and, as a result of the breach, the girl has lost
a good 'bargain', the damages are enhanced, and she may be
adequately rewarded by the Court. If the woman wishes the
world to know that her fiancé might have called her 'O Mis-
tress mine', she may also be awarded compensation for the loss
of her chastity. On the other hand, if an engagement, made one

night in an excited outburst of emotion, is broken with the dawn, when sanity returns, the aggrieved lady will not receive the same reward for her distress, for she will not really have suffered any loss. Nor will she receive much financial encouragement if her action is prompted by revenge. In other words, a girl may be awarded substantial damages if the man has behaved like a cad, but she will, as a rule, receive little financial solace when there have been no aggravating circumstances, and the man has behaved honestly, in refusing to contract a marriage which would be doomed to failure from the outset. When a man is rash enough to institute an action for breach of promise, he should not expect to receive much compensation. It is always open to him to seek elsewhere for 'the endearing elegance of female friendship', and his real loss will be loss of pride, unless he was making a money match, and that will never gain him sympathy in Court.

You may be married when you are sixteen years old, but if you marry under the age of twenty-one, you must first have the consent of your parents or guardian, or, if this is refused, the consent of the magistrates.

When you wish to be married, there are various ways in which you may make your 'Appointment with Fear'. If it is a religious ceremony, it will either follow the publication of banns or the issue of a licence. The clergyman who officiates at your church will make the necessary arrangements for banns, for a standard fee, but the total cost of the ceremony will depend on the contribution you decide to make to the officiating clergyman, and the expense you incur in supplementary celebrations.

If you wish to marry by licence, there are two types, called an 'ordinary licence' and a 'special licence'. An ordinary licence applies to a named place of celebration, and is valid for three months. It will be issued only after personal application by either party who has had his or her usual place of residence for fifteen days in the parish of that celebration. Your vicar will furnish you with the address of the nearest office at which your application may be made. The cost is about £2. A special licence is, normally, issued only in an emergency, when the ceremony has to be performed without delay. It costs £25 and can be obtained only through the Faculty Office of the Archbishop of Canterbury, after conclusive evidence of the emergency.

A Register Office marriage may be effected either by certificate or by licence. In the former case, either party may make personal application to the local registrar of marriages for each of the districts in which they have been respectively residing for at least seven days prior to the application. This involves two certificates, if the parties reside in different districts, and they will be issued after the expiration of twenty-one clear days, if no objection has been raised. Each certificate is valid for three calendar months from the date of the original application. The fee payable when the parties reside in different districts is 14s. 3d. It is 17s. 3d. when both reside in the same district.

If the marriage is to be by licence, only one notice is necessary, instead of the two notices required in the case of a certificate. A fifteen-day residential qualification is essential, and, either the parties must both live in the registration area, or one must reside in the registration area in which the notice is given and the other must reside in England or Wales. The licence may be issued at the expiration of one clear day, in the absence of any objection, and it is valid for three months from the date of application. The fee payable for the licence is £3 6s. 9d.

Before the passing of the Married Woman's Property Act 1882, the wife, after marriage, possessed few legal rights. Her property, in the absence of a marriage settlement, automatically became her husband's property, and she was deprived of most of her powers to enter into a contract. The marriage settlement, now little more than a faded memory, was usually regarded as an essential preliminary to middle- and upper-class marriages. From the husband's point of view, the capital monies settled on trustees, for the benefit of the wife, were intended to be a financial inducement which lightened the burden of supporting a wife. The wife, on her side, gained security from the settlement, as she was entitled to receive the income from the trust funds – but not to spend it in anticipation – for her own use and benefit. A dishonest or spendthrift husband was, moreover, prevented from obtaining control of

I

and wasting his wife's capital. Marriage settlements have, however, been out of fashion since successive Acts of Parliament have helped to create modern woman and her privileges, and even the restraint on anticipation was abolished in 1949.

Today every wife has substantially the same rights as her husband. She has, for many years, been able to own property, and also to carry on her own business, while the Law Reform (Married Women and Tortfeasors) Act 1935 entitles every woman to enjoy the privileges of bankruptcy – a reward for insolvency previously reserved solely for women who had carried on a trade or business of their own.

Wedding presents of a married couple, other than purely personal presents, are joint property after marriage. This means that neither of the parties may dispose of them without the consent of the other. In the event of separation or divorce, and unless the parties are able to reach an agreement on division, the only practical course is to agree to their sale, and an equal division of the proceeds of sale. They may not, however, be sold without consent of both parties, and the result is a deadlock if one of the parties refuses to agree.

Where questions arise of whether property belongs to the husband or wife, the Married Women's Property Act 1882 provides for a summary determination by the Court to decide what the true position is. It is not the Court's duty to decide how the husband and wife ought to have shared their wealth but to try to ascertain their actual intention in dealing with their property as between themselves, perhaps over a long period of time, although any settled intention is not easily held to have been varied. The Court may find that certain resources were expended with no other aim in mind than that of enriching generally the course of married life, in which case, the financial benefit, if any, is divided equally.

A wife is entitled to receive financial support from her husband, and if he fails to give her this support, she is entitled to pledge his credit, to enable her to purchase the necessaries of life. When compelled to resort to this method of acquiring her daily bread, she is known in law as an 'agent of necessity'. In this capacity she is entitled to purchase nothing beyond actual necessaries. She is not, however, entitled to contract as an agent of necessity if her husband is making her an allowance adequate to his means and their station in life. There is no exact definition of 'necessaries'. It depends on the husband's social and financial status, and other surrounding circumstances and may include even legal costs.

When a husband pays his wife a fixed sum each week for housekeeping, any money left over at the end of the week belongs to the husband. It cannot be retained by the wife for her own benefit, and if she saves some of it week by week, the Court may order her to repay all the savings to the husband if he sues her, because she has received the money as his agent, and it has never assumed any character other than money paid to an agent for the use of the principal. If, on the other hand, the husband makes the wife an allowance, and she undertakes to pay housekeeping bills out of the agreed allowance, the balance may belong to her. Whether the money is paid to the wife for her own personal use, or as an agent for the husband, is a question of fact in each case. In the former event the wife may retain the money; in the latter event she must return it on demand.

When husband and wife are living together, the wife will, generally speaking, be regarded as her husband's agent when she buys goods for the household. She is her husband's agent because it is customary for a married woman, living with her husband, to 'do the shopping', and it is therefore within the scope of her implied authority to purchase goods for her husband's account. The husband will, accordingly, normally be liable for the bills he receives for purchases of household goods, even although they do not fall within the description of 'necessaries'.

A husband sometimes inserts an advertisement in a newspaper to say that he will not be responsible for his wife's debts, and that she has no authority to pledge his credit. This does not affect his legal obligation to his wife. If he is making his wife a proper allowance, he is not responsible for her debts, but if he is not doing so he may be sued in the circumstances which have been specified.

When a husband fears that his wife is likely to pledge his credit when they are living separately, and she is in receipt of a proper allowance, it is prudent for him to notify every shop with whom he has opened an account that his wife no longer has authority to purchase goods for his account. Otherwise he may be liable to pay for goods purchased by his wife, unless he can satisfy the Court that the vendor knew, or ought to have known, that, for some proper reason, his wife's implied authority had been revoked.

Since the passing of the Law Reform (Married Women and Tortfeasors) Act 1935, a husband is no longer liable for his wife's torts or civil wrongs. If, accordingly, his wife calls a neighbour a 'thief', the husband cannot now be joined, as a defendant, in proceedings instituted by the neighbour to recover damages for the slander. For the same reason, the husband will not, normally, be liable if a wife driving her own car, on her own business, negligently knocks down and injures a pedestrian. He will, however, be liable if she is driving on his business, as in that event she is his agent.

If a wife is deserted by her husband, and he leaves her destitute, she has alternative ways of obtaining financial relief. She may take out a summons in the Magistrate's Court. The power of that Court to order maintenance is, however, limited, and the maximum sum it may order the husband to pay is £5 a week, with a further sum for each child under sixteen (and sometimes under twenty-one) of £1 10s. a week. If the husband is wealthy, this allowance is substantially less than her legal due, and she will therefore usually prefer to avail herself of her right to apply to the High Court. If no grounds exist for a divorce – a subject considered in the next chapter – a wife may apply for a decree, called 'restitution of conjugal rights'. A wife is always entitled to require her husband to render her 'conjugal rights', unless her conduct has been such as to afford her husband adequate excuse for refusal, or they have separated by mutual agreement. 'Conjugal rights' means shelter and the right of her husband's society, and upon the husband's default the Court may make an order, which theoretically requires him to comply with his obligations. Although it might often be more agreeable for a wife to apply for a divorce on the ground of desertion, she cannot take this step unless the desertion has lasted for a minimum period of three years. When she takes proceedings for restitution of conjugal rights, she must satisfy the Court that her petition is sincere. If she says in her evidence that she was delighted when her husband decided to leave her, and please, will the Court order him to carry out his proper legal obligation to support her, the Court will refuse her prayer, because her plea for restitution of conjugal rights is not sincere. No Court will, in fact, require a husband to obey the order to return.

Before 1949 the High Court had no power to hear a claim for maintenance except as part of some other application affecting the married status. The action for restitution of conjugal rights was the normal peg upon which the wife would hang her claim for maintenance. Since 1949 the action for 'restitution' has lost some of its importance, as a wife may now ask for maintenance in the High Court if her husband has wilfully neglected to provide reasonable maintenance, even although she has no grounds for other matrimonial proceedings. Another right which the Courts in recent years have decided a deserted wife may have, is that of continuing to live in the matrimonial home, although it may remain at the same time the property of the husband. The right is a limited one. The wife may find, for instance, that she is not allowed to remain to the prejudice of the husband's mortgagee or a purchaser of the property, even if aware of the desertion.

Since a husband who has left his wife will have little to gain from legal proceedings brought by her, and they will always involve him in substantial expense, it will be more prudent for him to make an amicable agreement to pay her a fixed allowance. No Court proceedings will then be necessary, and if the husband subsequently makes default under the agreement, the wife may sue for the amount due, or for damages for breach of contract. The wife must, however, be careful, if she enters into such an arrangement, not to come to any agreement to live separate from her husband, for if she does so she will be barred from bringing proceedings for divorce based on desertion at the expiration of three years. A mutual agreement to separate is almost always an absolute bar to a divorce on the ground of desertion, since the essence of desertion is a withdrawal from co-habitation, without cause, and against the wishes of the petitioning spouse.

The law treats marriage as a contract to which certain essential conditions are attached. On the breach of any one of these essential conditions, the other party may claim that the contract has been repudiated, and in due course may apply for the marriage to be dissolved. Unlike a business contract, the agreement may never be terminated by mutual consent. There is no more certain way of tightening the marriage bond than by husband and wife entering into an agreement to bring it to an end. Such an agreement, which will be considered in the next chapter, is known as a 'collusive agreement', and it is an absolute bar to a divorce.

Divorce generally will, as stated, be considered in the next chapter. Here we may observe that a wife is always entitled to apply for financial support when she presents a petition for divorce or for a judicial separation. So long as the marriage tie exists, the allowance which a husband may be ordered to pay to his wife is called 'alimony', except after an order for restitution of conjugal rights or maintenance, when the order for the allowance is called an order for 'periodical payments'. After the marriage has come to an end it is called 'maintenance'. There is an erroneous belief that a wife is entitled to a third of her husband's income when she receives alimony or maintenance. There is, certainly, no hard-and-fast rule, but, in general, a wife is entitled to one-fifth of the *joint* incomes by way of alimony *pendente lite* – i.e. pending suit – and to one-third of the *joint* incomes after a final decree has been made less her own income. This means that if a wife is earning her own living, or has any independent income, the amount of her income may be taken into account before calculating the amount of the husband's obligation. For example, if a husband is earning £800 a year, and his childless wife has an income of £200 a year, she will not, usually, be entitled to any alimony *pendente lite*, as she is already in receipt of one-fifth of the joint incomes. The proportion of one-fifth is, of course, a low one but the Court would not rigidly adhere to it, if for example the wife earned her own living due to her husband's meanness. It is based upon the theory that the wife is entitled to a bare minimum for her support, pending the disposal of the litigation. It is only after a final decree that the wife's permanent rights are assessed. When a husband is ordered to pay maintenance after a decree of divorce, he may also be ordered, if he has capital, to make a settlement which will secure part of the maintenance ordered to be paid. A settlement as security may also be ordered when a husband has wilfully neglected to provide reasonable maintenance for his wife.

Every order for maintenance, or alimony, will usually direct payment for joint lives or 'until further order'. This means that the payment must be continued until either the husband or the wife dies, unless there is any substantial change in the financial position of either party, when the Court has power to vary the amount payable. Even if the wife has remunerative employment when the final decree is made, and she does not require immediate financial support, she must make an application to the Court for an order for maintenance, if she wishes to safeguard her future rights. Unless her application is made within two months of the final dissolution of the marriage, she will be able to obtain an order at a later date only if she satisfies the Court that there were exceptional circumstances to explain her default in not making her application at the proper time. When, however, she is not in a position to ask for any substantial maintenance, the Court may make an order for a nominal allowance of 1s. a month. This gives her the right to apply for an increase if her financial position deteriorates, and she is later left either with a reduced income or with nothing at all.

If the husband is paying maintenance to his divorced wife under an order of the Court, her subsequent re-marriage is not, automatically, a ground upon which the order may be discharged or varied. It may be necessary for her former husband to prove that her financial status has improved, and that she is in receipt of an income, as a direct result of the second marriage, and unless he is able to do this he may not, necessarily, be able to obtain any modification of an existing order.

In calculating the sum which a husband may be ordered to pay his wife, usually no allowance is made in respect of income tax, and all the figures are computed on a gross basis. After the order has been made, however, the husband may ordinarily deduct income tax at the full standard rate before he makes each payment, unless the gross amount payable does not exceed £2 per week. If, accordingly, he is ordered to pay to his wife £30 a month, he will, in fact, pay her only £17 5s. when the current rate of tax is 8s. 6d. in the £. He must, however, sign and give his wife a certificate, on the appropriate Revenue form R185, as evidence of deduction of the tax, and to enable his wife to recover from the Revenue any balance due to her, after computation of her own liability for tax.

The calculations made on the one-fifth and the one-third basis, respectively, apply only to maintenance for the wife for her personal use. If there are children of the marriage, in the wife's custody, the husband may be ordered to pay additional sums for their maintenance. There is no rule upon which to calculate this additional amount. The general principle is that the children must not be allowed to suffer by reason of the dispute between the parents. The Court will normally order such a sum to be paid by the husband for each of the children of the marriage as will enable this intention to be carried into effect. Regard must be had, however, to the maximum sum which the husband might reasonably have been expected to pay for the children's maintenance, education, and support, if the marriage had not been broken up.

When a wife is the respondent or defendant to a divorce suit, she is usually entitled to apply for alimony *pendente lite*, in the same way as a petitioner. Since everyone is assumed by the law to have observed his or her legal obligations, a wife charged with a matrimonial offence is deemed to be innocent of the accusation until her guilt is established. The husband therefore cannot normally resist an application for alimony *pendente lite*. He may, however, do so when he is able to satisfy the Court that his wife is, in fact, being maintained by a corespondent. When the husband has obtained a divorce decree, he is no longer compelled to support his wife, unless she obtains an order for maintenance on compassionate grounds. As soon as adultery has been proved, she forfeits her legal right to financial support.

If an order for maintenance, or alimony, is not obeyed, an application may be made for its enforcement. Unfortunately, the legal machinery for enforcing such orders is slow and cumbersome. If the husband wishes to flout his obligations, and proves obstructive, the wife's lawyer may have a hard task. Frequently, if the husband is clever, the lawyer's efforts may prove abortive. A wife may regard a husband who fails to support her as a criminal. The law does not take the same view, and it is not easy to obtain an order to commit a man to prison when he ignores an order for payment of maintenance or alimony. Sometimes, indeed, it may be more advantageous to a wife to make the best of a bad job and set to work as she would do if her husband had died a pauper.

Magistrates' Courts have more extensive powers of enforcing their orders than the High Court. Moreover, Magistrates' Courts have power to make orders for maintenance on the ground of adultery, cruelty, and neglect, as well as on the ground of desertion and failure to maintain.

If, however, there are husbands who default, the majority recognize their financial obligations, even after divorce. It must also be remembered that although there are many virtuous wives, there are others who are only fit to be the 'mothers of dead dogs'. No law can be fair to all. In most respects the present rules for financing the wife are adequate to meet the normal, as distinct from the exceptional, case.

25

DIVORCE

'Fy! Madam, do you think me so ill-bred as to love a husband?'

Wycherley: *Love in a Wood*

IT is a fair guess that many readers will open the book at this chapter. If you are one of them, I hope you will immediately turn to the dedication which precedes the preface, in order to become one of those to whom the book is dedicated.

The principal grounds upon which a divorce or a judicial separation may be obtained are: (1) adultery, (2) cruelty, (3) desertion for three years or upwards, and (4) incurable lunacy of at least five years' duration. A marriage may be formally declared annulled, by decree, if it was, in fact, null and void from the outset, as, for example, when the ceremony was bigamous or had been celebrated between relatives within the prohibited degrees, or when one of the parties was under sixteen, the legal age permitted for marriage. A decree of nullity of marriage, as distinct from a divorce, but also operating so as to terminate an existing marriage, may be obtained if the marriage has never been consummated either on the ground of physical defect of one of the parties or by reason of wilful refusal on the part of the spouse against whom the proceedings are brought to agree to the consummation. Such a decree of nullity may also be obtained if proceedings are commenced within one year of the marriage on the ground that either party at the time of the marriage was of unsound mind, or that the respondent or defendant was, at the time of the marriage, suffering from venereal disease in a communicable form, or pregnant by some person other than the petitioner, the fact not being discovered by the petitioner until after the marriage ceremony, and thereafter voluntary intercourse not taking place.

There are scarcely any other grounds upon which a marriage may be terminated. Incompatibility of temperament is never a ground for divorce, and if husband and wife quarrel over trivialities, and irritate each other beyond all reason, their only alternative to 'gnawing domestic misery', unless it tends to cruel conduct by one or other or both of them, is to agree to separate by mutual consent. No petition for divorce may be presented to the Court to end such a marriage, while a separation agreement, as stated in Chapter 24, will bar any future divorce based on desertion, although not one founded on adultery.

Cruelty required to support a petition for divorce may be either physical or mental. *Physical* cruelty consists of calculated acts of physical violence which are dangerous to life or health. Continuous nagging, or constant abuse or neglect, or other deliberate and aggravating offensive behaviour (an intention to be cruel is not essential, but it may sometimes be decisive), which results in injury to health or causes fear for physical safety or health, may amount to *mental* cruelty. It is a question of fact whether the behaviour of the offending spouse reasonably deserves this description. For example, petty squabbling, for which each spouse may be partly to blame, is not cruelty. Insulting conduct may, however, amount to cruelty, if the effect is to cause injury to the other spouse's health. It is a matter of degree, but to amount to cruelty the conduct complained of must be grave and weighty. What constitutes mental cruelty is often difficult to decide.

Sometimes there may be insulting conduct by one or other of the spouses which may not amount either to physical or mental cruelty because there is no injury to health. The legal position in these cases is not satisfactory. Although the other party may then be justified in leaving the matrimonial home, and the marriage is broken up, neither party has any immediate right to a divorce. It is an example of what is known in law as 'constructive desertion', and no proceedings for divorce on the ground of desertion may be started unless and until there has been an uninterrupted period of desertion for three years immediately preceding the presentation of the petition for divorce.

'Constructive desertion' may also arise when a husband brings another woman into the house, to take precedence over his wife. She need not then remain. The husband's obligation is to provide a home for the wife, and to treat her as a wife, and he is not entitled to relegate her to the position of a house-keeper or domestic servant. If he does so, the wife may leave him, and even if she obtains no evidence of adultery she may proceed three years later for a divorce on the grounds of desertion, unless her husband has repented in the meanwhile, and has given his wife a sincere assurance that she will have no further reason to complain.

The party who seeks the dissolution of the marriage is called the 'petitioner', and the other party the 'respondent'. In a suit by a husband based on adultery, the other man is called the 'co-respondent'. When the wife is the petitioner, and she charges her husband with adultery, the other woman is called the 'woman named'.

Divorce proceedings cannot necessarily be brought in England merely because a matrimonial offence is committed here. Before the English Courts have jurisdiction to entertain the suit, it is normally necessary for the petitioner to prove that he or she is 'domiciled' in England, and that the marriage was celebrated at least three years prior to the date of the petition. Domicil is not the same as residence or nationality, although in the case of an English-born resident, English domicil may often be assumed as a matter of course. When, however, a petitioner for divorce, although not of English birth, seeks to establish English domicil, he must satisfy the Court that he has abandoned his domicil of origin, and intends to make England his permanent home, before his petition can be entertained.

The wife generally takes the same domicil as her husband, but not necessarily his nationality. Since 1 January 1949 a British woman who marries an alien no longer loses her British nationality, and any woman married prior to that date who by reason of marrying a foreigner lost her British nationality automatically re-acquired it. It is the wife's duty to live with her husband, wherever he may reside, and it would be illogical to allow her an English domicil if her husband were of foreign domicil. An exception is made in favour of a deserted wife, if her husband abandons his English domicil, and assumes a foreign domicil, after the date of desertion. In that event, proceedings for divorce, based upon any ground, may be brought by the wife in England. War-time legislation to give the Court jurisdiction, in cases where an Englishwoman might otherwise have been without a remedy after the breakdown of her marriage to a member of the allied forces not domiciled in England, lapsed in 1955. Nevertheless since 1950 it has been possible for a wife to petition for divorce in England, even if her husband is domiciled abroad, provided she has lived in England for a period of three years before commencing proceedings, but this concession does not apply if he is domiciled in Scotland, Northern Ireland, the Channel Isles, or the Isle of Man.

The provisions of the Matrimonial Causes Act 1950 which do not normally permit the presentation of any petition for divorce until three years have elapsed after the date of the marriage, are not to be confused with other provisions of the same Act, which prescribe three years as the minimum period of desertion required to support a petition for divorce based on that offence. No proceedings for divorce may ever be initiated until three years after the date of the marriage, unless leave to present the petition has been obtained from the Court. Such leave may be obtained only when the case is one of exceptional hardship suffered by the petitioner, or exceptional depravity on the part of the respondent, and a heavy burden is imposed on a petitioner who seeks to establish a case on either of these grounds. If, however, leave is granted, the petitioner may bring the proceedings, and prove the case, in the same way as in any other suit. The three years' limitation, however, does not apply to proceedings either for nullity of the marriage or for a judicial separation, as distinct from divorce.

A judicial separation may be obtained on almost the same grounds as a divorce. It is an order from the Court which relieves the petitioning spouse from the obligation of co-habitation. There is normally no advantage to either party in obtaining such a decree, for it leaves the marriage a skeleton, and divorce is the natural sequence to a broken marriage. There are, however, occasions when conscience will not permit a wife to ask for a divorce, and she is not compelled to do so. Moreover, as a result of the Inheritance (Family Provisions) Act 1938, a wife, judicially separated from her husband, may have a claim against his estate for maintenance after his death, although no similar right will accrue to a divorced wife.

In proceedings for divorce based on adultery, it is necessary for the petitioner to prove adultery, even although the suit is not defended. Sexual fidelity is an essential obligation of marriage, and breach of the obligation must be strictly proved, even in an undefended case, as the Court will not assume adultery has been committed merely because the respondent does not appear and defend the proceedings. Evidence of the parties having been seen in bed together is regarded as sufficient to establish adultery, but if such direct testimony is not available, the evidence brought before the Court must be more than sufficient to arouse suspicion. The Court may, however, infer adultery if strong evidence is given both of 'inclination' of the parties towards each other, and also of 'opportunity' when adultery might have been committed between them. It may be asked to grant a decree, if witnesses depose to acts of gross familiarity between the parties, and also frequent close association, on occasions when adultery might perhaps have been discreetly committed. The Court is, however, alive to current freedom of behaviour between the sexes, and will be slow to draw an inference of adultery unless this may be fairly and reasonably drawn after the whole of the evidence has been reviewed.

'Hotel evidence', as it is called, is the evidence which is frequently supplied by husband to wife, or *vice versa*, when one of them is anxious for a divorce. The husband may send the wife an hotel bill, showing that he has stayed the night with another woman, and when inquiries are instituted, evidence is usually obtained which confirms this. When the case is tried, a chambermaid or a waiter generally gives evidence that he saw the husband in bed with the other woman.

In all proceedings for divorce it is usually essential to have a witness who is able to corroborate the evidence given by the petitioner, even if the suit is not defended. A respondent cannot be compelled to admit adultery, but the Court will usually accept a confession on oath by the respondent if no other evidence is available and the respondent is willing to admit the allegations in the witness-box.

Although husband and wife must not make any agreement for a divorce, there is no legal objection to a letter being sent by the husband to the wife *after* he has committed adultery, in the hope and expectation of his wife then taking action. The wife will, however, be unsuccessful if she has told her husband that, if he will commit adultery and will provide her with the evidence, she, on her part, will commence divorce proceedings against him. If she does this, the agreement is known in law as a collusive agreement, and collusion is an absolute bar to a divorce. It may sometimes be necessary to distinguish between a promise and a threat. For example, if the wife thinks she is in love with another man, and proposes to spend a week-end with him, her husband might say: 'If you go off with Bill Carefree, I shall divorce you.' If that is construed as a threat, intended to deter, the law will regard it as praiseworthy. If, on the other hand, the same words are interpreted as an invitation to the wife to obtain her freedom by committing adultery, and if, in fact, she accepts the invitation, and spends the week-end with Bill Carefree, the parties commit the offence of collusion. The sequel may be disastrous to both, for when a divorce petition is presented, it must be accompanied by an affidavit, sworn by the petitioner, that there is no collusion between the parties. If the oath is untrue, and the Court subsequently ascertains that there has, in fact, been collusion, not only will the decree be refused, but the petitioner may be charged both with the offence of perjury – i.e. deliberately swearing a false oath – and also the offence of attempting to pervert the course of justice. A sad sequel to an unhappy marriage.

When a divorce decree is granted, the dissolution of the marriage is accomplished in two stages. The first is complete when the Court has heard the evidence and has pronounced a decree, called a decree *nisi* – the Latin word meaning 'unless'. The marriage may be brought to an end three months later, when the decree may be made absolute, 'unless' in the meanwhile there has been an intervention in the proceedings by a third party, to show cause why the decree should not be made absolute. When an intervention is entered, the intervener is usually a Government official, called the Queen's Proctor. It is his duty to investigate the *bona fides* of petitions for divorce. He is required to play the rôle of detective, and ascertain if the true facts have been presented to the Court. The Queen's Proctor is, for example, compelled by reason of his office, to intervene in order to ask for the decree *nisi* to be rescinded if he finds that husband and wife have brought the proceedings by mutual agreement. It takes all sorts to make a world, and the function of the Queen's Proctor is accepted by lawyers and the community without enthusiasm.

The usual period allowed to the Queen's Proctor in which to make his inquiries and intervene in the suit is the three months between decree *nisi* and decree absolute. This period may be abridged, or shortened, by the Court, in special circumstances – e.g. if one of the parties is expecting a child and wishes to marry before its birth, in order that it may be legitimate. Expectant mothers may always ask for leave to go to the head of the queue. Although the Court has power to abridge the time, it will not, however, do so without the consent of the Queen's Proctor. In practice, the Queen's Proctor is quite human, and in suitable cases he will assist the parties to bring about the desired result.

Collusion is not the only bar to a divorce.

If one party forgives the other for any matrimonial offence, and there is a reconciliation, or 'condonation' – i.e. forgiveness of the offence, and not a forgiveness based on any concealment or fraud – the innocent party is not entitled to decide at a later date to start divorce proceedings based upon any incident which has been forgiven. An effort by husband and wife to adjust their differences is always regarded by the law with benevolence, and the parties need not fear that these attempts will injure their prospects of divorce if they do not achieve their object. Divorce proceedings will fail, however, if the reconciliation becomes a *fait accompli* and there is a resumption of intercourse between husband and wife. In that event past offences are condoned, and any pending proceedings would have to be abandoned; for condonation, like collusion, is an absolute bar to a divorce. If, however, at a date subsequent to the condonation another matrimonial offence is committed by the party previously at fault, it will revive the earlier offence, and the innocent party may then take proceedings based upon both offences. For the purpose of reviving a condoned offence the fresh offence need not itself be a ground for divorce, but it must be sufficiently serious to override the condonation.

Collusion or condonation may always be pleaded as a defence to a petition for divorce. The respondent to a divorce suit is also entitled to plead, by way of defence, that the petitioner has 'connived' at the offence with which he is charged. If a wife encourages her husband to spend a week-end in the country with a girl friend, she is not entitled to complain to the Court if he commits adultery during his leave of absence. She will be said to have 'connived' at that adultery – i.e. she had encouraged it by her conduct. Connivance need not necessarily be direct encouragement. It may be tacit acquiescence so long as there is an *intention* to connive. It is connivance for a petitioner to stand by in silence when a prudent spouse, anxious to prevent adultery, would take some step to prevent it. Conduct 'conducing' to adultery may be another bar to a divorce. If John Doe treats his wife in so callous a manner as to throw her into the arms of Richard Roe for protection, and she then commits adultery with him, she may plead that her husband's conduct has 'conduced' to the adultery, and if the Court accepts her evidence, it may refuse to grant him a divorce.

The person against whom the decree is granted is colloquially called the 'guilty party'. The law assumes the other party to be innocent, but if, in fact, he or she is not entitled to a badge of innocence, the decree may be refused. Adultery by a petitioner does not, however, operate as an absolute bar to the divorce; it is called a 'discretionary' bar. In ordinary circumstances the Court might not, of course, know of any adultery committed by the petitioner, when the petition is not defended. To guard against 'deception', the Court requires a petitioner who has committed adultery to make a full confession and apply to the Judge who hears the case for the exercise of the Court's discretion in his or her favour. In order that there may be no misunderstanding about this particular matter, the Courts have imposed the duty on the solicitor who acts for the petitioner to ask his client (as delicately and as tactfully as he pleases) whether he or she has or has not been guilty of adultery.

There are certain saving graces about this distasteful practice. Although the petitioner must make the disclosure, the confession is lodged in Court, after signature, in a sealed envelope, and it remains there until it is placed before the Judge when he hears the case. The contents are not divulged, and it is not the practice to make any reference in Court to the name of any party mentioned in the discretion statement.

When both parties have committed adultery, John Doe may present a petition for divorce against Joan Doe, alleging adultery by her with Mr Careless, and Joan Doe may file an answer, denying the charge, and asking for a divorce against John Doe on the ground of his adultery with Miss Carefree. Both parties may deny the allegations, and at the same time ask for the exercise of the discretion of the Court. The Court will then usually tend to exercise its discretion in favour of the party who has had the lesser responsibility for breaking up the marriage, or it may exercise its discretion in favour of both parties and grant each the decree prayed for. Similarly, where each alleges cruelty against the other the Court may find that the case of each has been proved and grant decrees to both.

It must not be thought that the exercise of discretion by the Court in favour of an erring party is automatic. Every case is considered on its merits. Provided, however, the petitioner expresses sincere regret for the adultery, and there is a reasonable excuse for the lapse, and so long as it is consistent with public interest, the Court will usually adopt a benevolent attitude. It will do so on the assumption that full disclosure of the facts has been made by the party who asks for clemency. Little sympathy will be shown if it is ascertained at a later date, and after inquiries have been made by the Queen's Proctor, that the petitioner has not been frank with the Court. It should also be noted that the petitioner is not entitled to commit adultery after the date of the presentation of the petition, or even after the decree *nisi* has been granted.

If either party later wishes to re-marry, it is necessary to produce a certificate of the decree absolute which has been obtained. No Registrar may perform a subsequent marriage ceremony unless he is satisfied of the dissolution of the earlier marriage. The production of the certificate is the most satisfactory evidence of the validity of the dissolution.

Although the Marriage Act 1949 allows a man to marry his *deceased* wife's sister, he is not entitled to marry his *divorced* wife's sister during the lifetime of his former wife. Similarly, a woman is entitled to marry her late husband's brother but not her divorced husband's brother.

If a man or a woman goes through another ceremony of marriage while the first marriage is still in existence, the crime of bigamy is committed. It is a defence to a charge of bigamy that the defendant had not heard of the husband or wife, as the case may be, for a period of seven years, and had no reason to believe he or she was alive, or, alternatively, that he, or she, had a reasonable and *bona fide* belief in the death of the other. Any such defence does not, however, make the second 'marriage' a valid one, and any children of the second 'marriage' will be illegitimate. The Divorce Court has power to make an order presuming the death of a spouse, where reasonable grounds exist for believing him or her to be dead, or if he or she has not been heard of for seven years, and there is no reason to believe him or her to have been alive during this period. The order may be followed by a decree dissolving the marriage, but the petitioner must give full details of the steps which have been taken to trace the respondent, before the Court will condemn him or her to judicial extinction. If, moreover, the 'dead' person comes to life at any time before the decree is made absolute, the decree *nisi* will be rescinded upon the intervention of any party interested.

If either party has the misfortune to be married to a partner who is not quite sane, but not sufficiently insane to be classed as a lunatic, the position is very difficult. If the husband, in one of his moods of insanity, treats the wife with cruelty, she may nevertheless be refused a decree of divorce. One essence of legal cruelty is an understanding by the respondent of the acts which are said to amount to cruelty. On the other hand, it is recognized that a wife needs protection, and the only remedy may be by way of divorce for cruelty. If however, the husband's condition requires restraint, he may be certified by doctors, and removed to a mental home under certain conditions. This will not enable a spouse to obtain a divorce on the ground of insanity. No decree on this ground can be granted until the patient has been continuously under care and treatment, not commencing with voluntary treatment, for a period of at least five years immediately preceding the presentation of the petition, and unless there is medical evidence that there is no prospect of recovery. However, as already stated, if one spouse is of unsound mind at the date of marriage, proceedings for nullity may be commenced within one year of marriage.

A husband is normally liable for his wife's costs in divorce cases, and he may always be required by the Court to provide security for her costs, whether the wife is the petitioner or the respondent. A guilty wife may be ordered to pay costs if she has separate property, and if there is a prayer in the husband's petition asking for an order for costs against her. A co-respondent will usually be ordered to pay the costs of the proceedings if the petitioner is able to satisfy the Court that the co-respondent knew the respondent was a married woman when the adultery was committed.

A petitioner is always entitled to ask for damages against a co-respondent, but not against a woman named. When he does so, a claim for a specific sum must be included in the petition. The claim is usually made by a husband who feels that the co-respondent has broken up a happy marriage or who regards his wife as a commercial proposition, whose worth should be assessed by the Court. If damages are awarded, they are based upon the pecuniary loss which the husband has suffered, and the harm done to him in that status, and not upon the means of the co-respondent. Damages may, of course, be substantial if the co-respondent has really broken up a happy home, and may be trivial if the marriage had been reduced to a sham before the adultery was committed.

Divorce law presents many strange anomalies. They arise from the fact that divorce was previously a prerogative of the Ecclesiastical Courts. The Church has always regarded marriage as sacred, and a divorce could only be granted by a Private Act of Parliament. Indeed, until the Matrimonial Causes Act 1857, no court had power to try actions for dissolution of marriage. In 1957, when John Doe's views on 'freedom' differ from those of his ancestors, he may revile a system which prevents him from breaking the chains of marriage as easily as he would wish. He often doubts whether a shadow marriage is a burden which a 'civilized' man ought to bear. Perhaps if public opinion continues to progress at its present speed, either forward or backward (according to your personal view), existing anomalies in divorce practice may disappear in the course of years. It would, however, be rash to prophesy. The subject of divorce law reform is tricky. It has been before Parliament on many occasions, a great landmark being the Matrimonial Causes Act 1937 which was successfully piloted through the House of Commons by Sir Alan Herbert. Notwithstanding, penny-in-the-slot divorces may still fail to receive universal support, and M.P.s, following what they presumably believe to be public opinion, always seem reluctant to sanction any change in the law designed to facilitate dissolution of marriage. It is not necessarily reasonable for John Doe and his wife to describe divorce laws as 'cant' and 'hypocrisy' because they disagree with this view. The law *does* sometimes reflect the views of the majority, and John Doe and his wife, who live in a democracy, ought not to blame the law because they disagree with the majority.

A Royal Commission reported in 1956 on the laws of marriage and divorce, and reflected the dissension on the question of whether marriage is to be regarded essentially as a sacrosanct or an expedient institution. A crumb of comfort may be offered to some of those afflicted by these 'iniquitous' laws and the 'cold clatter of morality'. There is popular fancy for the escape method which is offered to a woman by changing her name. 'What's in a name?' In law, a natural British-born subject (but not an alien) is entitled to call himself by any surname which he may choose. He is not bound by his birth or baptismal certificate. If a woman wishes to change her surname, she may adopt the name of the partner with whom she has elected to live, without the formality of a marriage ceremony. This change of surname – but not of Christian name – may be effected by different methods. The orthodox procedure is complicated and expensive, and a married woman requires the consent of her husband. It also involves advertisements, oaths, and other legal paraphernalia. The simpler method is to execute a deed, called a 'deed poll', recording the abandonment of the old name and the adoption of the new. This deed can be prepared expeditiously by any lawyer, and when it has been executed and stamped with a 10s. stamp, the change is effective for all practical purposes. It is, however, frequently convenient to obtain one or more photostat copies of the deed which may be lodged with solicitors and bankers, to be produced as evidence of the change of name in the event of the loss of the original.

A Christian name may not legally be changed, since it is given at baptism, and is a matter which primarily relates to the Church membership of the holder. It may, strictly speaking, only be changed at confirmation or by Private Act of Parliament, but the law is, perhaps, more conservative than the practice, as no offence is committed if a natural-born British subject chooses to adopt a Christian name other than that with which he was endowed at birth.

The following statistics illustrate the rise in the number of divorces due to such diverse causes as the Matrimonial Causes Act 1937, the Second World War and the legal aid scheme – also the fall in their number as more settled conditions have come to prevail.

	1938	1947	1955
Petitions filed	9,970	47,041	27,656
Decrees Absolute	6,092	58,444*	26,262

* Some months elapse between the filing of the petition and the granting of the decree.

26

WILLS, INTESTACY, AND TRUSTS

'Can anyone do much for anyone else unless by making
a Will in his favour and dying then and there?'
The Way of All Flesh

THERE is no branch of the law which better illustrates the pitfalls open to the ordinary man, than that relating to wills.
Making a will or testament – the words now have a similar
meaning – is a job for a lawyer. An attempt to follow the instructions given on a sixpenny will form, procured from a local
stationer, frequently ends in the Law Courts. Home-made wills
have provided a rich harvest for lawyers, and a small sum spent
in obtaining professional advice in the preparation of a will
may frequently avoid litigation at a later date.

It is proper that wills should be highly technical documents,
for if the law were to admit informal directions for disposing
of property after death, it would give rise to many cases of
fraud. For example, your 'friend' John Doe might invite you
to a drink at the Red Lion, and ask you to sign a document
which he tells you is a petition for improving a car park. If
John Doe were a swindler, and the document was not a petition at all, but a will by which you bequeathed your estate to
him, it might lead to great injustice. This example may sound
fantastic, but every lawyer will tell you of people who are defrauded, because they sign documents before they read them.
Sometimes the swindler is caught, but not so easily when the
defrauded man is dead.

To ensure as far as possible that a man appreciates the nature
of his act, when he signs a will, the Wills Act 1837 requires
every will (with the exception of wills of those on active service with the Armed Forces, and of merchant seamen at sea)
to be in writing, and signed at the foot or end in the presence
of two witnesses. The 'testator' – i.e. the man making the will
– together with both the witnesses, should all sign the will in
the presence of each other, and unless the will is signed with
these formalities, it is void and of no effect. As a further safeguard against fraud, neither the witness of a will nor the

husband or wife of a witness may take a legacy or any other benefit under a will.

It is scarcely necessary to emphasize the desirability of making a will, if you have any definite wishes for the disposal of your property after your death. It is not a matter which should be put off for a more suitable occasion, as death does not await the pleasure of a man who procrastinates. 'Die, my dear Doctor, is the last thing I shall do', are famous last words.

When a testator makes his will he should appoint one or more persons, not exceeding four in all, to 'wind-up his estate' – i.e. to deal with his affairs after his death. They are called his 'executors', and an executor who later proves the will is the 'personal representative' of the estate of the deceased. The function of executors is more particularly described in the next chapter. Their office is often a thankless one, and if the testator does not know of any friend or friends willing to act, he may appoint either his solicitor, his Bank, or the Public Trustee. Banks undertake the duties on terms obtainable from any of their branches. The Public Trustee, who administers a large number of estates throughout the country, is a Government official set up by the Public Trustee Act 1906, an Act which regulates the terms and conditions upon which he acts.

If a testator wishes the whole of his estate to be distributed as soon as possible after his death, the will may be a comparatively simple one. A lawyer can record the testator's wishes in language which is easy to understand. If, however, the testator prepares the will himself, he cannot be expected to realize that words which are used in a colloquial sense do not necessarily have an identical dictionary meaning, or may have received judicial interpretation. A simple will might read, 'I leave all my money to John Doe'. The word 'money' ordinarily means a token of exchange or cash. It does not include stocks and shares or other property. Until some fifteen years ago, when the House of Lords delivered a judgement extending the ordinary meaning of the word 'money', a bequest of 'all my money' in a will almost invariably failed to give effect to the probable wishes of the testator, to dispose of *all* his property. The testator who wrote 'I leave all my money to John Doe' may have meant to say 'I leave all of which I die possessed to

John Doe'. It has in many cases proved unfortunate for John Doe that he did not say so. Moreover, even the decision of the House of Lords referred to does not necessarily mean that the word 'money' suffices to cover all property in every will. The House of Lords reached its decision on the facts before it, but affirmed its freedom from being bound by any narrow construction, so that when you dispose of all your property by will it is still inadvisable to limit yourself to the use of the word 'money'.

When a testator uses a word or phrase which has a different meaning from that which he thinks, it is not the duty of the law to try to decide what he intended. If the law operated in this way, it would give rise to more injustice than it would cure, for who is entitled to explain after a man's death what his wishes were really intended to be, when the words he has used in his will do not legally express those wishes? The method which is applied by the Courts – and it is the only safe and just method – is to construe the will according to the words which have been used. While, therefore, the Court is anxious, when legally possible, to give effect to the intention of the testator, it is generally not competent to add to or alter any of his words. The Court can give consideration to every word and every phrase which may throw light on the will's construction, but always it is the intention of the testator, and not the wishes of his relatives which must be construed. The Court cannot be expected to tamper with the chosen words when they indicate a meaningful, even if unreasonable intention.

The debts and funeral expenses of a testator must always be paid in priority to any legacies, so there is no special need to include a direction for their payment in the will. The testator should specify the particular bequests – i.e. legacies or money gifts, or gifts of specific chattels, which he desires to make, and he should give directions for the disposal of the remainder of his property, called the 'residue'. 'Residuary estate' comprises everything which is not otherwise specifically disposed of by the will.

When a testator makes a bequest he should exercise great caution before he attaches any condition to the payment, for the beneficiary is entitled to take the bequest free of the condition, either if it is repugnant to public policy or if it is too vague to be capable of any certain legal construction. Moreover, a testator should always be careful, when he makes a bequest, to be precise and exact in expressing his wishes. If you leave your estate 'to be divided equally between all persons living in Hemel Hempstead, Hertfordshire, who have red hair', the Court may say that your wishes are too uncertain to be fulfilled, since no two people may agree on the meaning of the expression 'red hair'.

If a bequest is void for uncertainty the proposed beneficiary will receive nothing. There is an exception in the case of bequests to charities. In such a case, and if your wishes are not clearly enough expressed to be determined with certainty, the Court has power to give directions for the money to be applied for purposes which appear, as nearly as possible, to carry out your wishes, on the principles of a legal doctrine called the *Cy-près* doctrine (French, 'near to that').

When we speak of a 'charity', we mean objects which are charitable in the legal sense, and there is no power to apply the *cy-près* doctrine except to bequests which are definitely charitable. What is or is not charitable depends primarily on whether it falls within the scope of an Act of Parliament passed in the time of Queen Elizabeth the First four centuries ago. While most charities are concerned with the relief of poverty or the promotion of education or religion, there are others which the Law recognizes on the ground that they benefit the Community generally, so long as they are not outside the purport of the Elizabethan statute.

A testator should not leave his property to be applied as his executors may think fit to 'charitable or other purposes', even if the latter are clearly defined. Many such purposes could be charitable as the word is normally understood, without being charitable within the strict meaning of the law. In a case which went to the House of Lords a bequest was held to be bad, since 'purposes charitable or benevolent' could not be held necessarily charitable. The executors had unfortunately already paid away the money in question, and a second lawsuit was fought, also to the House of Lords, to establish the right of the next of kin to receive repayment from the charities which had received the money. This case contains a moral, even for lawyers, since it serves to prove that the law insists upon precision, and the more precise and clear our thoughts and actions, the less likely we shall be to fall foul of the law.

If the testator leaves a wife and children surviving, he will frequently desire to make for the children financial provisions, which are not to come into force until after the death of his wife. In that event the will must contain specific directions which will prevent the distribution of the estate during the life of his wife. If you execute a home-made will leaving everything to your wife, and after her death to your children, your wishes cannot be legally carried out. You have left your property twice over: (1) to your wife, (2) to your children. The effect would be that your wife would be able to dispose of all your property during her lifetime, leaving nothing for the children. If you wish your children to benefit after the death of your wife, you must use words which are accepted by the law as having that effect. This is done by a procedure peculiar to English law called 'creating a trust'.

A trust is of great significance in English legal history, but unfortunately it is another of those tiresome, complicated stories, which cannot be compressed into anything simple, and I do not favour any attempt to achieve the impossible. It probably took its rise in the thirteenth century, when the Crown became jealous of certain religious bodies which were acquiring land, thus depriving the Crown of the profits extracted from private holdings. When the danger of confiscation loomed, these religious bodies arranged for their lands to be acquired by the landowning class, who would hold them for their 'use', and the practice became known as 'putting land to uses'. The landowner was the legal owner, and the religious body was the beneficiary – i.e. it was entitled to the beneficial occupation of the land. If we skip the intervening six centuries, we arrive at the present doctrine of 'trusts'.

Trusts may be expressly created by deed or other documents or even by word of mouth. Sometimes, the law will assume a trust to have been created. For example, if John Doe purchases a property in the name of Richard Roe, the latter will normally be deemed to be a 'trustee' of the property for John Doe – i.e. the law assumes that Richard Roe holds the property in trust for John Doe. On the other hand, if John Doe purchases property in the name of his wife Joan, the law will assume that the property is a gift from John Doe to his wife. Evidence may be given that these assumptions are not correct. In the former case Richard Roe may prove that the property does in fact belong to him, and in the latter case John Doe may prove that his wife really holds the property in trust for him.

A trust always imposes legal obligations on the trustees, and a 'breach of trust' – i.e. a failure to carry out the specified terms of the trust – is, accordingly, a breach of a legal duty. It will give rise to a right of action by beneficiaries – i.e. the persons who are entitled to benefit under the trust – and they may claim damages equivalent to any actual loss sustained by the breach. The general duties of a trustee will be considered in the next chapter.

When a testator sets up a trust in his will he usually, but not necessarily, appoints his executors to act also as the trustees. If the trust is in favour of the widow and children of the testator, the widow will frequently have a 'life interest' in the estate – i.e. directions will be given in the will for the income from the investments to be paid to the widow for her life, and for the trust funds to be realized after her death and divided among the testator's children.

Among the many rules which must be observed by a testator when he sets up a trust, and desires his wishes to be legally effective, are the 'Rules against Perpetuities and Accumulations'. If you settle or leave a sum of £500 to trustees on trust to accumulate the money for a period of 500 years, and at the end of that time to pay it to your most direct descendant, the result would be fantastic. Of course, this is an extreme case, but money accumulated at compound interest at 5 per cent will double itself in fourteen years, and at the end of even 300 years it would reach the astronomical figure of over one thousand million pounds. At the end of 500 years it would provide more than sufficient to pay off the National Debt!

To safeguard the community against absurdities of this

character, the law has laid down that a man may not provide for the accumulation of income for longer than twenty-one years after his death or impose any restriction on the disposition of his property (unless he is leaving it to a charity), which may conceivably last for longer than 'a life or lives in being and twenty-one years thereafter'. The lifetime of members of the Royal Family has been used as a yardstick in applying this rule, and when trusts are established to provide superannuation benefits for employees, it is not uncommon to provide that the trust will continue 'during the lives of the lineal descendants now living of his late Majesty King George V and for twenty-one years after the death of the last survivor'. Under a provision of this nature the trust might be expected to last for up to a hundred years. If the bounds permitted by the rule are exceeded, the trustees are not entitled to distribute the fund at the end of the permitted period, for the proposed trust is null and void from the beginning.

A trust usually gives directions as to the class of securities in which the capital funds, or trust monies, are to be invested, and unless such directions are given, all investments must be made in securities called 'trustee securities', which are designated by law as proper investments for trustees.

In making his will the testator should have due care for his legal and moral obligations. Although he is not bound to leave part of his estate to any member of his family, the Inheritance (Family Provisions) Act 1938, as amended by the Intestate's Estates Act 1952, entitles the Court, when the Testator has made no adequate provision in his will, to make an order for maintenance at the expense of the estate, within specified limits, in favour of a wife or husband, an infant child, an unmarried daughter, or a daughter or son who is incapable of maintaining himself or herself. A person entitled to make a claim under these provisions should apply to the Court within six months after the issue of the 'grant of representation' to the estate of the deceased, dealt with in the next chapter. When an application is made under the Act, the Court will only make an order in favour of the applicant, if it thinks fit to do so, after it has taken into consideration all relevant factors, including any personal reasons the testator may have expressed in writing, for excluding the applicant from receiving any adequate benefit under his will.

In the absence of express provision in a will or a trust, a trustee, other than the Public Trustee, is not entitled to any remuneration for his services, but he has a right to be reimbursed for expenses properly incurred by him in carrying out his duties. The Public Trustee has express power to charge fees, and Banks will agree to accept the office of trustee only if the document which appoints them includes a provision which allows them payment of their prescribed fees.

No alteration may be made in a will after it has been executed. If it contains erasures or alterations, they must all be signed both by the testator and the witnesses prior to its execution. If a testator wishes to make alterations after the will has been signed, he can only give effect to his revised desires by a new will, or by a document called a 'codicil'. This specifies the alterations he wishes to make, and a codicil must be executed with the same strict formalities as the will.

Adopted children will not take a share under a will leaving a gift to 'all my children' if the adoption order is of later date than the signing of the will. A codicil is insufficient to include such adopted child in the gift unless it specifically amends the will to include the name of the adopted child.

A will may always be revoked. Revocation is automatically effected by marriage, unless the will has been made, and is stated to be made, in contemplation of the marriage in question. Revocation may also be effected either by making a subsequent will which expressly revokes the earlier will, or by deliberate destruction.

As a will does not take effect until after the death of the testator, the will is normally construed as though it had been executed on the day on which the testator died. This means, that if John Doe has given Richard Roe a legacy of £100, and Richard Roe 'predeceases', or dies before, the testator, his legacy 'lapses'. It is not payable to his wife or family. There is a peculiar exception to this rule, if the legacy is to a direct descendant of the testator. If the descendant has died during the lifetime of the testator, leaving issue (but not otherwise), the legacy does not lapse, but is paid to the personal representative of the deceased descendant.

When a will sets up a trust in favour of children they will have either a 'vested' or a 'contingent' interest in the estate, dependent on the exact phraseology which has been used. If the benefit to the children is not to lapse if they die before it becomes payable – i.e. if the testator gives his widow a life interest, and after her death leaves the estate 'to my children living at the date of my death and if more than one in equal shares' – each child has a 'vested' interest in his share of the estate. This means that if a child dies during the lifetime of the widow, its share will be payable to its personal representative after the death of the widow. If, on the other hand, the actual words used give his widow a life interest 'and after her death to my children living at the date of my wife's death and if more than one, in equal shares', each child has a 'contingent', as distinct from a 'vested' interest, for the share or interest of each child is then contingent on its surviving the widow. From a practical point of view the difference is important. A beneficiary with a vested interest may sell or mortgage it, but he will not easily do so if it is contingent, unless he gives other security.

A man's property or estate falls into two classes, called real property and personal property. The former consists of freehold estates, described in Chapter 18, and the latter consists, generally speaking, of every other type of property, and all personal effects. Until the passing of the Law of Property Act 1925, there was a vital distinction between the two classes, for when a man died intestate – i.e. without making a will – before 1926, all his real estate passed to his heir at law, while his personal estate was divisible among his next of kin. His eldest son, if there was one, was the heir at law, but his wife and his children, if any, were the next of kin. However, since 1926 this distinction has virtually ceased to exist, and in the absence of a will, all property, both real and personal, is now divisible among the next of kin, whilst the heir at law receives no special privilege.

Before the estate is divided between the next of kin on an intestacy, the widow or widower, if there is one, is entitled to receive the personal chattels and effects of the deceased, which include furniture, jewellery, and clothing. In addition, the surviving spouse will receive a specific capital sum of money, with interest at 4 per cent from the date of death until payment. The amount of this sum may not be more than (a) £5,000 in the case where there is any issue of the marriage which reaches the age of twenty-one years; (b) £20,000 in the case where there is no such issue, but a parent, brother, or sister, (great) nephew or (great) niece who reaches the age of twenty-one years survives. The widow or widower has also a life interest in half the remainder of the estate in case (a), and an absolute interest in half the remainder in case (b). The life interest, when there is one, may generally be capitalized by the widow or widower, who also has a right, which in the majority of cases will be exercisable, to call for the deceased's interest in the matrimonial home to be allocated as *part* of the share mentioned previously.

The next of kin of anyone who has died after 1925 are defined by the provisions of the Administration of Estates Act 1925. They are, in order of precedence: (1) wife or husband of the deceased, (2) children, (3) father and mother, (4) brothers and sisters, (5) half-brothers and sisters, (6) nephews and nieces, (7) grandparents, (8) uncles and aunts, and children or grandchildren of a deceased uncle or aunt. If the death occurs after 1 January 1950 adopted children will rank in the same category as real children, whether the adoption order was before or after that date. If the deceased has died intestate, without leaving a relative within any of these eight degrees, the whole of the property, after payment of the debts, will pass to the Crown – i.e. the estate will fall into the communal chest. No relative who is not within the eight specified degrees is entitled to any share of the estate, and neither a woman living with a man to whom she is not married, nor an illegitimate child, has normally any legal right to a share of the estate. Since 1952 the Inheritance Acts may apply where the deceased has left no will; an innovation which may have the effect of benefiting the issue of any earlier marriage of the deceased. An illegitimate child is, however, entitled to participate in its mother's estate under the Legitimacy Act 1926, when its mother does not leave any legitimate issue.

The exact division of the estate among the next of kin is complicated, and may best be illustrated by examples.

Example 1. John Doe has died intestate leaving surviving him his widow, Joan, and three children, Anne, Bella, and Christopher, or A, B, and C. After payment of John Doe's debts, Joan Doe will receive the sum of £5,000 free of death duties and expenses, and also the personal chattels. The remainder of the estate is then divided into two equal parts, which may be called, respectively, the children's share and the widow's share. They are dealt with as follows:

(1) *The Children's Share*. This is divided equally between A, B, and C, provided they each attain the age of twenty-one, and they will therefore each receive one-sixth of John Doe's estate. If one of the children, A, had died during her father's lifetime, leaving two children, Margaret and Rachel, each of these children will take one-half of the one-sixth share which A would have received if she had survived. If A had died without leaving children, or leaving children all of whom die under the age of twenty-one, her one-sixth share would lapse, and B and C would take the children's share equally between them, and would each receive one-fourth of John Doe's estate.

(2) *The Widow's Share*. Disregarding her right to receive a lump sum representing the value of her life interest, or the matrimonial home in part satisfaction, this share is dealt with in quite a different manner. It must be invested in trustee securities, and the interest received from the securities is payable to Joan Doe during her life, and after her death the share becomes divisible among John Doe's children, in the same proportions as the children's share.

Example 2. John Doe has died leaving his widow, Joan, without children. He has, however, left other next of kin within the eight specified degrees. The widow will receive £20,000 (provided, of course, the estate is worth this much) and the personal chattels, as before, and she is entitled to half the remainder absolutely. The other half will go to his parents if both are living at his death, or if only one is living, then to that one. Should his parents no longer be alive then, if there are brothers and sisters, to them equally. If any brother or sister has died during his lifetime leaving children, the children

K

between them would be entitled to the share which their parent would have received if alive.

Example 3. If John Doe died leaving his widow, and no other next of kin within the eight specified degrees, the widow will be entitled to the whole estate absolutely.

'Let's choose executors, and talk of wills', by all means, but are you now satisfied that, although it is highly desirable for every man to make a will, it is not a job which anyone should endeavour to undertake personally?

27

EXECUTORS, ADMINISTRATORS, AND TRUSTEES

'Now for vexation, and exasperation, and endless trouble.'

Jane Eyre

AFTER the death of a testator, it is the duty of an executor, if he is willing to act, to assume the control and management of the estate and to take steps for its administration. It used to be the practice for the family lawyer to read the will of the deceased after the funeral. There is no obligation to do so, and in the majority of cases it is no longer the practice.

Although an executor has power to act as soon as the testator has died, he should take steps to establish his title as soon as possible. No executor is compelled to act if he does not desire to do so. He may sign a document called a 'renunciation', which will relieve him of any obligation to accept the office. He must, however, make up his mind promptly. If he has once intermeddled in the affairs of the deceased, it may be too late for him to renounce, and if an executor has taken on himself the burden of office, he is not allowed to resign or relinquish his duties.

An executor proves a will – i.e. establishes his title – by making an application to the Probate Registry for a grant of probate of the will. This application must be supported by an affidavit in which the executor undertakes to administer the estate in accordance with the law. He must also make an affidavit giving details of the estate, and schedules are attached setting out particulars of all the assets and liabilities. Details are given in Chapter 28 of the appropriate death duties payable to the Estate Duty Office. These formalities are usually carried out by a lawyer, but the executor may make a personal application for the grant. He will usually do so, however, only if the estate is small and he has plenty of time at his disposal. Personal applications should be made to Ingersoll House, 1 Kingsway, London, W.C.2.

If the deceased has not made a will, or if he has not appointed an executor by his will, no one is empowered to deal with his estate after his death until a grant, called a Grant of Letters of Administration, has been obtained. This grant is also issued out of the Probate Registry. If the deceased has made a will without appointing an executor willing or able to act, the application for administration with the will annexed is usually made by one or two of the residuary legatees – i.e. the persons entitled to share in the residue of the estate – but no grant will be issued to anyone under the age of twenty-one. If there is an intestacy – i.e. if there is no will – the application is usually made by two of the next of kin. In either event the administrators must make affidavits similar to those required from an executor, but, in addition, administrators are obliged to find two sureties willing to guarantee that the administrators will fulfil their legal obligations. The guarantee is given by a 'Surety Bond', which requires the sureties to pay penalties if the administrators do not carry out their legal duties. An administrator may find it invidious to ask friends to stand surety for him. If, however, he decides to ask them to do so, it may be embarrassing to refuse the request. The alternative course for the administrator is to ask an Insurance Company to give the bond. A number of insurance companies specialize in this business. But it entails expense, which may be avoided when an executor has been appointed.

When application is made for Probate the grant may be withheld because a 'caveat' has been lodged. A caveat, or caution, is a notice filed by someone who wishes to oppose the grant on one or other of a number of grounds. These include the following: (1) An allegation that the testator was not of sound mind and understanding when he executed the will, or that he did not appreciate the nature and contents of the document. (2) A claim that the will which is presented for probate is not the last will of the testator. (3) A claim that the will was not duly executed. (4) A claim that the will was procured by undue influence, which means that unfair, or improper, pressure was brought to bear on the testator in order to persuade him to make the will. All these may be grounds for rejecting a will which is offered for Probate.

When a caveat has been entered, and it is not 'subducted' –

i.e. withdrawn – Court proceedings must be taken to establish the validity of the will, and the Court must decide, after it has heard all the evidence, whether or not the will is a valid testamentary instrument.

The onus of upsetting any will is, generally speaking, placed upon the person who impeaches its validity. It is necessary to satisfy the Court by positive evidence, and not by mere hearsay or suspicion, that the testator did not understand or appreciate the nature of his acts, and that the disposition of his property did not represent his free and independent wishes. Unless these facts are proved, the will will usually be admitted to probate, subject to formal proof of due execution in accordance with the requirements described in the last chapter. It will be observed that there is nothing in these limitations which precludes a person of unsound mind from making a will, on condition that the will is made during a lucid interval – i.e. when the testator understands and appreciates the nature of what he is doing.

As a general rule, the production and lodgement in the Probate Registry of the original will is essential before Probate is issued. If, however, the original will has been lost or accidentally destroyed, the Court may make an order, giving leave to prove a copy. In such circumstances the Court will require to be satisfied not only that the copy is a true copy, but also that the original will was duly executed and has not been revoked.

Both the Grant of Probate and Letters of Administration are known as a Grant of Representation, and the executor or the administrator is described as the 'personal representative' of the estate of the deceased. After a Grant of Representation has been obtained, the personal representative must take steps to administer the estate, and his first duty is to pay the debts and funeral expenses.

When an estate is 'insolvent' – i.e. when there are insufficient funds to pay all the debts, let alone the legacies – the unfortunate legatees get nothing, as debts must always be paid in priority to legacies. Special rules exist as to the distribution of an insolvent estate. These provide for the priority in which payment of the debts is to be made, and also the circumstances in which an executor may 'prefer' – i.e. pay one debt in priority to another, or in some cases 'retain' a debt due to himself. These rules are complicated, and any person named as an executor would be wise to renounce the office, if there is any likelihood of the estate being insolvent, unless he wishes to take on a waggon-load of trouble. Proceedings to administer an estate in bankruptcy may be taken by a creditor in proper cases, but any payment made by the administrator prior to the commencement of such proceedings will not, generally speaking, be invalidated by such a course.

In order to protect a personal representative against claims of creditors, after he has completed his administration of the estate, it is necessary for him to insert a notice in the *London Gazette*, which is an official publication, and also in a newspaper circulating in the district in which the deceased had his residence, requiring creditors to notify their claims within a specified period – usually two months. If they do not do so, they may subsequently be barred, and there will be no liability on the personal representative.

After payment of the debts and funeral expenses (and the cost of a memorial stone may not be included as part of the funeral expenses, unless express provision has been made in the will for payment) the personal representative should proceed to deal with any bequests left by the will. When a specific article, such as 'my grandfather clock', is given to Richard Roe by a will made by John Doe, and the clock has been sold or given away between the date of the will and John Doe's death, so that it no longer forms part of John Doe's estate, Richard Roe gets nothing, and he is not entitled to compensation for his loss.

In cases in which there are sufficient assets to pay the debts, but insufficient to pay all the legacies in full, the specific legacies – i.e. the bequest of specific chattels, must first be dealt with, and, thereafter, all the pecuniary legacies must be treated on an equal footing, and must 'abate' rateably. One year from the date of the death is normally allowed for payment of legacies.

When the bequests have been discharged, the personal representative is left with the duty of disposing of the residuary estate. Final accounts must then be prepared. Chapter 28 gives particulars of further affidavits and accounts which are required, and the further duties which must in many cases be paid. When this business has been completed the estate may be finally distributed, and any land or houses comprised in the residuary estate will be 'vested' in the beneficiaries – i.e. the title-deeds will be formally made over to them.

When a trust is created by a will, the duties of the trustee commence, and the duties of the personal representative end, when the funds are 'appropriated' or allocated to the purposes of the trust, if the duties of the personal representative have otherwise been complied with.

Although trusts are frequently created by will, they may, as stated in the previous chapter, be created in other ways, and the rights and obligations of a trustee are largely regulated by the Trustee Act 1925. If you are asked to act as a trustee you would be wise, before you agree to do so, to ascertain precisely what is involved. The duties should never be undertaken lightly, for many burdens are imposed upon every trustee. Here are some of them:

(1) A trustee must make himself familiar with the terms of the trust, since, in general, he is only entitled to act in accordance with the express powers which are given to him.

(2) A trustee is not entitled, as a general rule, to appoint an agent to act in his place. This rule is modified by allowing him to employ qualified agents in proper cases, and also in certain other circumstances when he requires professional advice. For instance, he may employ a solicitor to undertake legal work, an estate agent to negotiate the sale of property, or a stockbroker to carry out the sale of investments.

(3) A trustee is not entitled to act without the concurrence of his co-trustees, if any, nor may he permit his co-trustees to act without his concurrence. If they do so, and a loss results, he may be held liable for a breach of trust, unless they have acted without his knowledge, and without any negligence on his part.

(4) A trustee must act with strict impartiality towards all the beneficiaries, and must not favour one at the expense of another.

(5) A trustee is not permitted, either directly or indirectly,

to make any profit out of his office, unless the trust deed expressly allows him to receive remuneration. If he does so in other cases he may be called upon to pay over any profit he has made to the beneficiaries.

(6) A trustee is under a duty to exercise vigilance over the property of the trust. This means that he must always act with prudence, and if he has a turn for speculation, it is no excuse for him to say that he only dealt with the trust property in the same way as he would have dealt with his own affairs.

(7) A trustee may invest the trust property only in such investments as are authorized by the terms of the trust, or, if no particular securities are specified, he must limit his investments to those which are authorized by the Trustee Act 1925.

(8) If property is lost, or has depreciated in value, as a result of default on the part of the trustee, he may be compelled to make good the loss. The Court, however, has power in a proper case, in which a trustee has acted honestly and reasonably, and ought fairly to be excused for any loss, to relieve him from some or all of this personal liability.

(9) A trustee is always under an obligation to render a full account of his stewardship to his beneficiaries.

(10) A trustee is not entitled to purchase for himself any of the trust property, even although he is prepared to pay a fair price. To permit a trustee to do so would obviously facilitate fraud by a dishonest trustee.

(11) If a trustee once accepts the office – and of course he is not under an obligation to do so, unless he so desires – there are a number of cases in which he cannot retire from the trust without the consent of his co-trustees, although he may be removed by the Court if he acts improperly, or becomes bankrupt, or becomes unfit to act.

In general, a trustee has no power to resort to the capital funds of the trust if the income in insufficient to carry out all the objects of the trust. He may, however, do so in any case in which the trust instrument gives him the power, and when there are infant beneficiaries there are express powers given by the Trustee Act 1925 which permit him to make advances out of capital for their benefit, under certain defined conditions. This Act also gives powers to trustees to apply income, which would otherwise be accumulated, to maintain beneficiaries in need.

A trustee may often find himself perplexed as to how he should act in any given circumstances. He should then seek professional advice, and in proper cases he is entitled to apply to the Court for directions, which may be given at the expense of the trust. He is not entitled to do so, however, if reasonable prudence clearly indicates the course which he should adopt.

The Courts do not allow the terms of trusts to be altered simply because change would be advantageous, for example, to avoid payment of heavy death duties. However, where all the parties benefiting under a trust are over twenty-one years and in full possession of their faculties, the trust may be wound up by unanimous agreement, the funds distributed and the trustees relieved of all further duties.

The number of individual trustees has diminished in recent years. The Public Trustee, acting under the regulations of the Public Trustee Act 1906, and Trust Corporations, including the larger Banks, have all served to relieve individuals from personal responsibility. The nomination of one of these corporate bodies to act as trustee in place of individuals is frequently a wise policy, since it eliminates the difficulty which may always arise on the death of an individual trustee. The rules under which the Public Trustee acts may be obtained from the Public Trustee Office in Kingsway, London, while the conditions under which a Bank will accept nomination, are contained in booklets published by each of the Banks.

Trusts are part of a branch of the English law known as equity, and the administration of trusts falls within what is known as the 'equitable' jurisdiction of the Courts. This was formerly of great importance, but the note on 'Equity' in Appendix 1 explains the circumstances in which equity has now lost most of its distinctive features.

28

TAXES AND DEATH DUTIES

'Alas, regardless of their doom,
The little victims play!
No sense have they of ills to come,
Nor care beyond today.'
Thomas Gray

*Note: The figures given in this chapter are those applicable
after 5 April 1957*

THE most profitable of all taxes, from the point of view of the
State, is Income Tax, which is regulated each year by a Finance
Act founded upon 'the Budget'. The Finance Acts deal with
taxation from 6 April in one year to 5 April in the following
year, and the scope of the various taxes tends to fluctuate year
by year in accordance with the current economic and political
aims of the Government in power. But revenue has to be
raised, and the basic or standard rate of Income Tax has shown
a fairly obdurate stability over the past decade. From April
1946 to April 1951 it was 9*s*. in the £; from April 1951 to
April 1953 9*s*. 6*d*. in the £; from April 1953 to April 1955 9*s*.
again, and since then 8*s*. 6*d*. in the £.

Income Tax is payable not on the whole of your income but
on your 'taxable' income, and you are entitled to certain allowances or 'reliefs' before your taxable income is arrived at.

If you have earned income, which covers wages, salaries,
and pensions and also the profits of any trade or business you
carry on yourself, you are entitled to *Earned Income Relief*. This
is computed on your total earned income less any annual payments (such as ground rents, mortgage interest, or Bank and
Building Society interest) which you have to make out of your
earned income. Annual payments of this nature are treated as
being made out of unearned income, so far as this is available,
and your earned income for the purpose of calculating the
Earned Income Relief will only be reduced to meet the balance
of any annual payments which cannot be met from your unearned income. For example, John Doe earns £1,000 a year
and pays interest of £100 a year on a mortgage of his house.

He has no unearned income. His Earned Income Relief will be based on an earned income of £900. Richard Roe, on the other hand, earns £800 a year, but has unearned income of £200 a year. He also pays mortgage interest of £100 a year. In his case the interest payment is set against the £200 unearned income, and he will be entitled to Earned Income Relief on the whole of his £800 earned income.

The Earned Income Relief is two-ninths of your total earned income, with a maximum high in the surtax range. Your total earned income includes any earned income of your wife, but if your wife is a wage-earner you will also be entitled to an additional special allowance amounting to seven-ninths of your wife's earned income with a maximum of £140. This is known as *Wife's Earned Income Allowance*, and is technically an additional personal allowance.

An allowance corresponding to the Earned Income Relief is given on unearned income when a taxpayer or his wife is over sixty-five years of age and their combined income from all sources does not exceed £700 a year. This is known as an *Age Allowance*. Marginal relief can also be claimed where the total income is in excess of £700, and it is advisable to make a claim for Age Allowance when, in the case of a single person or a widow or widower, the total income is less than £1,078 and in the case of a married man when the amount of the joint income is less than £1,050 all unearned. Total exemption is given when the maximum income does not exceed respectively £250 and £400.

Every income-tax payer is entitled to a *Personal Allowance*. If you are single or a widower it is £140 for the current financial year; if you are a married man it is £240. Normally a husband is liable for tax on the whole of his wife's income, but where a wife is not living with her husband the wife may be separately assessed and charged as if she were unmarried. When husband and wife are divorced, or living apart under a deed of separation, or are separated in such circumstances that the separation is likely to be permanent, each is separately assessed so that the husband cannot claim the married man's allowance of £240. Instead, he will be regarded as a single man and will receive only a single man's personal allowance of £140. The separated or divorced wife will also be entitled to a separate personal allowance of £140 as if she were an unmarried woman. It thus appears that the Government allows a bonus of tax on £40 for immorality. Apart from the case where the wife has earned income, a married couple have a joint personal allowance of £240. If the same man and woman decide instead of marrying to live together 'in sin', each is entitled to a personal allowance of £140, so that their combined allowances will be £280. A curious result!

There is a *Child Allowance* of £100 for every child under eleven, £125 for every child over eleven, but for any child over sixteen who, at the beginning of the tax year, is receiving full-time instruction at a university, school, college, or training establishment or is in apprenticeship or vocational training for not less than two years, £150. The allowance is not given if the child has income in its own right (excluding scholarships or similar educational grants) exceeding £100 a year. The Child Allowance for income-tax purposes has nothing to do with the allowance paid by the Government since August 1946 in respect of every child after the first who is under school-leaving age, now 8s. a week for the second child and 10s. a week for subsequent children.

If you are maintaining a widowed mother, a mother-in-law, or a relative who is incapacitated by old age or infirmity, you may also be entitled to a *Dependent Relative Allowance*. The amount of the allowance depends on the total income of the relative. The maximum is £60, which is paid when the relative's income is £105 a year or less. When it exceeds this figure the allowance is reduced by the amount of the excess, so that if the income of the relative were £165 a year or more no allowance could be claimed. A similar allowance may, in certain circumstances, be claimed towards the maintenance of a relative living with you who does not fall into the category of old or infirm.

If your daughter lives with you and is maintained by you because you or your wife is old or infirm you can claim an allowance of £40 for her. Special consideration is also given to a widower or widow who keeps a female relative or other person as a housekeeper. The *Housekeeper Allowance* is £60, and it is also available in certain circumstances to a married or single man or woman who employs a resident housekeeper to look after children for whom the Child Allowance is claimed.

Allowances are made in respect of *National Insurance Contributions* and *Life Insurance Premiums*. In the latter case the extent of the allowance varies with the size of the premium; if the premiums you pay are more than £25 a year, the allowance given is two-fifths of the premium; if the premium is under £25 p.a. the allowance is on the amount of the actual premium up to a maximum of £10. You are also entitled to relief on any interest you pay to a Bank on an overdraft or to a Building Society on a mortgage, but as mentioned earlier your earned income allowance may be reduced by such payment. Your earned income allowance may also be reduced by the National Insurance contribution allowance, if you have no income taxed at the highest rate.

In some cases, such as in the payment of ground rent or interest on a mortgage, you are bound to deduct income tax at the standard rate before making the payment. In doing so you are acting as an unofficial collector for the Inland Revenue, and you have to account to them for the tax. If you are yourself entitled to tax relief on the amount of the annual payment, as you will be, for instance, in the case of mortgage interest if it is paid out of taxed income, whether earned or unearned, you will be allowed to retain the tax you have deducted. Otherwise you will have to pay it on demand to the Inland Revenue. The person to whom the payment is made is entitled in either case to ask you for a certificate of deduction of tax. This will save him from having to pay tax again on the same money, and if he is not liable to tax at the standard rate, he can claim the appropriate rebate.

When all the permitted allowances have been deducted from the gross income of the taxpayer and his wife, the balance remaining is called the *Taxable Income*, that is to say the income upon which tax is payable. The whole of this taxable income is not, however, charged at the full standard rate of 8s. 6d. in the £. The first £60 is charged at 2s. 3d. in the £, the next £150 at 4s. 9d. in the £, and the next £150 at 6s. 9d. in the £. Any taxable income over £360 has to bear income tax at the full standard rate of 8s. 6d. in the £.

Where a taxpayer's total income from all sources does not exceed £300 a year his tax liability will be reduced by an amount equal to tax at the standard rate on two-ninths of his income. In other words, he will receive the benefit of the Earned Income Allowance, at the standard rate of tax, whether he has earned income or not. There is marginal relief where the income exceeds £300 but is less than £397 a year.

If your gross income exceeds £2,000 a year, you come into the surtax range. Surtax is really an additional income tax. On the first £500 of income over £2,000 the surtax is 2s. in the £, and it rises by degrees to 10s. 6d. in the £ on incomes of more than £20,000. Earned Income Relief may reduce surtax liability, as has been mentioned.

An example may help to explain the very intricate system of taxation and allowances.

John Doe is married with two children of seven and nine and one child of seventeen receiving full-time instruction at a technical training college. He earns £1,100 a year as an engineer and receives approximately £47 a year (18s. a week) from the Government as Family Allowance for the younger children. This Family Allowance is treated as Earned Income, so that his earned income is £1,147 a year. His wife Joan Doe also works part time and is paid £135 a year, which brings their total earned income to £1,282 a year.

In addition, John Doe has an income of £200 a year under his uncle's will (received without any deduction of tax at source), and £15 a year as interest on a post office savings account.

He has bought a house which is assessed under Schedule A (see p. 175) at £60 a year, but he has had to raise £2,000 on a mortgage and pays interest at 6 per cent less tax. He has also insured his life for £2,000, so that the mortgage can be paid off if he should die before he has repaid all he has borrowed, and he pays a life assurance premium of £80 a year.

John Doe's income-tax liability will be calculated as shown on the opposite page.

John Doe will thus have to pay to the Inland Revenue the

sum of £155 18s., but he will be allowed to retain the tax he has deducted in paying his mortgage interest, because he has paid tax on £148 of his income at 8s. 6d. in the £. This will amount to £120 at 8s. 6d., i.e. £51. The income tax actually borne by John Doe will therefore be £155 18s. less £51, i.e. £104 18s.

		£	£
Earned Income:			
Salary – John Doe			1,100
Joan Doe .			135
Family Allowances			47
Total Earned Income			£1,282
Unearned Income (including £50 Schedule A Assessment for house)			265
Total Income from all sources			£1,547
Less Allowances and Reliefs:			
National Insurance Contribution (John Doe only)		12	
Earned Income Relief (2/9ths of Total Earned Income)		285	
Wife's Earned Income Allowance (7/9ths of wife's salary)		105	
Personal Allowance		240	
Child Allowance (2 children under 11 years, 1 child 17 years old receiving full-time education		350	
Life Assurance Relief (2/5ths of premium) .		32	
Post Office Savings Interest (up to £15) .		15	
			1,039
Taxable Income			£508

Tax Payable:	£	s.	d.
£60 at 2s. 3d.	6	15	0
£150 at 4s. 9d.	35	12	6
£150 at 6s. 9d.	50	12	6
£148 at 8s. 6d.	62	18	0
Tax payable to Inland Revenue . .	£155	18	0

How are these calculations worked into the scheme of 'Pay as You Earn' or P.A.Y.E.? P.A.Y.E., which was introduced in 1943, is not a substitute for income tax but a system designed to facilitate collection of the tax. The employer acts as the agent of the Inland Revenue. He is bound to deduct the appropriate amount of tax from the wages or salaries of his employees and to pay it over to the Inland Revenue. But no employer could be expected to work out in detail the tax liability of each member of his staff, and the actual assessment is made by the Inspector of Taxes. The employee is given a code number based upon the Inspector's estimate of the allowances, other than Earned Income Relief, to which the employee will be entitled during the following year. The estimate and thus the code number can be adjusted at any time before or during the tax year concerned to take into account changes in allowances.

The fixing of the code number is only the first stage in the P.A.Y.E. calculations. Your employer must know how much to deduct from your wages or salary each pay day. For this purpose every employer is given a series of tax tables from which he can calculate the proportion of the allowances which are due on each pay day, including the Earned Income Relief, and the tax payable by the employee. The system is worked on a cumulative basis. For instance, if you are paid monthly the calculation in the second month of the tax year will be based on your salary for both the first and the second month. The tax tables will show your employer the tax due for these two months, and the tax payable for the second month will be arrived at by deducting from this figure the tax already paid for the first month. If your allowances have increased or you have been away sick the tax due at the end of the second month may be less than the amount you have already paid in tax for the first month. In that case your employer must pay you the difference.

The P.A.Y.E. system works fairly smoothly in practice, and although it may be one further cause of headaches to employers, the average taxpayer is relieved to know that when he has received his wages or salary he has no further tax demands to meet in respect of his earnings.

Income tax is levied under a number of different headings or Schedules, known as Schedules A, B, C, D, and E.

Schedule A is the tax levied on the annual value of property – namely, lands and property such as houses – of which the taxpayer is the owner. This has been dealt with in Chapter 16 and above.

Schedule B is a tax levied on the occupation of land, except where the land is used for the purposes of husbandry (farming) or some other commercial purpose. The assessments are based on one-third of the annual value.

Schedule C. This schedule deals with tax on dividends, interest, annuities, etc., payable in the United Kingdom, out of public funds or out of the public funds of any other country. Income tax is deducted at the source in respect of income which arises under this schedule – i.e. the taxpayer only receives the net amount after deduction of tax.

Schedule D is tax collected on income from trades and professions (including farming), and also Bank and Post Office interest, and interest on certain Government securities, such as War Loan, from which tax is not deducted at the source. It also includes tax on income derived from foreign securities and possessions, excess rents, furnished lettings, and all other income not assessed under any other Schedule. Every trader must submit annual accounts to the Revenue, in order that his tax liability may be assessed under Schedule D. If he fails to render accounts he may be assessed at such figure as appears reasonable to the Income Tax authorities. He has a right of appeal from an arbitrary assessment, but if he appeals, he must show that the figures upon which he has been assessed are incorrect, and he can, normally, do this only if he has accounts to submit which will prove the correct figures.

Schedule E. This is tax levied on income from employment, pensions, etc. All tax payable under this Schedule comes within the scope of P.A.Y.E., and is now deducted at source.

There is a right of appeal from every assessment for income tax. The appeal is generally heard before a tribunal presided over by experts called Special Commissioners. If aggrieved at their decision, the taxpayer may appeal to the High Court on any question of law. The decision of the Commissioners is, however, final on questions of fact.

If you receive all your income from dividends on stocks and shares of companies, income tax will, as you have seen, be deducted before payment. In such a case, you will not have received the allowances to which you are entitled. You may, however, make a claim to the Inspector of Taxes for an appropriate refund of the overpaid tax. A similar application may be made if you have received only part of your allowance. The necessary form to enable you to apply for the refund may be obtained from your local Inspector of Taxes. He will also give you assistance in completing it.

When in 1941 personal allowances were cut, the Government promised that the loss sustained would be repaid to each taxpayer after the War, and to implement this promise, Post-war Credit Certificates were issued for each of the years 1941–2 to 1945–6 inclusive, showing the amount payable to each taxpayer, as soon as the Government considered it expedient to do so. Since 1946 repayment of Post-war Credit Certificates has been made to men when they attain the age of sixty-five and to women when they become sixty, or to the estate of a deceased person at such time as the qualifying age would have been reached.

The most prolific source of Revenue after income tax and surtax is that which flows from estate, i.e. death duties. Prior to April 1946 these duties were levied on the estate of everyone who died leaving property of a value in excess of a gross sum of £100, but by the Finance Act 1946, every person who died on or after 10 April 1946 was entitled to total exemption if his estate did not exceed £2,000. The rate of duty on the estates of persons dying after 29 July 1954 is 1 per cent of the net value of an estate over £3,000 and not exceeding £4,000, 2 per cent of an estate over £4,000 and not exceeding £5,000, 3 per cent of an estate over £5,000 and not exceeding £7,500, 4 per cent of an estate over £7,500 and not exceeding £10,000. Thereafter the scale rises more steeply and reaches 75 per cent in the case of an estate in excess of £750,000. The duty is payable on the value, as at the date of death, of all property, both real and personal, left by the deceased, and also on settled property, whilst interest at the rate of 2 per cent is charged on the amount of the duty, from the date of death until the date of payment. Estate duty on all property except land and buildings must be paid before a Grant of Representation can be obtained, and as it is not permissible to deal with the assets of a deceased person before the issue of the Grant, it is often expedient to arrange for an advance from Bankers of the necessary sums. Duty payable on land need not, however, be paid immediately, but may be deferred and paid by instalments over a period of eight years, or in some cases the land itself or part of it may be surrendered to the Government on account of death duties due on the whole estate. Country mansions have been acquired in this way.

Some of the formalities required in order to obtain a Grant of Representation to the estate of a deceased person were described in Chapter 27. For Estate Duty purposes, a list of the assets, together with their respective values, calculated as at the date of death, is scheduled to an affidavit, called the Inland Revenue Affidavit. This affidavit also contains details of the debts and funeral expenses of the deceased, and after it has been sworn by the person making the application for the grant, it is submitted to the Inland Revenue. The Revenue then calculate the amount of the Estate Duty payable on the net value of the estate – i.e. after deduction of the debts and funeral expenses.

Legacy and Succession Duty was formerly payable in addition to Estate Duty, but it was cancelled altogether by the Finance Act of 1949 in respect of a death occurring not before 30 July 1949.

After the legacies have been paid, the personal representative may be in a position to wind-up the estate. It frequently happens, however, in the course of the administration that additional assets come to light, or other assets are found to have been over- or under-valued. In all these cases another affidavit, called a 'corrective affidavit', must be filed giving details of the items which require correction. The additional duty must then be paid, or overpaid duty reclaimed, as the case may be.

If the deceased has made any gift for public or charitable purposes within one year before the date of his death, estate duty is chargeable on the value of the gift. Other gifts, if any, which have been made at any time during the last five years of his life are also subject to payment of estate duty, unless they do not exceed an aggregate sum of £500. Such gifts will not, however, be liable for estate duty, if they were part of the reasonable normal expenditure of the deceased. For example, if the deceased had been in the habit of making one of his children a voluntary allowance of £150 a year, none of the five annual instalments paid by him during the last five years of his life would attract estate duty. Gifts made in consideration of marriage are also exempt.

If the deceased has made a settlement of property during his life, and has retained any interest in the settled property which ceases on his death, or from the termination of which a benefit accrues to some other person, duty will be payable on the value of the settled fund on his death, as it is classed as property which passes on death.

The rate of duty which is payable on any estate is assessed on the 'aggregate' value of all the property which 'passes on the death'. For example, if John Doe dies leaving an estate which consists of a freehold house valued at £3,000 and personal estate valued at £6,500, the gross value of the estate will be £9,500. If the debts and funeral expenses are £800, the net personalty will be £5,700 and the value of the estate for duty purposes will be £8,700. If, however, John Doe had made a gift of £1,000 to one of his children two years before he died, and had also settled a sum of £5,000 on another child several years previously, providing for the settled fund to pass to the child for its own use and benefit absolutely on John Doe's death, both of these amounts must be 'aggregated', or taken into account, before the appropriate rate of duty is assessed. In that event, the aggregate value of the estate for duty purposes will not be £8,700, but will be £8,700 plus £1,000 plus £5,000 (or the market value of the settled property at the date of John Doe's death) – viz. £14,700 in all. Estate Duty on an estate of £8,700 is at the rate of 4 per cent, but Estate Duty on an estate of £14,700 is 8 per cent. Estate Duty at the rate of 8 per cent will therefore be immediately payable on £5,700, being the value of the net personalty. Payment on the sum of £3,000, being the value of the realty, may, as stated, be deferred, whilst the estate will not be liable for the duty payable on the gift of £1,000, or on the duty payable on the settled property. In the former case the duty is payable by the beneficiary of the gift, and in the latter case the duty is payable out of the settled fund.

While most of us are pestered with direct and indirect taxation and nearly always feel that we are up against a brick wall, many firms and companies and wealthy individuals spend large sums on obtaining expert advice to minimize tax and death duty liability. Tax dodging has come in the popular view to mean not contravening the law but going round it. The Royal Commission on the Taxation of Profits and Income which published its final report in the summer of 1955 advocated no great reforms in the law of Income Tax, but listed ninety recommendations for changes in detailed respects. Among these are suggestions that expenses allowable for wage-earners and salaried workers should be *reasonably* and not only *necessarily* incurred, that Schedule A assessments of house property should be capable of annual revision, that everyone in business should keep at least simple accounts and that a wife should sign the part of her husband's return relating to her own income. The members of the Commission were not unanimous in all their conclusions, and in any case there is a gap which is sometimes a gulf between the report of a Royal Commission and a change in the Law.

Our forefathers felt at least as bitterly about taxation as we do. This is what Sidney Smith, who died a hundred years ago, had to say on the subject of American taxation at that time: 'The schoolboy whips his taxed top – the beardless youth manages his taxed horse, with a taxed bridle on a taxed road; and the dying Englishman, pouring his medicine, which has paid 7 per cent, into a spoon which has paid 15 per cent – flings himself back upon his chintz bed, which has paid 22 per cent – and expires in the arms of an apothecary who has paid a licence of £100 for the privilege of putting him to death.'

Table of Some of the More Usual Stamp Duties and Taxes

Agreement under hand, not chargeable under any other heading	6d.
Agreement under Seal. *See* Deed.	
Bill of Exchange payable on demand or within three days after date or sight – any amount . . .	2d.
Bills of Exchange, other than above, and other than Foreign Bills of Exchange	1s. per £100
Bills of Exchange – Foreign	6d. per £100
Companies – Capital share duty . . .	10s. per £100
Loan Capital	2s. 6d. per £100
Cheques	2d.

Contract note for the sale or purchase of Stocks and Shares:

 Transactions under £100 . . . . . 1s.

 Transactions in excess of £100 on a rising scale up to £1 in respect of a transaction of £20,000.

Conveyance on Sale of Property . . . £2 per £100

 (Where the price does not exceed £3,500 and is so certified in the document, stamp duty is 10s. per cent, up to £4,250 £1 per cent, up to £5,000 £1 10s. per cent.)

Deed of any kind, not chargeable under any other heading . . . . 10s.

Estate Duty. *See* Text of this chapter.

Income Tax. *See* Text of this chapter.

Lease – exceeding 35 years . . . . £2 per £100 of rent

Lease (Counterpart) . . . . . 5s.

Legacy Duty. *See* Text of this chapter.

Marriage Licence. *See* Chapter 24.

Mortgages . . . . 5s. per £100

Power of Attorney . . . . . 10s.

Promissory Note . . . . . 1s. per £100

Receipts – £2 or upwards . . . . 2d.

Settlement (other than a voluntary Conveyance) . 5s. per £100

Transfer of Stocks and Shares and other Securities unless otherwise adjudicated . . . £2 per £100

Note.—Agreements under hand and deeds must, generally speaking, be stamped within thirty days of execution, or they are subject to a penalty.

29

CRIMINAL PROCEDURE AND THE
FUNCTION OF THE JURY

> '*The Inquisitor (blandly):* Master de Courcelles, the Maid
> alleges that she paid handsomely for the Bishop's
> horse, and that if he did not get the money, the fault
> was not hers. As that may be true, the point is one on
> which the Maid may well be acquitted.
>
> *Courcelles:* Yes, if it were an ordinary horse, but the
> Bishop's horse! How can she be acquitted for that?
> (He sits down again, bewildered and discouraged.)'
>
> Bernard Shaw: *St Joan*

A CRIME is an offence against the community. The Criminal
Law and the Civil Law are two separate branches of our judicial system, and both consist of a mixture of Common Law and
Statute Law, which frequently overlap. When a crime is committed, it is the prerogative of the Criminal Law to punish the
offender, in order to protect the community, and not to provide a remedy for the injured party. Murder, arson, forgery,
theft, and the rest of the criminal catalogue are not specifically
dealt with in this book, and, although crime marches on, it is
to be hoped that John Citizen will be satisfied to view these injuries to the community from a safe seat in the jury box. Some
Sunday newspapers will always provide lurid colour in their
reports of the more salacious type of crime, if this is what you
desire.

This chapter is limited to the background of criminal procedure. It may not only help you to understand the legal steps
which lead a defendant to the dock, but may also assist you to
understand your function, if you are summoned to sit on a
jury in a criminal case.

The scales of justice are often said to be unfairly weighted
against the defendant in a criminal case. It is alleged that all the
resources of the State are employed against him, in order to
secure a conviction. This does not, in fact, present a true picture of criminal administration. The legal machine may not
have a soul, but when you deal with crime, sentiment is easily
misplaced. You are dealing with offences committed by a

member of the community who would in many cases scorn
pity, and would not thank you for expressing in public your
private view that he is a 'poor devil'. This, however, does not
mean that justice is not tempered with mercy.

In theory, the State or 'Regina' – i.e. the Queen – is the pro-
secuting authority in every criminal case. 'Reg. *versus* Doe' or
'Reg. *versus* Roe' will be the name of the case where John Doe
or Richard Roe is charged with a criminal offence. Legally, any
member of the community may set the Criminal Law in motion for certain offences. In these cases he will have the assistance of the State machine in marshalling the evidence, but he
must be prepared to sign the charge sheet and give evidence in
Court. If he wishes, he may instruct his own solicitors and
counsel to conduct the prosecution. A private prosecution always involves a certain amount of danger, however, for if it
fails there is a risk of a civil action being brought by the accused man for damages for malicious prosecution, a class of
action referred to in Chapter 15. An Act of Parliament has
abolished private informers, but this does not affect the right
to bring a private prosecution. What the Act did was to end
the right, which a private prosecutor had in some cases, to
claim for himself the penalty which the offender was bound by
law to pay. The State will itself usually institute a prosecution
when the mischief directly affects the Government, or the welfare of the community. For example, if the police catch a burg-
lar, they will usually prosecute him. If, however, an employer
has a dishonest employee who has been guilty of embezzlement – i.e. the appropriation of money which belongs to the
employer – the latter is usually expected to institute a private
prosecution, if he wishes criminal action to be taken. He is entitled, however, to wonder why he should be compelled to do
so, when he pays rates for a police force and taxes for a Director of Public Prosecutions.

When the Criminal Law is once set in motion, it is not, as a
rule, permissible to withdraw a charge. Indeed, it is not even
lawful to hold out a promise not to institute proceedings if restitution is made of stolen property, and for this reason it is an
offence to offer a reward for its return, stating that 'No questions will be asked'. This contrasts with proceedings in a Civil

Court, which may always be abandoned or compromised on terms.

Incidentally, it may here be noted that if you find a valuable article you are not allowed to keep it, and if you do so you may be prosecuted for theft. Your duty is to take it to a police-station.

There are a large number of safeguards designed to secure fair treatment of a man accused of a crime. They will facilitate his acquittal, unless the facts proved against him, by evidence, establish his guilt beyond all reasonable doubt.

It is, of course, ridiculous to suggest that innocent men are never convicted of a crime. No legal system operated by man can secure such a result, and we must be alive to the fact that either you or I may at any time be caught in the machinery of the law, and convicted of an offence which we have never committed. Such a contingency does not justify condemnation of a system which is necessarily subject to human judgement, and if this complacent view exasperates a victim who has been found guilty of a crime which he has never committed, it is an incontrovertible fact. Nobody blames the law when lightning strikes and causes irreparable injury to an innocent man. An act of God is accepted as inevitable. We do not always appreciate that an act of man may be equally inevitable, when it is a sequel to fallible human intelligence. In addition to inevitable human limitations, there is also the danger which arises when a judicial official regards the evidence of every police-constable as 'testimony from heaven'.

Under the English legal system every man is deemed to be innocent until he is proved to be guilty. Other nations have other systems, but the majority of English people would undoubtedly prefer ten guilty men to be acquitted as a result of this assumption, than allow one innocent man to be condemned by the 'wild justice of revenge'. The effect of the system is to deprive the police of power to subject any person to what are known as 'third degree' methods, when they intend to charge him with the commission of a crime. If a defendant wants to 'talk', he is permitted to do so, but nothing in the way of a confession may, generally speaking, be used in any proceedings subsequently brought against him, unless it can first be proved that he was warned, in clear terms, and before making the confession, that it might subsequently be used in evidence.

Lawyers rate highly our constitutional right of liberty, and it is the rule, rather than the exception, for a prisoner – i.e. a man deprived of his liberty – to be released on bail until his trial takes place. He will usually only be refused bail for good reason. A man on trial on a charge of murder is always remanded in custody, for he would have no incentive to surrender himself to his bail to undergo a trial which might deprive him of any further interest in freedom, if not life itself. Bail may also be refused in any case when there are reasonable grounds to suspect that the prisoner will not attend to stand his trial. This danger may always exist if the prisoner has no fixed address, for in such a case it may not be difficult for him to find shelter with associates in the underworld. Bail may also be refused if the police suspect that the prisoner will tamper with the witnesses and induce them through fear, or otherwise, to withhold the truth.

Bail may also be refused in a grave charge, such as rape, or some big financial case, where a very large sum is involved, unless someone stands 'surety' in a substantial sum. 'Surety' is a security which is given, by recognizance or bond, by a third party, to secure the defendant's attendance at the trial, when he is granted bail. If John Doe is remanded on bail, conditional on his finding a surety for £50, it means he must find a friend who is worth that sum, and is willing to stand bail for him. If John Doe does not subsequently attend to stand his trial, the bail may be 'estreated' – i.e. the surety may be ordered to forfeit the sum of £50. In cases of stealing, or receiving stolen goods, which have not been recovered, bail is usually only granted on a 'surety' for a sum up to or nearly equal to the value of the missing property.

It is not necessarily the mark of a good citizen to deplore the occasions when a prisoner is remanded in custody before he has been proved guilty of the offence with which he has been charged. The conception may outrage your feelings, but to set a man at liberty with little assurance of his attending to stand his trial, is to permit sentiment to dominate intelligence. The refusal of bail does not in any way affect the subsequent trial, and if a prisoner is aggrieved by the refusal to grant bail, or if bail is only offered at an excessive sum, he has a right of application to a High Court Judge. When an application of this kind is made, it is considered of such importance that it usually takes precedence over all other business before the Court on that day.

In every criminal case the prosecution must prove by evidence that the defendant is guilty of the offence with which he is charged. Unless the evidence brought before the Court satisfies the jury that the charge has been proved beyond all reasonable doubt, the defendant is entitled to be acquitted. For this reason there is nothing unethical in a barrister undertaking the defence of a defendant, even although the latter has privately confessed his guilt. The English Criminal Law only recognizes the guilt of a defendant when the offence has been proved by evidence, given in accordance with strict rules of procedure. A defendant is always formally asked whether he wishes to plead 'guilty' or 'not guilty' to the charge made against him and, unless the defendant elects to put forward a plea of 'guilty' in open Court, nothing may be assumed against him. Every fact must be strictly proved. If he does plead guilty, or when he has been found guilty, the prisoner can ask for other similar offences to be taken into consideration. This does not enable the Judge to give a heavier sentence, but does ensure that the prisoner will not later be brought to trial for such offences so taken into consideration. In a murder case the Court is always reluctant to accept a plea of 'guilty', and will exert its influence to induce the prisoner to plead 'not guilty', in order that the jury may hear the witnesses, and be satisfied that their evidence justifies the Court in pronouncing sentence, which for certain kinds of murder remains the death sentence.

When criminal proceedings are initiated, the defendant is usually charged on a warrant or a summons. The former authorizes the arrest of the defendant. In all cases of felony (defined below) the police have power of arrest without a warrant. Normally, a man who is arrested is entitled to demand particulars of the offence with which he is charged, and he must be brought before a magistrate within twenty-four hours of his arrest. Otherwise a civil action may be brought by the prisoner for false imprisonment. A summons is issued in less serious cases, and a defendant is then required to attend the Court to answer a specified charge on a specified date. If he fails to appear, a warrant may then be issued for his arrest.

Before a defendant is brought before a jury, the prosecution must call evidence to prove a *prima facie* case of guilt at a preliminary inquiry. This preliminary inquiry takes place at a Magistrate's Court or a Court of Petty Sessions, and the general functions of this Court are considered in the next chapter. The Court is presided over by a paid magistrate in London and in the larger towns, and by at least two unpaid magistrates called Justices of the Peace, or J.P.s, in other areas. They hear the evidence brought to support the charge, and decide whether it is sufficient to justify a committal for trial. It is not necessary for the defendant to put forward any defence. He is entitled to do so, but as the only purpose of the preliminary inquiry is to arrive at a preliminary decision, he may be frequently advised to 'reserve his defence'. Criticism is sometimes offered a system which is said to require a defendant to undergo two trials. This criticism is founded on false premises, as there are not two trials. The preliminary hearing is *not* a trial, but is conducted for the benefit of the defendant. Unless the Court is satisfied that a *prima facie* case has been established, he is entitled forthwith to be discharged, and in such a case he is never placed on his trial at all. The preliminary hearing may be held with the public (including press reporters) excluded from the Court, but this is not the general rule.

In certain cases of a minor character the defendant has no right of trial by jury. All other cases are called 'indictable offences', and some of them, such as murder, manslaughter, rape, bigamy, and forgery, must always be tried on indictment before a jury. There are, however, numerous indictable offences, such as larceny, receiving, false pretences, and certain kinds of indecency, when a defendant may be dealt with in the Magistrate's Court, if he so wishes, and if the Magistrate's Court considers it a proper case for summary trial. But if he claims his right of trial by jury, he is entitled to it, and in such cases, after the preliminary inquiry has taken place, he is committed to the Sessions or Assizes, if a *prima facie* case is established.

English Law classifies crime either as treason, felony, or misdemeanour. Treason is an attack upon the safety of the State, or the Queen as its head. The distinction between felony and misdemeanour is hard to define, and in serious need of revision. Broadly speaking, crimes of gravity, such as murder, manslaughter, theft, embezzlement, and forgery, are classified as felony, and lesser offences are called misdemeanours, but the changing character and habits of the community through the years have resulted in many strange anachronisms in these classifications. For example, riots, bribery, perjury, and many serious frauds are all grouped under the heading of 'misdemeanours'. Whatever the nature of the offence, however, it must be precisely specified in the 'indictment' when a defendant is committed for trial.

In a case of gravity the Court may give directions for a defendant to be represented by solicitor and counsel, at the expense of the State, if he himself is unable to pay for their employment. It is sometimes suggested that lawyers who accept this task are no match for leading members of the Bar who may be briefed on behalf of the Crown. This charge is not a fair one. In many cases, eminent members of the Bar undertake the defence, and few prisoners who are so defended have reasonable grounds to contend that it is not adequately conducted, even if they are subsequently found guilty.

A defendant may be tried at the Central Criminal Court, at Assizes (in Liverpool and Manchester at the Crown Courts), or at Quarter Sessions. The Central Criminal Court, or the 'Old Bailey', as it is usually called, has general jurisdiction to try defendants in respect of offences committed, roughly speaking, in the Greater London area or outside of England. Cases of exceptional importance from other parts of England may also, on occasion, be tried at the Old Bailey. The Court is presided over either by a High Court Judge or by one of a number of Judges who have been specially appointed. Assizes are held at the County Towns in England and Wales three or four times a year. They are usually presided over by a Judge of the High Court, who travels from London, and they have jurisdiction to deal with civil as well as criminal cases. The Crown Courts at Liverpool and Manchester are presided over by a full-time Recorder. These Courts replace Assizes for their particular areas. A Recorder is a judicial officer. County Quarter Sessions are composed of Justices of the Peace, usually presided over by a paid Chairman, who is a lawyer, and cases at Borough Quarter Sessions are tried by a Recorder, who is usually a practising barrister.

When a defendant is sent for trial, he may be committed either to the Old Bailey or Sessions in London, to Assizes or Quarter Sessions outside of London, or as mentioned to the Crown Courts. Although the less serious offences are usually tried at Quarter Sessions, there is, in general, no hard-and-fast rule, and sometimes it is a case of expediency as to which Court is likely to give the defendant an earlier trial.

When a defendant is brought up for trial he is placed in the hands of the jury – normally twelve men or women, but reduced during the war to seven. All natural-born British subjects, being men or women between twenty-one and sixty-five, are liable to serve as jurors, if they fulfil the necessary qualifications. Most property-owners or ratepayers are qualified, but members of certain professions are exempt from jury service. The names of all qualified persons are marked on the electors' lists, which may be inspected in Town Halls and Public Libraries. If your name is on the list, and you have not had it removed, you are compelled to serve if you are summoned to sit on a jury, even if you are over sixty-five years of age. You are, however, entitled to receive a fee as a contribution towards expenses and loss of earnings.

When you are on a jury, and you take your place in the witness-box, you will be sworn, without fear or favour, to try the issue joined between 'Our Sovereign Lady the Queen and the prisoner at the bar'. The jury are not lawyers, and are not asked to decide upon questions of law. It is their function to try issues of fact, and the law is left to the Judge. It is his duty to safeguard the defendant, by refusing to allow any evidence to be heard which is not given in strict accordance with the rules of evidence. In criminal cases these rules operate almost entirely in favour of the defendant. Hearsay evidence is never admissible. Richard Roe as a witness must not say, 'I was told by Mr Doe that he saw the prisoner take the stolen jewellery'. The only person who is entitled to give this evidence is Mr Doe himself. The reason is that every witness must submit himself to cross-examination – *i.e.* examination by the opposing Counsel – in order that the truth of his statements may be tested. If Richard Roe were permitted to give evidence of statements made to him by John Doe, Counsel would have no opportunity of testing the truth of the statements.

When John Doe says, 'I saw the prisoner take the stolen jewellery', his evidence is called direct evidence. When he says, 'I saw the prisoner leave the premises, and a few seconds later I heard the jeweller call out that a diamond brooch had been stolen', the evidence is called circumstantial. It is frequently impossible to obtain direct evidence of a crime, and circumstantial evidence – i.e. evidence from which it is fair to draw inferences of fact – is admissible, even although the same weight is not to be attached to it as to direct evidence.

Another rule of evidence, particularly applicable to criminal cases, does not allow anything to be said during the course of the trial as to any previous conviction recorded against the defendant, or to suggest he is of bad character, unless he himself has put his character in issue by giving evidence of good character, or has attacked the character of a witness for the prosecution. This rule is imposed to protect a defendant of bad character from the prejudice of a jury learning of a previous conviction. If such evidence were allowed it would tend to relieve the prosecution of its bounden duty to prove the guilt of the defendant in respect of the specific charge for which he is on trial. For the same reason, the failure of the defendant to give evidence in his own defence must not be criticized by Counsel, but the Judge may comment unfavourably on it in his summing up, provided such comment does not amount to a misdirection to the jury. Nor may the prosecution normally refer to any statement by the defendant confessing his guilt, unless, as previously stated, it is abundantly clear that, when it was made, the defendant fully appreciated the possibility of its subsequent use in evidence. It is entirely his prerogative to give evidence if he so desires, and there is no obligation upon him to do so.

When the evidence has been concluded, the jury will hear speeches from the Counsel engaged in the case, and after Counsels' speeches have been delivered, the Judge will 'sum up' the case to the jury. This means that he must summarize the evidence, and direct the jury on the matters which they have to take into consideration, before they arrive at their decision.

The jury must always endeavour to remain impartial, and to keep an open mind, until the conclusion of the case. After the summing-up, and when they retire to consider their verdict, they should endeavour to arrive at unanimity, as otherwise they must be discharged from giving a verdict, and the trial will have been abortive. In considering their verdict, it is not part of the function of a jury to take into consideration the consequences of a verdict of 'guilty'. The punishment which follows the verdict is a matter for the Judge, acting according to defined rules. The jury, however, have the right to make a recommendation to mercy if they so desire, and in a case in which a plea is made and supported by evidence that the prisoner was insane, they may return a verdict of 'guilty but insane', meaning that he was unable to understand and appreciate the nature of his acts at the time when the crime was committed.

If a jury disagrees and is discharged, a fresh jury may be convened to re-try the case. If the second jury fail to reach agreement, the Crown will almost invariably withdraw the prosecution.

Since the jury are entitled to find against the defendant only if there is evidence to support the finding, it is the duty of the Judge, as a matter of law, to withdraw a case from the jury, or to direct them to return a verdict of 'not guilty', if there is no evidence to support a verdict of 'guilty'. If, however, there is some evidence to justify conviction, it is for the jury to decide whether the evidence satisfies them, beyond all reasonable doubt, that the defendant is guilty of the offence with which he has been charged. There is no such thing in law as 'giving the defendant the benefit of the doubt'. When a Justice of the

Peace expresses himself in this way, he shows his lack of legal training, for if there is insufficient evidence to justify conviction, the defendant is entitled to acquittal as of right, and not as a benevolent favour.

If a defendant is found not guilty, he is entitled to his immediate discharge, and the case is finished and cannot be reopened. The prosecution is not entitled to appeal from the verdict, and if new evidence comes to light on the following day, there is nothing to be done about the matter. A defendant may never in any circumstances be tried a second time for an offence of which he has once been acquitted.

If a verdict of guilty is returned, the case is not, however, necessarily at an end. A convicted prisoner is entitled to appeal to the Court of Criminal Appeal, on a question of law. He is also permitted to appeal on the ground that his sentence is excessive, although in that event the Court may increase the sentence, if they do not agree with his views, and consider that the trial Judge has been unduly lenient. A prisoner is not, however, permitted to appeal when he disputes a finding of fact, as facts are for the jury to decide, and it is not ordinarily the function of any Judge to reverse the decision of a jury. The prisoner is entitled, however, to contend that the Judge 'misdirected' the jury – i.e. that he did not put the case properly before them – when he delivered his summing-up, or he may appeal on the ground that evidence was improperly admitted, or that during the course of the trial the Judge arrived at an erroneous decision on a question of law. It is also permissible for him to submit that there was no admissible evidence on which it was possible for the jury to find a verdict of guilty. For example, suppose the jury had returned their verdict on the evidence of Richard Roe, as the only witness, and his evidence had been that he was told by John Doe that he had seen the prisoner stealing the jewellery. This, as stated, is inadmissible evidence. No Judge would admit it, except in a moment of mental aberration, and if he had, in fact, done so, the Court of Appeal would upset the verdict. In some cases an appellant may argue that the verdict of the jury was perverse. He may contend that, on the evidence, no reasonable body of men could possibly have returned a verdict of 'guilty'. As, however, the Court of

Appeal does not interfere with a verdict when there is properly admissible evidence on which the conviction could be founded, it will be very slow to allow an appeal in such a case. It will not do so merely because it might itself have arrived at a different decision. It is the privilege of a prisoner to be tried by his equals, and he is not entitled to appeal from their verdict, if it does not suit him, provided the rules governing the trial have been strictly observed.

An appeal from the Court of Criminal Appeal will lie to the House of Lords in exceptional cases only. Leave to appeal must be obtained from the Attorney-General, the principal Law Officer of the Crown, and it will be granted only in a case which involves a point of law of exceptional public importance.

We may summarize a prisoner's position by describing the protection given to him as 'the seven safeguards', viz.:

(1) The prisoner is deemed to be innocent until he is proved to be guilty.

(2) The prosecution must prove its case by admissible evidence, and not by assumptions.

(3) The prisoner may not ordinarily be placed upon trial, unless a preliminary hearing has established a *prima facie* case of guilt against him.

(4) The prisoner may ask for free legal defence in any case of gravity, if he is himself unable to afford the expense.

(5) No evidence adverse to the character of the defendant may generally be placed before a jury, and no adverse comment may be made by Counsel, if the prisoner elects not to give evidence in his own defence.

(6) The verdict of the jury must be unanimous.

(7) The prisoner has a right of appeal on a question of law.

When all these are taken into consideration, is it reasonable to say that the key turns too easily to confine the prisoner within the four walls of his cell?

The Criminal Justice Act 1948, while making several important amendments in criminal procedure, completely revised the rules relating to punishments. Whipping, Hard Labour, and Penal Servitude were abolished. Corrective Training was introduced for the reform of those whose past record justified such remedial treatment, while Preventive Detention was instituted for habitual criminals. Prisons without bars have proved successful in dealing with many criminals.

30

THE ADMINISTRATION OF JUSTICE

'Law and Legal Procedure have always been a mystery
to the uninitiated, a snare to the unwary, and a red rag
to the unhappy man possessed of reforming zeal.'
Viscount Buckmaster

JUSTICE in England is administered in a number of different
legal Courts, and, almost without exception, every Court is
open to the public. In many instances, the jurisdiction of the
several Courts overlaps, and a cursory survey must, accordingly, leave entangled many of the intertwined threads.

We considered in Chapter 29 the function of the Petty
Sessions, or the Magistrate's Court as it is now officially described, although it is still colloquially called a police court,
when acting as a Court of preliminary inquiry. A Magistrate's
Court has, however, jurisdiction in many other matters. For
example, it deals with almost all petty criminal offences, including such 'crimes' as minor infringements of the motor-
ing laws, 'drunks', and other offences punishable by fines or a
term of imprisonment not exceeding three months. Much of
this criminal business is artificial in character, for some of the
laws introduced for the welfare of the community bring defendants to police courts who are by no means 'genuine criminals'. Indeed, many motorists, who have never killed a pedestrian, regard it as an insult to be charged with exceeding the
speed limit in a built-up area. In similar manner some drug-
gists who sell patent medicines are pained at being required to
consider the health of their customers, as a result of regulations contained in the Public Health Acts. The Food and
Drugs Acts also create many criminal offences designed to
catch those who sell adulterated milk and impure foods, which
are not in accordance with the descriptions under which they
are sold. When we are all saints, these enactments will no
longer be necessary, but as many of us are still sinners, the law
deems it proper to restrict our power to inflict harm on our
fellows, and when we commit offences of this type we are
charged at a Magistrate's Court.

In addition to their criminal jurisdiction, Magistrates' Courts have limited powers of trial in specified civil matters. These include disputes arising in certain cases between landlord and tenant, and between employer and employee, and in totally different categories, applications for affiliation or bastardy orders, and a large number of matrimonial disputes, when a wife is asking for maintenance or a separation order.

The Justices who sit to administer justice in the Magistrates' Courts, outside of the London area and the larger cities, are always unpaid. They have not necessarily any legal knowledge, and are often appointed as a reward for political services. It is reasonably argued that it is bad policy to leave the administration of justice in the hands of a layman. It would be equally illogical to leave the navigation of a ship in the hands of a company director, and no one of intelligence would advocate such a course. In defence of the system, it is said that the majority of offences brought before a magistrate are of a trivial character, and turn on questions of fact, as distinct from law. It is therefore contended that it is not essential for a magistrate to be a lawyer. If this argument were sound, it would suggest that many actions in the High Court might also be tried without the assistance of a qualified Judge, since a substantial percentage of them raise issues of fact, as distinct from issues of law. The argument is unsound because a trained legal mind is more capable of sifting relevant from irrelevant facts, and it is to be deplored because it suggests that there is one law for cases of minor importance, and another law for those which involve serious issues.

When questions of law arise in a Magistrate's Court, the J.P.s are usually guided by an official called the Clerk of the Court. He is normally a solicitor, who has an intimate knowledge of the business of the Court, and a prudent J.P. leans heavily on his clerk when legal problems are involved. The system, however, inevitably results in a travesty of justice at times, for however anxious the amateur may be to prove his wisdom and benevolence, courtesy cannot be a substitute for knowledge.

A Royal Commission was appointed in 1946 to consider the reform of the lay magistracy, and many lawyers hoped that the

Commission would recommend the abolition of the practice of appointing an irresponsible amateur to a position of judicial authority. The report of the Commission was a disappointment from this point of view. The proposal that paid legally-qualified magistrates should be appointed was rejected, largely on the ground of expense. However, some of the Commission's recommendations for improvements in the system were brought into effect by the Justices of the Peace Act 1949. These include the provision of courses of instruction for lay magistrates and the fixing of a maximum retiring age of seventy-five.

An appeal lies in many cases from the decision of a magistrate to 'Quarter Sessions'. This is the Court referred to in the preceding chapter, which tries many criminal offences. Appeals from a Magistrate's Court are not, however, always heard at Quarter Sessions. If a question of law is involved, the magistrates may be asked to 'State a Case' for the opinion of the High Court. This means that they must prepare a statement of the principles upon which they have based their legal decision. The 'Case' is submitted to a Court called the Divisional Court presided over either by two or by three High Court Judges. They will decide whether or not, in their view, the magistrates have correctly interpreted the law.

The County Court is a Court of civil jurisdiction. There are over 400 of them throughout England, and they sit in the more populated areas, presided over by a Judge who has been selected from among practising barristers. They have jurisdiction to try actions when the amount in issue between the litigants does not exceed £400, and they have jurisdiction in probate matters, where the net value of an estate is less than £1,000. They are also empowered to settle disputes relating to land of an annual rateable value not exceeding £100, and to deal with all cases arising out of the Rent Restrictions Acts. They may try other actions, with the consent of the parties, even when the amount involved in the dispute exceeds the prescribed limits, and some County Courts also have jurisdiction in Bankruptcy and Admiralty business. Although, however, the County Courts deal with a wide range of disputes, they have no power to try actions of libel and slander, breach of promise of marriage, or seduction.

Actions in a County Court, commenced by a document called a 'Plaint', are usually tried within two or three months. On the date fixed for trial, the parties will attend with their lawyers and their witnesses. The arrangements are not always perfect, however, as a case may be adjourned for want of time, when other actions are fixed for hearing on the same day and at the same time. This is a practice which has prevailed in nearly every Court in the country, for it is one of the principles which dominates the English legal system that a litigant and his lawyers must wait upon the pleasure of the Court. However, in the High Court, a recent innovation is the introduction of a system by which it is possible if the parties are in agreement, to fix an appointment many months in advance for the trial, and in the County Court a day, or several days, may sometimes be set aside for a particular case. It is to be hoped that the system introduced in the High Court will prove a success, and that the waiting period between the fixing of the appointment and the trial will not become too lengthy.

County Courts in their present form were established in the year 1846 as Courts for the poorer class of litigant. Today, however, County Court litigation is, unfortunately, not always economical, although costs are on a substantially lower scale than those allowed in the High Court.

Any appeal on a question of law lies from the decision of a County Court to the Court of Appeal, but leave to appeal must generally be obtained when the amount involved in the dispute does not exceed £20. In some cases an appeal on a question of fact is allowed.

The Supreme Court of Judicature, or the High Court of Justice, has its headquarters in London – the 'Law Courts'. The High Court is divided into three main divisions, which are called the 'Queen's Bench Division', the 'Chancery Division', and the 'Probate, Divorce, and Admiralty Division'. Probate work is linked with divorce work, as both were previously undertaken by the Ecclesiastical Courts, which alone had jurisdiction to deal with wills and matrimonial disputes. Admiralty work, previously left adrift on the uncharted ocean of the law, has now found an anchorage with the Probate and Divorce Division, where it is tied up alongside of matrimony. A soldier who altered the heading of his divorce petition 'Probate, Divorce, and Admiralty Division', by substituting the word 'Military' for 'Admiralty', was not devoid of intelligence.

The Queen's Bench Division deals principally with actions which arise out of contracts and torts – i.e. Common Law actions. Attached to this Division are the Divisional Court and the Courts of the Official Referees. An *Official Referee* is deputed to deal with cases which involve a mass of detail or complicated accounts, and he is not to be confused with the *Official Receivers*, who are Bankruptcy and Company liquidation officials. The Chancery Division has taken the place of the Courts of Equity described in Appendix 1. They usually try actions dealing with the construction of wills, settlements, and other documents, the administration of trusts, and disputes which relate to mortgages or the sale of land. Bankruptcy business and Company business (including the liquidation of Companies) have also been assigned to the Chancery Division.

In many instances there is overlapping between the Chancery and the Queen's Bench Division. Actions relating to copyright may, for example, be commenced either in Queen's Bench or in Chancery. There is no hard-and-fast rule, but, broadly speaking, the influence of the old practice which made damages the particular province of the Common Law still prevails. Accordingly, a litigant usually commences his copyright action in the Queen's Bench Division when he hopes for substantial damages. If, however, his principal aim is to establish his legal right – the survival of the earlier function of Equity – he usually brings the proceedings in the Chancery Division.

There is an unconditional right of appeal to the Court of Appeal from a final judgement of the High Court. The Court of Appeal, which normally consists of three Judges, does not hear the witnesses again, but it reviews all the evidence which has been considered by the trial Judge. It will, usually, be slow to upset a judgement which is based upon findings of fact, for the trial Judge has had the advantage of hearing and seeing the witnesses in the witness-box, and it is never easy to assess the value of evidence when it is read in black and white. Occasions, however, do arise when the Court of Appeal decides that undue weight has been given to irrelevant evidence, and if it is of the opinion that the Judge has arrived at an erroneous conclusion of fact, or has drawn untenable inferences from the evidence, it may reverse his decision. In many instances, when a judgement has been based upon the exercise of discretion, the Court of Appeal will be reluctant to interfere, and it will not do so unless the discretion has been exercised upon wrong legal principles. For example, when a petitioner in a divorce suit has himself committed adultery, he is not entitled to a decree as of right, but only if the Judge exercises his discretion in his favour, and if the Judges refuses to do so, the Court of Appeal will not normally interfere. If, however, it can be shown that the Judge manifestly acted upon wrong principles in arriving at his decision, it may be persuaded to do so. For example, if the Judge had refused Joan Doe a decree of divorce in a discretion case, because he was under the mistaken impression that she wished to live in adultery with Richard Roe, a married man, when, in fact, Richard Roe had been divorced by his wife, and intended to marry Joan Doe, the Court of Appeal might be asked to allow an appeal. It could do so on the ground that the Judge had exercised his discretion on a wrong principle.

When an appeal is based upon alleged errors of law, the question of discretion does not arise. Full consideration will be given to the judgement from which the appeal is made, but the legal issues will be investigated afresh, without any bias in favour of the existing judgement.

An appeal from a decision of the Court of Appeal lies to the House of Lords. In some cases such an appeal may be made without leave, but in others, the leave of the Court of Appeal or of the House of Lords must first be obtained. This will usually be granted, if substantial issues are at stake, or if there has been a marked divergence of views among the Judges themselves. It will not, however, be so readily granted if all the Judges have been unanimous in their judgements.

The House of Lords is the final appeal tribunal of the United Kingdom. The Court usually consists of five Judges who have been appointed peers, and are known as Law Lords. Technically, the hearing of an appeal is a sitting of the House of Lords. When the arguments in the case have been

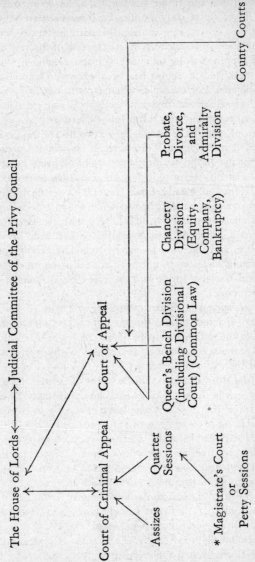

The House of Lords ←——→ Judicial Committee of the Privy Council

Court of Criminal Appeal   Court of Appeal

Assizes   Quarter Sessions

* Magistrate's Court or Petty Sessions

Queen's Bench Division (including Divisional Court) (Common Law)

Chancery Division (Equity, Company, Bankruptcy)

Probate, Divorce, and Admiralty Division

County Courts

* In certain cases an appeal from a Magistrate's Court on a question of law may be heard by a Divisional Court.

considered, the Law Lords do not deliver judgement. The Lord Chancellor, who presides, 'moves' that the appeal be allowed or dismissed, as the case may be. The other Law Lords then speak to the motion, and either support it or oppose it. The majority verdict will decide the issue.

There is another appellate court, known as the Judicial Committee of the Privy Council which deals with appeals from the Appeal Courts of the non-self-governing countries of the Commonwealth, as well as from the Supreme Courts of Australia, New Zealand, Ceylon, Ghana, and the Isle of Man and the Channel Islands, the last two territories being part of the British Isles but not of the United Kingdom. This Court is usually composed of five Law Lords, or four Law Lords and a distinguished colonial jurist. They never deliver a formal judgement, but after they have expressed their views, they 'humbly advise Her Majesty' to allow or reject the appeal.

Among the specialized Courts is the Restrictive Practices Court set up by the Restrictive Trade Practices Act 1956 which has a jurisdiction concerned with those business practices which, under the Acts, are held to restrict free competition between firms in a particular industry or trade. Cases are brought before the Court by the Registrar of Trading Agreements, whose duties in this respect are directed by the Board of Trade, so that the Court may decide whether any particular practice is to be held consistent with the public interest and therefore legal. The Court cannot be said to be either civil or criminal. Its impact on economic life is as yet unknown.

The following figures which relate to the year 1955 sketch the extent of the business conducted in the main courts. The figures also illustrate the 'popularity' of the County Courts as compared with the High Court, which has grown since 1955, in view of the extension of jurisdiction under the County Courts Act 1955 and the availability of legal aid for County Court actions since 1 January 1956.

1. County Courts:
   Total proceedings commenced 730,768
   Actions tried 24,185
   (Some 700,000 actions settled by consent or on admission, in default of appearance or defence, struck out, withdrawn, or paid.)

2. High Court, Queen's Bench Division:
   Total proceedings commenced 58,700
   Actions tried (including Assizes) 2,289
       Chancery Division:
   Actions and Matters disposed of in Court . . . 1,385
       (Many more cases are disposed of in Chambers not
       open to the public.)
          Probate, Divorce, and Admiralty Division:
   Probate: Actions tried 79
       (for Divorce see p. 278)
3. Court of Appeal:
   Appeals set down from County Courts . . . 163
   Appeals set down from Q.B. Division . . . 247
   Appeals set down from Chancery Division . . . 39
4. House of Lords:
   Appeals set down 33

The diagram on p. 330 may help to clarify the links connecting the courts, but does not include a number of courts of specialized or local importance.

31

TRIALS AND ARBITRATIONS
THE FUNCTIONS OF A WITNESS

> ' "Little to do and plenty to get, I suppose?" said
> Sergeant Buzfuz with jocularity.
> "Oh, quite enough to get, sir, as the soldier said ven
> they ordered him three hundred and fifty lashes,"
> replied Sam.
> "You must not tell us what the soldier, or any other
> man said, sir," interposed the Judge; "it's not evi-
> dence." '
>
> *Pickwick Papers*

EVERY action in the High Court is initiated by the issue of a
formal summons to the defendant called either a 'writ of summons', or an 'originating summons'. This usually contains a
short *précis* of the nature of the complaint and the 'relief'
which the plaintiff proposes to ask the Court to grant. Legal
proceedings must always be commenced within a definite
period from the date when the cause of action arose. For an
ordinary contract this period is six years, and a similar time
prevails in many other instances. An action if damages are
claimed for personal injuries must, however, be brought within three years of the date of the cause of action. On the other
hand, mental disability, infancy, and sometimes fraud generally have the effect of delaying any period during which time
is held to run. The subject is dealt with basically by the Limitation Acts 1939 and 1954, the latter statute repealing the rule
which allowed only one year's delay for an action to be
brought against a Public Authority.

A writ must be personally served upon the defendant, unless
he has authorized a solicitor to accept service of the proceedings on his behalf. A plaintiff is not entitled to relief before a
writ has been served, except in cases of emergency. An *ex parte*
injunction, as it is called, i.e. an injunction obtained without
previous notice to the defendant, is granted only when irreparable injury might otherwise be caused.

If the defendant does not, in due course, 'enter an appearance' to the proceedings, the plaintiff is frequently entitled to

judgement. Entering an appearance is, however, a purely formal step, amounting in effect to a formal acceptance of the challenge contained in the plaintiff's writ. The defendant does not have to make a personal appearance in Court at this stage, and his solicitor will normally arrange, as a matter of course, to get his client's name entered as a defendant on the Court record. Even if he has no real defence to an action, a defendant will often enter an appearance in order to gain time. He is perfectly entitled to do this, but the longer the action goes on the higher the costs which the unsuccessful defendant will be required to pay. If you are being sued for money which you undoubtedly owe, it will be cheaper to pay as soon as the writ is issued rather than allow legal proceedings to take their full course.

When the claim can be assessed in terms of money, the plaintiff can apply for immediate judgement before the case proceeds any farther. The application must be supported by an affidavit, a statement made on oath and sworn before a solicitor who has been granted a Commission to administer oaths. A client is never permitted to swear an affidavit before his own solicitor, even if the solicitor is himself a Commissioner for Oaths. This practice is presumably adopted to avoid the risk of a conspiracy between the solicitor and his client to swear a false affidavit. The application for 'summary judgement' will be heard not by a Judge, but by a senior official of the Court called a 'Master' in London and a 'Registrar' in the provinces. The defendant, if he wishes to resist the application, will normally file an affidavit in opposition, and if the Master or Registrar considers that the contents of the affidavit would, if true, afford an answer to the claim, or even a case for legal argument, he must give the defendant leave to defend the action. It is not the function of the Master or Registrar to decide the strength or weakness of the defendant's case, and he has no power to do so.

If the action is not ended in its early life by a summary judgement, there are a number of interlocutory proceedings which must take place before the action is entered for trial. These relate to what are called the 'pleadings' – i.e. the particulars of the claim and the defence – 'discovery' – i.e. the disclosure by each party of all the documents in his possession which have any bearing on the issues in the action – and other incidental matters. All these are subject to strict regulations, and the rules of procedure in the High Court, which consist of over seventy principal 'Orders', govern every step in an action. When you are informed that the annual publication of these orders with notes and annotations, results in a volume of nearly 4,000 pages, with another volume as a case citator and index, you will understand why lawyers who are concerned with Court work are not immune from headaches!

When you are involved in litigation outside of London, your action may be tried at Assizes. If your case is to be heard in London and your action has been entered for trial, you take your place at the end of the queue, and several months may elapse before you reach the head of the list. Like the patient housewife, however, your turn will eventually come, and, in the meanwhile, your solicitor will have delivered a brief to the Counsel who is to argue the case on your behalf, and you will probably have had one or more conferences with him. A notice is published at the Law Courts each evening of actions which are to be tried on the following day. When your case is in the list, and the Judge has disposed of other actions, if any, which are set down to be heard before him at precisely the same time on precisely the same day, your case will be called by the Clerk of the Court, and if you are the plaintiff, you will probably see your Counsel rise from his seat. As a general rule, the onus of proving a case rests upon the plaintiff, and it is therefore usual for plaintiff's Counsel to open the case and to outline to the Judge the nature of the complaint and the evidence which he proposes to tender on his client's behalf. If you are excitable, you should not be disappointed if your Counsel appears to be cold and unemotional. A prudent Counsel will never present an exaggerated case which cannot be supported by the statements of his witnesses.

When Counsel has finished his opening address, he will call his first witness into the witness-box.

Laws lay down precepts or rules for the governing of the community and the adjustment of disputes. The laws may be excellent, but unless there is an efficient system for their administration, they may be of little practical value. In England, the witness-box is the foundation upon which the system has been built. In every trial the evidence which is produced and tendered to the Court from the witness-box is the keystone of the system. The rules of evidence and the procedure for giving evidence apply not only in the High Court in London or on Assize, but also in every County Court, Magistrate's Court, and judicial arbitration. Inferior Courts tend to be less formal than the High Court, but the basic principles are the same.

Before a witness gives his evidence he must take an oath: 'I swear by Almighty God that the evidence I shall give the Court will be the truth, the whole truth, and nothing but the truth'. If the witness has no religious belief at all he must be allowed to 'affirm'. In many instances, however, truth cannot be expressed in words. It is abstract and not concrete. If you are a plaintiff, and your action has been brought to recover damages for injuries sustained in a street accident, there may be an issue of fact as to the speed of the car which has knocked you down. It cannot be equally true to say that the car was travelling at 10 m.p.h., and that the car was travelling at 30 m.p.h. You may give evidence that the car was travelling at 30 m.p.h., and you may have an honest belief that your evidence is true. The driver of the car may give evidence that it was travelling at 10 m.p.h. with a similar honest belief. If you substitute the words 'fast' and 'slow' for exact speeds, you will be no nearer the truth, since both terms are relative. You will not be determining the truth, and you will not be making any attempt to clarify the issue of fact. You can never be sure of arriving at the truth, for even if the driver were able to produce a photograph of the speedometer reading at the precise moment of the impact, no one could say whether or not the speedometer was recording accurately at that moment.

For these reasons, it would be more satisfactory if the oath were not administered in such uncompromising terms, and if a witness were permitted to qualify his oath by the addition of the words 'to the best of my honest belief'. If a witness is determined to give false evidence, it is disturbing to think he may quieten his conscience by the reflection that the oath which he is obliged to take requires him, before God, to achieve the impossible. The same criticism applies to every affidavit that is sworn.

Evidence, as intimated, is usually the central feature of an action. A witness may attend Court voluntarily, or he may be compelled to do so by 'subpoena' – i.e. he may be served with a summons which requires him to attend, and if he has been paid 'conduct money' to bring him to Court, and he fails to appear, he may be charged with contempt of Court. After the trial he is entitled to a witness fee and his expenses.

It is advantageous for a witness to understand and appreciate his duty to the Court, before he goes into the witness-box. There are some good witnesses, and many bad ones. Here are some suggestions which every witness might usefully note.

(1) It is the duty of a witness to recount facts and not, generally speaking, to express opinions, unless he is an 'expert witness' – i.e. a witness called to testify on a technical matter, of which he has expert knowledge. It is true that on occasions a reply is necessarily a matter of opinion, as in the case of the witness who is asked whether a car was travelling at a fast or a slow speed. His answer is only able to reflect his personal view, and the Judge will normally attach little weight to his opinion. If, on the other hand, you are the witness, and are able to say: 'The near mudguard of the car hit the plaintiff's left thigh', you are deposing to a fact. It may not be true, of course, because you may be mistaken, but if you are able to speak precisely as to a fact, and your evidence is not contradicted, the Court may be expected to accept it, unless there are other grounds for rejecting it.

(2) A witness should remember that it is not his function to make speeches. It is his duty to answer the questions which are put to him by Counsel or the Judge. If he is able to answer 'yes' or 'no' to a question, so much the better. If that answer is complete in itself, it is not necessary to add anything more. An answer such as 'Absolutely yes' or 'Definitely no' should always be avoided. Such answers are as unimpressive as a speech. A Judge is not a simple-minded person. More likely than not, he will form an unfavourable view of the witness

who tries to impress him. You would probably do the same if you were in his place. When you meet a stranger, you will not think much of him if he commences to brag of his achievements, or to bore you with some dull personal reminiscence, before you have been five minutes in conversation with him. A Judge will favour the evidence of a witness who answers questions simply, without evasion, and without making long and irrelevant speeches. It is never the function of a witness to display his character. He is not an actor. He is a cog in the machinery of the law.

(3) Every witness should direct his mind to the question which is asked of him, before he gives his answer. If a question cannot be answered in a word, the reply should be directed to the question, and should not be an elaborate explanation of something which has not been asked. A witness who fences with questions asked of him may be reprimanded by the Judge, and when this happens, the witness may be sure that he has created a bad impression. The truthful answer may damage the case which the witness is hoping to establish, but an untruthful or evasive answer will generally do even more harm. If the Judge does not believe the witness is telling the truth, his evidence will always injure the party on whose behalf it is given, and may make a substantial contribution towards the loss of the case. If a witness wishes his evidence to be believed, he must satisfy the Judge he is doing his best to tell the truth. It is never advisable to try to deceive the Court.

(4) You should endeavour not to allow prejudice to influence your replies. This is very difficult. If there were no prejudice, the task of arriving at the facts would be greatly simplified. We may 'smack against the rock of prejudice' in many ways. For example, each of us makes a number of mistakes daily. On these occasions there is an inevitable tendency to pretend the fault is not entirely ours. Someone else has been partially responsible, or we may prefer to claim that 'the cup has come to pieces in our hands'. The pedestrian knocked down by a car is rarely ready to admit any responsibility. The driver of the car will be equally unwilling to accept liability. One blames the other, and the attempt to 'pass the baby' aggravates the prejudice which each feels against the other.

Pride, closely associated with prejudice, also plays its part in such a case. When we know we have made a mistake, pride makes us obstinate and does not permit us to admit it. We do not realize how easy it is to disarm an opponent by the simple words, 'I made a mistake. I'm sorry.' We fight shy of such an admission, and the more the accusation is pressed, and our fault brought home to us, the more obstinate and prejudiced we become. On such occasions, many a witness, cross-examined by a clever Counsel, has been so swayed by prejudice as to give answers which no reasonable man would believe to be true.

(5) Avoid exaggeration. Exaggeration is frequently a symptom of indignation, but evidence of indignation is never proof of the case which a witness seeks to establish. Moreover, an indignant witness is seldom impressive, since indignation may be so often simulated, consciously or unconsciously, in order to conceal shortcomings.

(6) Hearsay evidence being inadmissible, the witness must not make statements as to what he was told by a third party.

(7) Speak clearly and not in a whisper, and face the Judge when you answer questions, even though they are put to you by Counsel.

After a witness has been examined by his own Counsel, he will be cross-examined by the Counsel for the opposing party. After his cross-examination has been concluded, his own Counsel is entitled to re-examine him in order to clarify any answers given in cross-examination which may be capable of better explanation.

After the first witness has concluded his evidence, the plaintiff's Counsel will call his other witnesses, and when they have concluded their evidence, the plaintiff's case is said to be closed.

The defendant's Counsel will then open his case, and may outline his defence before he calls his witnesses. His witnesses will be subject to the same examination and cross-examination as the plaintiff's witnesses, and after their evidence is concluded the defendant's Counsel will argue his case before the plaintiff's Counsel has the last word.

In their final speeches each Counsel endeavours to persuade the Judge to his point of view. In many cases, however, the issue has already been decided before the last witness has left the witness-box. If the case is one which turns on issues of fact, the Judge will have formed his own impression of the veracity of each of the witnesses. The most eminent Counsel is unlikely to be able to persuade him to change his opinion. Although it is the duty of a Judge to keep an open mind until the last word has been spoken, it is also his duty to decide the case on the evidence, and he must not be influenced by the seductive oratory of Counsel.

If issues of law, as well as issues of fact, are involved, the decision of the Judge must, of course, depend in part on the skill with which Counsel presents his arguments in support of his legal submissions. In such a case it may be truly said that a case is never lost until it is won. A final speech made by Counsel for the plaintiff frequently rescues an apparently lost cause.

The system of trial may not be perfect. A witness, nervous through no fault of his own, will always be at a disadvantage. No one, however, has yet found any better procedure. It certainly would not be satisfactory to excuse a witness from giving evidence because he is too timid to face Counsel. To yield to the desires of a nervous witness would undermine the system, and make it impossible to conduct judicial proceedings with any pretence of efficiency.

After a judgement has been obtained, there are a number of ways in which it may be enforced, always bearing in mind that 'you can't get blood out of a stone', and if a defendant is ordered to pay a sum of money, and is without means, no lawyer knows of any magic formula which will enable the plaintiff to enjoy the fruits of the judgement. If, however, a defendant has 'prevaricated, or said nay', the more usual methods taken to enforce the judgement are (1) to levy execution on his goods, (2) to institute bankruptcy proceedings, (3) to 'garnishee' his banking account, if his Bankers are known. Chapter 7 has dealt with Execution and Chapter 21 has dealt with Bankruptcy. 'Garnishee' is a procedure by which the judgement debtor's banking account is attached. If there are any funds standing to his credit, the Court may order them to be diverted, for the purpose of satisfying the judgement either in whole or in part. There are other steps which may also be taken to enforce a judgement, but they are not so frequently employed.

Arbitration is an alternative procedure to litigation, and it may take place when both parties agree to adopt this form of procedure for the settlement of their disputes.

Contracts frequently include a clause which provides for reference to arbitration of any dispute arising between the parties on matters arising out of or incidental to the contract. In such cases the decision of the arbitrator is usually final and binding on the parties. Sometimes a clause of this kind provides for the appointment of an arbitrator by each party to the dispute, with the right to the two arbitrators to appoint an umpire in the event of disagreement. This involves additional expense, which will be avoided if the submission provides for the appointment of a sole arbitrator. Every agreement to arbitrate is called a 'submission', and although the Court has power to make an order staying legal proceedings commenced by a party who has agreed to submit disputes to arbitration, it will not compel a litigant to arbitrate if he has not so agreed.

Arbitration, as an alternative to litigation, has both advantages and disadvantages. It is particularly appropriate in dealing with disputes which arise between parties to a commercial contract. It enables them to dispose of the dispute without publicity which may be harmful to both. It is also in many ways more expeditious than litigation, for an early hearing can be obtained, and the parties may be reasonably sure that the trial will take place on the fixed date. The advantages are, however, sometimes outweighed by the disadvantages. For example, the general belief that it is cheaper to arbitrate than to litigate is often erroneous. In many cases an arbitration is substantially more expensive than a lawsuit. The principal item which contributes towards the increased expense is the arbitrator's fees, and in some cases those of the umpire. A skilled expert, appointed to act as an arbitrator, may properly charge substantial fees for his services, but there is no corresponding item payable when an action is tried before a Judge.

There may also be a disadvantage in arbitration when difficult questions of law are involved. Either party is entitled to require the arbitrator to 'state a case' for the opinion of the High Court. This corresponds to the procedure referred to in Chapter 30, when a Magistrate 'states a case'. When this is done, it involves the added expense of what is, in effect, a second hearing of the dispute. Moreover, although provision may be made in some cases for the appointment of a qualified lawyer to act as arbitrator, there may be other instances in which the arbitrator has no legal training, and no experience in conducting a trial. Sometimes, also, he may know nothing of the duty of 'cold neutrality' which his position imposes upon him.

The rules which govern arbitrations are laid down in the Arbitration Act 1950. These rules are designed, as far as possible, to assimilate the procedure to that of a trial in the High Court, for every arbitration is and must be conducted as a judicial proceeding. As a general rule, each party will be required, before the hearing, to deliver particulars of the claim, and the answer to the claim, in the same manner as in a High Court action, in order that the issues may be clearly defined. Each party will also be required to disclose to his opponent, before the trial, all relevant documents, so that neither party will be taken by surprise at the hearing. Although it is not essential to instruct lawyers on an arbitration, it is usual to do so, unless the dispute is of a trivial character, or the arbitration is being conducted informally, according to practices which are customary in certain trades.

After the arguments have been concluded, it is customary for the arbitrator to notify each party when he has arrived at his decision, and he will require payment of his fees before handing over or 'publishing' the award. The award, which must be stamped with a 10s. stamp, will, however, frequently direct the losing party to pay the costs, including the arbitrator's fees, and if the winning party has already made the payment, he is then entitled to claim reimbursement from his opponent.

If the losing party to an arbitration refuses to carry out the terms of the award, an order may be obtained from the High

Court to compel him to do so. An award of an arbitrator, lawfully published, is as effectual as an order of the High Court, and the Court will always make an order for its enforcement, unless there has been fraud or irregularity in the conduct of the arbitration.

When you are engaged upon litigation or arbitration you need never fear that negotiations for settlement of the dispute will prejudice your case if no compromise is reached. Letters headed 'without prejudice' which contain proposals for compromise may never be disclosed to the Court, and when negotiations take place it is always the practice to conduct them 'without prejudice'.

Finally, if you do not wish to instruct a lawyer to represent you in an action, you are always entitled to conduct your litigation in person. Although, in these circumstances, the Court will give you every consideration and will allow you latitude not given to Counsel, you are bound to have a very uphill task. Not even a genius can expect to master the technicalities of litigation without training or experience.

32

COSTS

'The first thing we do, let's kill all the lawyers.'
King Henry VI, Part 2

LEGAL charges do not consist exclusively of solicitors' costs. They may also include barristers' fees, witnesses' fees, and Court fees. Many people, when they speak of heavy legal charges, have the impression that all the money goes to solicitors. They forget, or do not know, of the other expenses included in the bill.

The costs which a solicitor is entitled to charge his client are regulated by Statute. The Law Society – the body which regulates the activities of solicitors (but not barristers) – adopts a critical attitude towards any who agree, except from charitable motives, to carry out work at less than the approved rates. The Law Society is sometimes spoken of as the strongest Trade Union in England, and it has power to take disciplinary action against any solicitor who infringes the law or is guilty of professional misconduct.

In non-contentious matters, that is to say matters which are not of a kind associated with litigation, solicitors' charges are a lump sum, and not an itemized account. Taken into consideration, in arriving at 'the fair and reasonable' amount which represents the maximum that a client is obliged to pay, are the complexity of the questions raised, the skill and responsibility required in dealing with them, the documents prepared and perused, the time and trouble expended and a number of other factors set out in the Solicitors' Remuneration Order 1953.

For conveyancing transactions, there is an *ad valorem* scale of charges which applies. The costs for sales, purchases, mortgages, and leases of properties are based upon the amount of money involved in the transaction. The scale of costs allowed for transactions relating to registered land is on a much lower basis. The Solicitors' Remuneration Act 1881 originally fixed the scale which has been altered several times since, although hardly keeping pace with the fall in the value of money since 1881, notwithstanding increases in the sale price of property since then. Some specimen extracts are set out at the end of this chapter showing the charges allowed to solicitors when registered and unregistered property is bought, sold, leased, and mortgaged.

The Solicitors' Remuneration Act regulates solicitors' charges for litigation or Court matters. The standard rates were increased 33⅓ per cent after the First World War and in 1944 were raised to the level of 50 per cent above the 1881 rates. The cost of living has increased during the last seventy-five years many times more. In some cases, a detailed itemized bill of costs may be replaced by one for a lump sum.

A client receives professional services from his solicitor in return for the fees which he pays. In the great majority of cases legal business is completed to the satisfaction of both parties. A conscientious lawyer will do his best for his client, and the client will have confidence in his solicitor. The client will be wise, however, to remember, when he takes legal advice, that he ought to accept it, even if it is unpalatable, for it will be based on years of practical legal experience, which he himself does not possess. In all cases of difficulty and doubt Counsel's opinion may be taken, and although this will not reduce the matter to certainty, it will afford additional clues to the best solution. If, in fact, the client has no confidence in his lawyer, he is always at liberty to seek other advice, and the sooner he breaks the relationship, the better it will be for both parties. Clashes of temperament may occur between lawyer and client, in the same way as between other members of the community, and neither should feel aggrieved when they part company in such circumstances. In an exceptional case, if there has been some default on the part of the solicitor, the client may have a claim against him for damages for negligence. If the default is of a more serious and of a fraudulent character, the client may seek redress from The Law Society. If a solicitor abuses his responsibility, The Law Society will not only, as stated, call him to account, but will also, in appropriate cases, in which there has been fraudulent conversion of the client's money, allow compensation to the client who has been victimized.

There are black sheep and defaulters among every section of society. They are part and parcel of the community. When, however, your neighbour is robbed or defrauded, it is not usually your concern. After you have expressed your sympathy, you usually forget the incident, and you do not undertake to reimburse him for his loss. Solicitors, however, are no longer satisfied to adopt a complacent attitude when a fraud is committed by a member of their own profession. In 1942 they set up a fund to provide compensation to members of the community who had been defrauded by their solicitors. Every Trade Union is properly jealous of the rights of its members, but is there any Trade Union in the country, other than The Law Society, which will stir from its groove in order to reimburse a member of the public for a loss resulting from the fraud of one of its members?

The operation of the state legal aid system which is dealt with in the next chapter should help you to appreciate that solicitors are not primarily concerned with 'fleecing' their clients, as a few uninformed members of the community seem to think. In fact, a solicitor usually regards his duty to his client as a trust, and it is inaccurate to imagine that the practice of the law enables lawyers to make a fortune. When they die rich, their wealth has usually been accumulated as a result of other business interests. In Chapter 34 a few particulars are given of the long and expensive training which a solicitor must undergo, in the interests of the community, before he is permitted to practise. A solicitor who has invested many years of his life in training for his profession is entitled to a reasonable return for this investment.

It used to be the practice for a solicitor to endorse every account which he rendered to his client with the forbidding expression 'This is my bill', and this terse observation was followed by his signature. Unless a bill of costs was so signed he was not able to enforce payment. Even today it is necessary for a solicitor to sign his bill to his client, unless it is accompanied by a signed covering letter.

The custom of rendering a detailed bill of costs dates back to the period when lawyers were among the few members of the community who were able to read and write. Their services were retained as 'attorneys' to write letters for their clients. An itemized bill of costs was subsequently rendered, charging for each attendance on the client, and every letter written on his behalf. No charge was made, however, for considering the client's position, or for coming to a decision as to the best course to adopt in any particular case. The reasonable client will not cavil at a reasonable fee. A client who lacks appreciation is entitled, however, to object to pay a penny beyond what The Law Society may, on application, consider 'fair and reasonable' for the work done and further, a solicitor must draw his client's attention to his right to apply to The Law Society before sueing him on the bill. As has been mentioned the position is different now for non-contentious matters and also for many contentious ones.

Every client who receives a bill of costs and considers it excessive is entitled to have it 'taxed'. This means he may apply to the High Court for the bill to be scrutinized by a Court official called a 'taxing officer'. If more than one-sixth of the amount of the bill is taxed off by the taxing officer, the solicitor must pay the expenses of the taxation. If less than one-sixth is taxed off, the client must pay the additional charges of the taxation. In some cases the fraction of one-sixth is replaced by one-fifth. Any disbursement charged in the bill will be disallowed, unless it was either paid before delivery of the bill or is expressly noted as unpaid in the bill and paid before the completion of the taxation.

When you embark upon litigation, it is unfortunate that there are too many unknown factors involved to enable your solicitor to give you a reliable estimate of the maximum costs which you may incur. A solicitor cannot even estimate his own charges with any semblance of accuracy, as they will depend upon the amount of work involved – i.e. the number of hours during which he will be engaged in the course of conducting the case and preparing for trial – while in many cases the disbursements may exceed the amount of the charges.

This chapter is more about solicitors than barristers, because most of your legal associations will be with a solicitor. Barristers have little personal contact with the layman, for they are not allowed to interview clients, except in the presence of a solicitor. A barrister must, however, be briefed in every High Court action, as no solicitor has the right of audience before a High Court Judge in open Court. Counsel, as barristers are called, are classified either as Queen's Counsel, popularly called 'Silks' (from the nature of the gown which they wear), and Junior Counsel, a distinction which is more particularly described in Chapter 34. Barristers occupy a curious legal position. They have no legal right to remuneration, because fees payable to barristers have, from time immemorial, been regarded as gratuities. As a result of this fiction, a barrister may never sue for an unpaid account. Moreover, a layman will never receive a bill from a barrister. The 'fee note' will always be sent to the solicitor, who is under a moral obligation to pay, and if he fails to do so, after he has been placed in funds by his client for the purpose, he may be reported to The Law Society. A barrister would also, in most cases, refuse to accept any further brief from a defaulting solicitor, unless he received payment of his fees in advance.

Counsel's fees are frequently much heavier than solicitors' charges. Leading members of the Bar demand and receive remuneration far in excess of any allowed to solicitors, and there is no limit to the fee which Counsel is entitled to require before he accepts a brief. Of course, there is no obligation to employ expensive Counsel. There is, however, a popular idea that if you employ 'learned and expensive' Counsel, you are more likely to win your case. This idea is not always erroneous; it is not necessarily always true.

It would be unfair to be too critical of Counsel who demand a premium on brain. Most of us wish to exploit our earning capacity to the full, and if someone is willing to pay us £18 a week, we will rarely be willing to accept employment at £14 a week. Moreover, it is nearly always possible to brief a competent barrister to conduct a case at a fraction of the charges required by the fashionable 'Silks'.

When a Queen's Counsel is briefed, he is not allowed to appear in Court without a Junior Counsel. This involves additional expense, and the burden is increased by a rule which entitles the Junior Counsel to receive two-thirds of the brief fee paid to Queen's Counsel, except when the brief fee exceeds

150 guineas. In defence of the system, it is fair to observe that Junior Counsel has a great deal of work in the earlier stages of an action, and he may receive only nominal remuneration for his labour if the action is settled before the trial. The two-thirds rule accordingly enables him to gain on the swings what he has lost on the roundabouts. Nevertheless, critics of the system are able to make a substantial case, which it is not easy to answer.

Court fees make only a small contribution to the expense of litigation, but witness fees may prove a heavy burden. When a case appears in the list for trial, the parties, the lawyers, and the witnesses must all be available. When, however, the trial is not reached, because earlier cases in the list have not been disposed of, the time which is wasted must be paid for. The High Court has recently taken steps to alleviate the situation a little; it has been of the utmost inconvenience to the legal profession.

The award of costs in every action is in the discretion of the Judge who tries the case. Although it is usual to order an unsuccessful litigant to pay his opponent's costs, a Judge may deprive either party of costs for good cause – e.g. an action may be dismissed without costs if the successful defendant has adopted a defence which is devoid of merit, but offers a technical answer to the claim.

Not every unsuccessful litigant is in a position to pay costs, and some efforts have been made to meet this contingency. A defendant to an action brought in the High Court for damages in respect of a tort, but not a contract, is usually entitled to apply for an order to remit the action for trial to the County Court, upon the production of evidence that it is improbable the plaintiff will be able to pay costs awarded against him if the action fails. The usual practice is to make the order to remit, unless the plaintiff gives security for a specified sum, to meet this contingent liability. A plaintiff resident out of Great Britain may also be ordered to give security for costs in any action in the High Court, and a similar order may be made against a Limited Liability Company when it brings an action, if proof is furnished of its probable inability to pay costs if unsuccessful in the litigation. Other than in these specified cases, however, there is, as a general rule, no power to order a plaintiff to give security for costs, and a defendant can never be ordered to give security in respect of his defence. If you desire to sue a flea, you must accordingly be prepared to find as a result that you have only caught a bite.

If you lose an action and are ordered to pay the taxed costs of your opponent, such costs are usually described as 'Party and Party' costs, and it does not necessarily mean that you will be ordered to pay the fancy fees charged by a fashionable Counsel who may have been retained by your opponent. When the taxing master taxes the costs, he will allow the successful litigant only such expenses as were necessarily incurred in the conduct of the litigation. Fees paid to Counsel whose services are at a premium will frequently be substantially reduced on taxation, and there are nearly always a number of items which the taxing master will strike out as not having been incurred as a strictly necessary expense. Such items are known as 'solicitor and own client' charges, and the successful litigant will have to bear them out of his own pocket.

Costs in the County Court are on a much more modest scale than costs in the High Court. They vary according to the amount involved in the dispute. The lower scale is applicable to actions under £10, and the fees which a solicitor earns for his professional services in such an action are much less than the amount which a bricklayer earns for work occupying a similar time. Members of the community who are involved in petty disputes cannot afford to pay high fees, and, in spite of all that is said to the contrary, the law does try to offer them justice. It is always necessary to remember, moreover, that the law for cases which involve small amounts of money is the same as the law which has to be applied if £10,000 is at stake, and as you will observe from the table on pp. 331–2, only a small percentage of actions are started in the High Court, since the great majority are brought in the County Courts.

A well-known London newspaper once wrote in a leading article: 'The high cost of litigation has been an abuse in England ever since Magna Carta enjoined that "justice shall not be delayed or sold".' An even greater authority observed, 'It is a popular error to imagine the loudest complainers for the public to be the most anxious for its welfare' (Burke).

There are admittedly a number of deficiencies in the legal system which offer an easy target for criticism. Let us see what sort of argument lawyers are able to put up in answer to a charge that the costs of litigation are excessive.

1. The public would be the first to suffer from cheap litigation. Lawyers, as well as their clients, must eat bread and butter, and they also enjoy a piece of cake. If they were unable to earn sufficient to provide these sweets of life, they would look elsewhere. Lawyers do not set themselves above human failings, and if you underpay the legal profession, you will unlock the door which leads to temptation and corruption.

2. Litigation is bound under all circumstances and conditions to be a waste of time to the litigants, since they must always be prepared to devote time to their lawyers' requirements if they wish their cases to be thoroughly prepared and presented. Every dispute which is settled amicably is, accordingly, so much time saved, and in so far as the prospective expense of litigation has contributed to the settlement, it is a point in its favour.

3. Cheap litigation would be of great encouragement to dishonest claims brought by those who had nothing to lose. 'Blackmail' is the colloquial expression used by most litigants when they are sued by a man of straw. This, of course, is not the right term, since the essence of blackmail, one of the most serious criminal offences, is the attempt to extort money or other valuables by threats (usually of exposure of an offence alleged to have been committed by the threatened man). Doubtless, however, the expression represents the opinion of the man 'threatened' with legal proceedings in respect of what he considers is a worthless claim, and American lawyers will testify to the number of fraudulent claims pursued in a country in which law costs little to the plaintiff if he loses his lawsuit.

4. Expensive litigation does not act as such a serious deterrent as is popularly represented. In addition to the channels available to poor litigants, both in the High Court and the County Court, referred to in the next chapter, there are nearly

always lawyers available who are willing to undertake litigation for poor litigants if the lawyers believe that there is a good cause of action. Although lawyers are never permitted to conduct litigation on a speculative basis – i.e. to make an agreement with their client which permits them a percentage of any money recovered – it is not improper for a solicitor to conduct an action for an impecunious client, and to recover his proper legal costs if the action is successful.

5. The County Court scale of costs in small disputes is almost invariably within the means of all litigants.

6. English history has been built on compromise, and democracy is itself a compromise. A system which encourages compromise cannot be entirely devoid of merit.

After stating these arguments, it should be observed that a very low percentage of all legal work consists of litigation. In other business dealt with by solicitors there is not the same startling disproportion between subject-matter and costs. They are normal transactions, but it is a commonplace throughout life that the normal passes without notice and without comment. It is the unusual and exceptional which attracts attention, and it is the unusual and exceptional case which has done much to contribute to the complaint that legal costs are excessive.

To lessen the risk of becoming liable to pay a heavy bill of costs as a result of unsuccessful litigation, I would, as a last general exhortation, urge John Citizen, as a layman, not to assume that the law is what he would like it to be, and not to follow his own inclination on a legal matter. To pursue a false trail based on such a belief often leads to disaster, for there are many real and assumed grievances for which no legal relief can be given. On such occasions there is one and only one prudent course to adopt – viz. to cut your loss. If you do not do so, but fall instead into the grievous error of 'running your head against a brick wall', it may not always crack your skull, but it may leave you with a severe headache for the rest of your life.

Scale of Costs allowed in Conveyancing Business under the Solicitors' Remuneration Act 1881
(now subject to an increase of 50 per cent):

1. *Sale and Purchase of Freeholds and Leaseholds*
(*Titles not registered*)

Vendor's Solicitor. For preparation of contract, deducing titles to property, and perusing and completing Conveyance:

Purchaser's Solicitor. For perusal and completion of contract, investigating title to property, and preparing and completing Conveyance:

30s. per £100 for the first £1,000 of purchase price.

15s. per £100 for the second and third £1,000 of purchase price.

7s. 6d. per £100 for the fourth and each subsequent £1,000 up to £10,000 of purchase price.

3s. 9d. per subsequent £100.

These charges do not include either the additional costs allowed to a solicitor if he actually negotiates the sale or the costs of any mortgage.

2. *Leases*

Lessor's Solicitors. For preparing, settling, and completing lease and counterpart.

Where the rent does not exceed £100; £7 10s. per cent on the rental, with a minimum of £5.

Where the rent exceeds £100 and does not exceed £500: as above, with an addition of £2 10s. in respect of each subsequent £100 of rent.

Where the rent exceeds £500: as above, with an addition of £1 in respect of each subsequent £100 of rent.

Lessee's Solicitor. For perusing draft and completing, one-half of the amount payable to the lessor's solicitor.

Note: There is a custom in London and some other parts of the country which requires a lessee to pay the charges of the lessor's solicitors as well as his own.

M

3. *Scale of Costs Allowed in Regard to Registered Titles*
Vendor or Purchaser's Solicitor.

£4 up to and for £200; £4 10s. up to £300; and £1 10s. for each additional £100 up to and for £1,000.

£1 per £100 for the second and third £1,000 of purchase price.

10s. per £100 for the fourth £1,000 of purchase price.

7s. 6d. per £100 for each subsequent £1,000 up to £13,000.

5s. per £100 for each subsequent £1,000 up to £17,000.

4s. per subsequent £100.

Fees are payable to the Land Registry on a sliding scale additional to the legal charges.

33

LEGAL AID

> 'Whereas it has long been known and declared that the poor have no right to the property of the rich, I wish it also to be known and declared that the rich have no right to the property of the poor.'
>
> John Ruskin

FOR many generations it has been a tradition of solicitors and barristers to give voluntary and gratuitous help in legal affairs to the poor in the same way as doctors have used their medical skill without reward for the benefit of the poorer sections of the community. The assistance given by the legal profession in this way has included advising persons on legal problems, defending them in criminal matters, and conducting civil litigation on their behalf.

Solicitors and barristers throughout the country have for many years formed panels and have attended at Poor Man's Lawyer Centres to give legal advice to those persons who are unable to pay normal professional fees. In suitable cases steps are taken through the Centre to place applicants in a position to obtain legal redress.

The profession have also acted under legal aid, defence, and appeal certificates for poor persons charged with criminal offences to ensure that no person shall be prevented through poverty from having his defence fully argued before the Court. Persons granted legal aid in criminal matters are not required to pay anything towards their legal costs.

Civil litigation (that is to say non-criminal proceedings) in the High Court is an expensive matter, and the profession have long given their services gratuitously to enable poor persons who would otherwise have been unable to obtain redress in the Courts to bring or defend proceedings in the High Court under a scheme known as the Poor Persons Procedure. Under this scheme a poor person might apply for a poor person's certificate to bring or to defend or to be a party to civil proceedings in the High Court. Application for such a certificate was made to a Poor Persons Committee made up of solicitors who gave their services gratuitously. If a certificate was granted the poor person was assigned a solicitor and counsel, and he was liable to pay only the actual out-of-pocket expenses, excluding office expenses, incurred in the conduct of his case. Neither solicitors nor barristers received anything at all in respect of the services they gave to the poor person in conducting his case in the High Court. During the twenty-five years that The Law Society and the Provincial Law Societies administered the Poor Persons Procedure over a quarter of a million applications were dealt with by Poor Persons Committees and approximately 140,000 cases were undertaken by the profession. The majority of the poor persons' certificates issued related to matrimonial proceedings. The normal legal costs of an undefended divorce suit are in the neighbourhood of £60 to £80. While you may criticize the expense of obtaining release from an unsuccessful marriage, you cannot criticize the solicitor or barrister who undertook the conduct of a poor person's divorce, and thereby not only forwent his fees but was also, in fact, out of pocket. In the past those who have been assisted have all too seldom realized that not only have the lawyers given their services voluntarily and gratuitously but they have also been involved in personal expense in so doing, barristers often in their travelling expenses, and solicitors in overhead expenses of their offices, which have amounted for each undefended matrimonial cause to the sum of approximately £15.

A special branch of the work connected with the Poor Persons Procedure was that undertaken by the Services Divorce Department set up by The Law Society during the Second World War. Solicitors were employed whole-time in this Department to conduct matrimonial causes of Service men and women up to the rank of Sergeant or Petty Officer. The Services Divorce Department, when it was superseded in September 1950 by the present Divorce Department, had had assigned to it over 64,500 cases for petitioners, respondents, or co-respondents, and had obtained over 52,000 decrees absolute.

During the Second World War the Navy, Army, and Royal Air Force started legal-aid schemes under which lawyers gave free legal advice to members of H.M. Forces not above the rank of Sergeant or Petty Officer, whether serving in England or abroad. These Services legal-aid schemes worked in close co-operation with the Services Divorce Department and the Poor Persons Committees, and sailors, soldiers, and airmen were thus enabled not only to obtain legal advice on a variety of legal problems but also help in preparing their applications for Service poor persons certificates. By the end of 1945 over 122,000 applicants had been given legal assistance under these schemes.

A Committee, known as the Rushcliffe Committee, was set up by the Government in 1944 to examine the facilities available for legal aid and legal advice for the poorer sections of the public. That Committee made sweeping recommendations to widen the scope of the facilities then available. Their recommendations were embodied in the Legal Aid and Advice Act 1949, which, with the Regulations made under the Act by the Lord Chancellor and a document called the Legal Aid Scheme made by The Law Society under the powers contained in the Act, now provides the framework for a comprehensive scheme of legal aid and advice available to those of moderate means throughout the country.

The Poor Persons Procedure provided assistance only in connexion with High Court cases, and a poor person's certificate could only be granted to members of the community with an income of less than £4 a week and with capital possessions which did not exceed £100. The new Legal Aid and Advice Act 1949 provides for legal assistance in the conduct of all classes of civil litigation in the High Court (except certain specific classes of case, of which libel, slander, and breach of promise of marriage are the most important), in the County Court and the Magistrate's Court. Further, legal aid under the 1949 Act is made available to persons with a 'disposable income' not exceeding £420 a year. There is no definite capital limit, but if the applicant for aid has assets exceeding £500 he may be refused legal aid under the Act. The disposable income and disposable capital of applicants for legal aid are determined by the National Assistance Board, who make a number of deductions from the gross income or capital, for example, in respect of income tax, maintenance of dependants, and, in certain cases, rates and rent. Accordingly, the financial limits have been substantially extended from the days of the Poor Persons Procedure. One of the basic principles of the new Legal Aid Scheme is that persons receiving legal aid should pay towards their own costs such amount as they can afford. Accordingly, if Joan Doe's disposable income is less than £156 a year and her disposable capital does not exceed £75 she will obtain assistance free, and will not even have to pay her own disbursements as was necessary under the Poor Persons Procedure. On the other hand, John Doe, whose disposable income and capital exceeds the above amounts, will have to make a contribution towards his own costs in accordance with the amount which he has been assessed as being able to afford. The contribution is on a sliding scale, and may be met out of income and capital, if any, and provisions are made to enable the contribution to be paid by instalments. When a civil-aid certificate, as it is called, is offered under the scheme, the applicant is told what will be his maximum contribution towards his own costs and, if the contribution is to be paid by instalments, the amount of the instalments and whether they are to be paid weekly or monthly. Where the assisted litigant is successful and costs are recovered from the other party to the proceedings, the assisted litigants will probably receive repayment of his own contribution. Under the Poor Persons Procedure a poor person was only in exceptional circumstances liable to make a payment towards the costs of the other side if he was unsuccessful, but under the Legal Aid and Advice Act an assisted person may be liable, if he loses his action, for the costs of the other side. The Act and Regulations expressly provide, however, that before making an order for costs against an assisted person the Court must decide what is a reasonable amount for him to pay having regard to all the circumstances, including the means of all the parties and their conduct in connexion with the dispute. Further, in deciding the amount that the assisted person can pay, the Court will not normally consider as part of the assisted person's assets his dwelling-house, household furniture, and the tools and implements of his trade.

Legal aid is provided by solicitors and barristers who have

volunteered to go on panels for the different classes of legal proceedings. They are remunerated out of the Legal Aid Fund, which is administered by The Law Society, and receive in relation to High Court work 85 per cent of their normal remuneration.

The responsibility for the administration of this great scheme is vested in The Law Society. England and Wales have been divided into twelve Areas, and The Law Society has appointed in each Area an Area Committee consisting of twelve solicitors and four barristers. Each of these Committees is responsible for the administration of the Legal Aid Scheme in its own Area, and they in turn have each appointed a number of Local Committees consisting of solicitors and barristers by whom applications for civil aid certificates are considered. Applicants must satisfy the Local Committee on the evidence produced that they have 'reasonable grounds' for bringing or defending the proceedings. The addresses of the Local Committees may be obtained from the offices of the National Assistance Board and from Citizens' Advice Bureaux, or may be seen in the current Law List, which is normally available in any Public Library.

The Legal Aid and Advice Act 1949 also makes provision for the administration by The Law Society of a legal advice system throughout England and Wales. Under this scheme a member of the public will be able to obtain legal advice on payment of a nominal sum of 2s. 6d., and provision is made for even this sum to be waived in special circumstances. A person seeking legal advice may, however, be required to satisfy the Legal Adviser that he or she cannot afford to obtain legal advice in the ordinary way. Special provision is also made to enable members of the Armed Forces of the Crown to obtain legal advice both in England and abroad.

Finally, the Act deals with legal aid in criminal matters by modifying the Acts of Parliament relating to the provision of free legal aid in criminal matters, so as to secure that, if there is any doubt whether or not a person charged with a criminal offence is eligible for legal aid, the doubt shall be resolved in his favour and he shall be granted legal aid.

The Legal Aid and Advice Act 1949 can be brought into

operation in parts, and at the present date, 1957, those parts
of the Act which relate to proceedings in civil matters instituted in the High Court or County Court are in force. The
provisions of the Act enabling legal aid to be given in civil
matters in Magistrates' Courts, and for the provision of a comprehensive legal advice system have yet to be implemented.

34

HOW TO BECOME A LAWYER

> 'Johnson observed that "he did not care to speak ill of
> any man behind his back, but he believed the gentleman
> was an Attorney." '
>
> Boswell: *Life of Johnson*

BOTH branches of the legal profession in England – viz. barristers and solicitors – are open equally to men and women. Barristers are treated as the senior branch of the profession, and they have more glittering prospects than solicitors, for Judges are always appointed from their ranks. Barristers are also qualified to accept many high political appointments, including those of the Attorney-General and the Solicitor-General, the two principal legal officers of the Crown. The principal official appointments open to solicitors are in the Civil Service or with Local Authorities and Public Corporations.

The principal function of barristers is to plead cases in Court. As ancillary thereto, it is the practice for them to advise on legal problems of particular complexity, and to settle the formal documents called 'pleadings', which are prepared in every action, and which set out the facts relied upon by each of the parties to the suit, so as to define the issues to be tried.

In order to become a barrister it is necessary to pass certain legal examinations, and also to become a member of one of the four Associations, called Inns of Court. They are Gray's Inn, Lincoln's Inn, Inner Temple, and Middle Temple, and they were all founded many centuries ago. Their affairs are administered by Senior Barristers called 'Benchers'. When a student joins his Inn, he must keep at least twelve terms before he can be 'called to the Bar'. There are four terms or 'Sittings' in each year; Michaelmas Term runs approximately from October to Christmas; Hilary Term from January to Easter; Easter Term from Easter to Whitsun; and Trinity Term from Whitsun to the end of July, when the Long Vacation starts. A student keeps a term by dining six times in the Hall of his

Inn, although a University student need only dine three times each term.

Farington in his diary (17 November 1797), reports an occasion when '16 Benchers dined to-day in the Inner Temple Hall – about 30 Barristers and Students – The Benchers have a table covered with luxuries – They pay only 1/6 each. ... No Vegetables are allowed to Roast meats. They are paid for separate. Port wine is charged 3/6 a bottle.' A student should not rely upon finding similar conditions today.

Apart from dining, the student has also to pass certain legal examinations before he is entitled to be called to the Bar. Many students will have already taken a University course in law or some other subject before embarking upon a career at the Bar, and they may get exemption from some of the preliminary examinations. All students have, however, to pass the Bar Final Examination.

Just before or immediately after call to the Bar, it is usual to obtain practical experience in the profession by reading in Chambers as a pupil, i.e. studying in the office of a practising barrister who will be known as the pupil's 'Master in law'. When the student has been called to the Bar, he may appear professionally, in wig and gown, in any Court. A barrister frequently devotes himself to some special branch of the law. If his particular choice is the Common Law, he will usually appear in the Queen's Bench Division, and if he has specialized more particularly in matters of Equity, he will usually be seen in the Chancery Courts. Almost every chapter in this book has dealt with a subject on which a barrister may wish to specialize, but in whichever Court a barrister practises, he has no direct contacts with his lay client, and it is this feature which robs the work of much of its human interest. All his work must come to him through a solicitor. He is not even permitted to interview the client, except in the presence of his solicitor.

When a barrister receives instructions from a solicitor he is said to receive a brief, but he may have to wait a long time for his first brief, for, like a solicitor, he is never allowed to advertise for work. There are also strict rules of etiquette which govern his relations with solicitors, and he is not permitted to visit a solicitor in the solicitor's office, unless he is doing so in respect of his own personal affairs.

After a barrister has practised for ten years as a Junior Counsel, he is entitled to apply to be made a Queen's Counsel, or to take 'Silk', as it is called. Queen's Counsel are regarded as the leaders of the profession, and the Judges are usually appointed from their ranks.

Although the ultimate prospects open to a barrister are virtually unlimited, only a very few are outstandingly successful, and many prefer not to practice at all but to go into some other occupation where legal knowledge and training are helpful. The most desirable qualifications for a good barrister are a capacity for hard, concentrated work, a crystal-clear mind, an ability to seize on the essential points in an argument, a ready wit, and ease of expression. Needless to say, a pleasant personality is also an asset, as in every other profession or business. A barrister usually remains a member of his Inn for the whole of his life, and he may be disbarred for grave offences.

Even when he is possessed of the necessary attributes, a barrister is by no means assured of success. The commencement of his career is inevitably an uphill struggle. Briefs do not fall like manna into the chambers of an unknown barrister. If he has connexions among solicitors, he is, of course, more likely to receive briefs, and a young prospective barrister who, perhaps, knew his Gilbert and Sullivan, has been heard to observe that he always believed in courting the daughters of solicitors! However, even this will not avail him, if he is not able to turn opportunity to his advantage by skill and ability.

Three years' training, followed by a further protracted period of waiting for briefs, during which he still continues to earn nothing, is not a cheerful prospect. You will not be wise to contemplate the career of a barrister, therefore, unless you have ample resources, and a private income sufficient to keep you from starvation during the lean years. There is scarcely such a thing as 'taking a job' when you have passed your final examination, unless you propose to abandon the possibility of an active career at the Bar. A few lucky barristers, who devote themselves to theory, may obtain work from legal publishers, but for the rest they must rely upon their own skill and ability to obtain briefs.

Although it is the practice for a number of barristers to share chambers, partnership or anything resembling partnership is not permitted. Crumbs may, however, from time to time fall into the lap of a young barrister who shares chambers with a busy junior with more work than he can digest. In these conditions a fledgling may assist a busy junior to prepare a case for Court, and he is then said to 'devil' for him. He may also take over a brief when the barrister chosen for the case is too busy to accept it himself, but this practice is not so prevalent as formerly. Most solicitors prefer to know the qualifications of the barrister who is to appear for them in Court. They do not like their cases to be conducted by a fledgling. If the Counsel who has received the brief is too busy to attend to it, the solicitor prefers to choose his own substitute. In normal times the supply of keen barristers exceeds the demand, and most solicitors usually know a number of competent juniors.

The work of a solicitor is of a totally different character from that of a barrister, although many of the essential qualifications are similar. A solicitor must also be prepared to work hard, and he will usually be successful in his profession only if he is conscientious and ready to put the interests of his client before his own.

Every prospective solicitor must enter into 'articles of clerkship' with a practising solicitor before he can start his career. The consent of The Law Society must also be obtained before he may enter into his articles. The normal term of articles is five years, but this period is reduced to four and a half years when a student has passed the General Certificate of Education with the required number of passes at the advanced level or has passed other specified examinations, subject to certain conditions. The period is further reduced to four years when a student has taken certain courses at a recognized Law School, and to three years if he has taken a degree at a British University.

Before he is able to make a start, a student must, of course, find a solicitor who is willing to give him his articles, and a premium of £300 or more is sometimes required for this privilege. Moreover, the clerk must not expect to receive much remuneration during the period of his articles, if he has come straight from School or University. It is, however, becoming increasingly frequent for solicitors' clerks to enter into articles with their principal after they have had ten years' practical experience of the law, and they may then qualify after three years' articles. It is not unusual for a solicitor to offer a competent clerk free articles in such circumstances, whilst the solicitor will also continue to pay the clerk his usual salary during his articles.

Three examinations must normally be taken: The first is a preliminary or general-knowledge examination, and there are a number of instances in which exemption may be claimed in respect of the 'Prelim'. The Intermediate Examination tests the progress which a student has made in general legal knowledge, and also includes Book-keeping and Accounts. The Final Examination is decidedly 'stiff', and questions are asked which range over the whole field of law. Except for graduates in law or solicitors' clerks who are entering the profession under the ten-year rule, the student must attend for one year at a recognized Law School before he can take the Final Examination. A high standard is required in all these examinations, and the percentage of failures is substantial.

In addition to the premium on the articles there is considerable expense involved in becoming a solicitor. The examination and tuition fees may amount to £60. After qualifying, the practising solicitor will require a practising certificate, for which an annual fee of £4 is payable. There is also a contribution of £10, which every established solicitor is required to make annually to the Compensation Fund referred to in Chapter 32, and it is always advisable for a solicitor to become a member of The Law Society, even although this is not compulsory. Membership of the Society costs £5 5s. a year for London members and £3 13s. 6d. a year for country members.

These expenses will suggest that every boy and girl should seriously consider the prospects before deciding to enter into articles, even if keen on the law. He (or she) will often do better to obtain a post as a junior clerk in the office of solicitors of repute. Good work is usually appreciated in such an office, and there is nothing derogatory in starting on the bottom rung of the ladder. A diligent clerk, who wishes to qualify as a solicitor at a later date, can usually do so without financial strain, for the reasons which have been explained. Parents may make a useless sacrifice when they insist upon their son entering into articles as soon as he leaves school, because they think he will then have a chance in life which they themselves never enjoyed. Of course, they will usually have no difficulty in placing him in articles, if he has intelligence. They may even find a solicitor ready to give him articles without payment of any premium. When, however, he has qualified, at heavy expense, he will still be at the bottom of the ladder. A newly admitted solicitor, without practical experience, will usually command a salary lower than a clerk with several years' practical experience. It is vanity to make a boy a solicitor, unless he either has real prospects of being able to build up a practice on his own *clientèle* or wishes to take an official appointment.

Although the higher judicial posts are not open to solicitors, there are other compensations. If you have a real interest in law and the administration of justice, every day has its own interest. Some aspects of the law are, of course, more interesting to the theorists than to the practical man. Conveyancing or the transfer of property does not offer the same excitement as litigation. On the other hand, you may not like excitement, and there are many other fields open both to the practical man and the theorist.

Solicitors must be men of integrity. The high degree of responsibility which attaches to the profession is recognized by the fact that a solicitor is an 'officer of the Court' – i.e. the High Court. For practical purposes this means that the Court is his governing authority, although control is usually exercised by The Law Society, some of whose extensive powers were considered in Chapter 32. As large sums of money may be daily passing through the hands of solicitors, strict regulations have been laid down relating to solicitors' accounts, and they are designed to avoid lax methods which can so easily lead to dishonesty. Every solicitor is obliged to keep his clients' money in a separate banking account, and not to mix it with his own or his office funds. He is also obliged to keep proper books of accounts, which must be audited every year, and if complaint is made to The Law Society of default by a solicitor in respect of any financial transaction, the Society has power to investigate his books and to require him to attend to answer complaints. If found guilty of professional misconduct, the Society may impose penalties, suspend him from practice, or even strike his name from the Rolls.

It is, perhaps, necessary to add that, while it places him under this strict discipline, the law is also jealous of his rights, and it is not only an offence for any layman to hold himself out as a solicitor, but it is also an offence for any unqualified person to prepare a deed, as distinct from an agreement, for reward.

A final word of advice to a prospective solicitor – male or female. If you are leaving school and are attracted by the prospect of discovering whether the iron curtain which is supposed to separate the law from the layman is or is not only a blind, don't rush into articles, but ascertain first whether your interest in the law is of a passing or of an enduring character. If you seek employment as a junior clerk with a firm of repute you can leave your job without harm to yourself or to anyone else if you find that you can't 'stick' the law. On the other hand, if you want to stay the course you will already have made a start. Given a fair share of good fortune, you will have begun a career which holds out prospects sufficient to satisfy all but the most exacting ambitions, and at the same time you will have the opportunity, if you are conscientious, of being of real service to the community.

EQUITY

WHILE the Common Law of England was largely built up by the application of common sense, the early English Courts had very limited powers, and they could only be exercised according to fixed rules, for all legal procedure was rigid and inflexible. If a man suffered a legal injury, he could have no remedy at Common Law unless his request for redress could be prepared according to these strict rules. Generally speaking, they were framed upon the principle that money was a cure for every legal injury. Unless compensation was the foundation of a claim, there were few cases in which the Common Law had power to give it consideration.

The community, however, discovered in course of time that money was not the cure for all ills. There were many cases in which it did not yield the required remedy. If John Doe insisted upon a persistent infringement of his neighbour's legal rights, the neighbour would want to abate the nuisance, and an award of compensation would not achieve this end. This was not the only type of grievance which could not be remedied by the Common Law. There were many others, and in each instance the suitor had to look elsewhere for redress.

To meet this situation a practice arose of preparing a petition addressed to the King praying justice for the complaint. If this petition was presented in due form, it was handed to an official of the King's Court, called the Lord Chancellor. Although the law was administered by the Judges, they could not deprive the King of his supreme prerogative of doing 'equity' – i.e. right or justice – to his subjects, and the Lord Chancellor was accordingly given power to remedy grievances. When the Lord Chancellor exercised these powers they were described as being 'equitable', as distinct from 'legal', because they were founded on 'equity' as distinct from 'law'. In course of time, more and greater demands were made upon equity, and, as a result, it gradually introduced its own series of rules and set up its own Courts. Complications then ensued, and resulted in competition, fierce at times, between the rival Courts. Courts of Equity regarded themselves as superior to Courts of Common Law, as they claimed to be able to remedy any legitimate injury. For instance, equity invented the legal devices known as an 'injunction' and 'specific performance', both of which have been dealt with in the text, while it also took control of all disputes which arose out of trusts.

Some may think that equity sometimes used its powers maliciously, as, although it could never directly overrule any decision of the Court of Common Law, it did have power to grant an injunction, in suitable cases, to restrain a litigant from continuing with his Common Law action. This state of affairs continued until the Judicature Act 1873. This Act fused the two systems, and merged all the Superior Courts of the country in the Supreme Court of Judicature. Justice is now administered as one whole, and equity is no longer able to make independent regulations to suit particular grievances, for it must only operate in strict accordance with Statute and precedent. On the other hand, the Courts still maintain what is termed their 'equitable jurisdiction', and although this is usually administered by the Chancery Division, its jurisdiction is not exclusive.

Equity has played an important part in the development of English Law. Today, when it has become assimilated into the legal system, a layman may go through life without feeling its impact. For example, if he acts as a trustee, and commits a breach of trust, an offence which would formerly have brought him into conflict with equity, he may now expect to feel the full weight of ordinary legal procedure brought to bear against him.

JOHN DOE AND RICHARD ROE

'Jove and my Stars be praised! Here is yet a Postscript.'
Twelfth Night

'John Doe' and 'Richard Roe', who figure so often in this work, are, as already stated, fictitious legal characters. This brief account of their life is involved, and unless you feel prepared for concentration, you may prefer to take their lives for granted and omit this postscript.

John Doe and Richard Roe originally appeared as plaintiff and defendant respectively in numerous lawsuits brought for the possession of property from the time of the Stuarts until the Common Law Procedure Act 1852 swept away one of the most extraordinary of legal fictions.

It happened in this way. In early days the Courts had power to adjudicate on disputes only if they were instituted in accordance with set forms. Those which related to disputes regarding the ownership of property were of a most complicated and cumbersome nature. They were, moreover, so beset by traps, e.g. a description of a garden as an orchard would be sufficient to throw the plaintiff out of Court, that they became too dangerous for the average litigant. There was, however, a less complicated procedure for settling disputes regarding ownership, if a claim of trespass was made under a lease. The Court could settle a dispute, either as between a landlord and a tenant, or between a tenant and a trespasser. Accordingly, if William claimed freehold land in the occupation of his neighbour Henry, but considered it too hazardous to bring proceedings against Henry to recover possession of the disputed land, he would grant a lease of the land to George, who would today be called a 'stooge'. It was George's function to make a token entry on the land, and to remain there until there was a trespass by a stranger, Charles. George, as tenant, would then start proceedings of ejectment against Charles, as trespasser. These proceedings might, of course, be taken without Henry's knowledge, but the Court required formal notice of the litigation to be served on any person actually in occupation of the disputed land, and in this way Henry would be informed of the action. Henry then had the right to apply to intervene in the Suit, and he was permitted to do so, on condition that he admitted that George had actually entered on the land, under the lease granted to him by William, and that Charles had trespassed on the land. He was entitled, however, to dispute William's right to have granted the lease to George, and this plea made it necessary for William to prove his title to the land. If he was able to do so, it followed that Henry had no title to the land. Conversely, if William failed to establish his title, *he* had no right to the land. In this way the real issue as to the ownership of the land between William and Henry was decided by the Court.

In practice, the procedure was obviously most cumbersome and inconvenient, so an ingenious scheme was devised to enable a fictitious plaintiff to replace George, and a fictitious defendant to replace Charles. The former was called John Doe, and the latter was called Richard Roe. In these proceedings John Doe claimed (1) that the freeholder, our friend William, the real claimant, had granted him, John Doe, a lease of the premises for a term of years; (2) that he, John Doe, had entered into possession of the premises under the lease, and (3) that the defendant Richard Roe had wrongfully entered on the land and ousted him from possession. When Henry, the rival claimant, was notified of these proceedings he was permitted to intervene in the suit, and to be substituted as defendant for Richard Roe on condition that he admitted (1) the fictitious grant of the lease to John Doe, (2) John Doe's fictitious entry on the land, and (3) the fictitious trespass by Richard Roe. He denied, however, that the grant of the lease was a valid lease, and would contend that the freeholder, William, had no title to grant the lease. This issue was thus decided between the parties, as before, but without the necessity of actual lease, actual entry, or actual trespass.

And that was that! When John Doe and Richard Roe, like good old soldiers, faded away in 1852, after new and simplified legal forms had been introduced, they received no funeral oration. There were 'No flowers by request', but there are still a few lawyers who may say, 'Thanks for the memory'.

INDEX